Third Edition

Study Guide for
Shapiro
Multinational
Financial
Management

Prepared by
Andrea L. DeMaskey
University of Nevada—Reno

Allyn and Bacon
Boston   London   Sydney   Toronto

CONTENTS

PREFACE

The purpose of this **study guide** is to help you develop an understandin of the conceptual framework within which the key financial decisions of t multinational corporation can be analyzed.

This **study guide** follows the chapter outline of **Multinational Financia Management**. In each chapter of the study guide you will find a chapter summary, a listing of key terms, and questions and problems as well as selected questions and problems from the text for study purposes.

I would like to thank Alan Shapiro and Cary Tengler for their comments and guidance in the preparation of this study guide. Special thanks are also extended to the secretarial staff of the Managerial Sciences Department in the College of Business at the University of Nevada, Reno, and to Rebecca Fallow, in particular, for her word processing assistance preparing each chapter of the study guide.

Andrea L. DeMaskey
Managerial Sciences
College of Business
University of Nevada, Ren

February, 1989

CHAPTER 1

INTRODUCTION
MULTINATIONAL ENTERPRISE AND
MULTINATIONAL FINANCIAL MANAGEMENT

Summary: This chapter traces the evolution of multinational corporations and the interrelationships of international finance as a field of study and the role of the international financial manager.

I. The Rise of the Multinational Corporation

   A. The classical theory of international trade is based on the idea of <u>comparative</u> <u>advantage</u> which states that each nation should specialize in the production and export of those goods that can be produced most efficiently while importing those goods that other nations can produce most efficiently.

   B. The following assumptions underlie this theory:

      1. Goods and services can move internationally.

      2. Factors of production, such as capital, labor, and land, are immobile.

      3. Only undifferentiated products are traded.

   C. International mobility of certain factors of production provide the basis for the existence of the multinational enterprise.

   D. The distinguishing characteristic of the true multinational corporation is its emphasis on group, rather than individual, performance.

   E. Firms have become multinational by:

      1. Exploiting the raw materials that could be found in foreign countries - <u>raw</u> <u>material</u> <u>seekers</u>.

      2. Going overseas to produce and sell in foreign markets - <u>market seekers</u>.

      3. Seeking out and investing in lower-cost production sites overseas in order to remain cost competitive both at home and abroad - <u>cost</u> <u>minimizers</u>.

II. The Process of Overseas Expansion

    A. Firms become multinational by degree, with foreign direct investment being a late step in a process that begins with exports.

    B. The internationalization process is the unplanned result of a series of corporate responses to a variety of threats and opportunities abroad that appear at random.

    C. Thus, the multinationalization of firms can be seen as the inevitable outcome of the competitive responses of members of oligopolistic industries; that is, industries which consist of several companies that recognize their mutual interdependence. Each member of the oligopoly tries to both create and exploit product and market imperfections internationally and, simultaneously, attempts to reduce the perceived competitive threats posed by other members in the same industry.

    D. The _evolutionary approach_ to expanding overseas can be viewed as risk-minimizing response to operating in a highly uncertain foreign environment. By internationalizing in phases, a firm ca gradually move from a relatively low risk-low return, export-oriented strategy to a higher risk-higher return strategy emphasizing international production.

    E. The foreign expansion sequence consists of:

        1. Firms faced with highly uncertain demand abroad will usually begin _exporting_ to a foreign market. The advantages of exporting include:

            a. Reduced capital requirements and start-up costs.

            b. Low risk.

            c. Immediate returns.

            d. Potential learning is great (present/future supply, demai conditions, competition, channels of distribution, etc.).

        2. As uncertainty is reduced through increased communication wit customers, the firm might establish its own _sales subsidiary_ and new service facilities.

3. With increased assurance of supply stability, firms may choose to establish their <u>production</u> <u>facilities</u> <u>overseas</u>. This move, which demonstrates greater commitment to the local market, offers the following advantages:

   a. Keeping abreast of market developments.

   b. Adopting product and production schedules to different tastes and conditions.

   c. Providing more comprehensive service and support to local customers.

4. Whenever a firm decides to produce abroad, it will eventually be faced with the question of whether to establish its <u>own</u> <u>affiliate</u> or to <u>acquire</u> an existing concern. While the cost of acquiring an ongoing company is very high, the following advantages may make such a move worthwhile:

   a. Speedy transfer of highly developed but underutilized parent skills.

   b. Ready-made marketing network.

   c. Gaining knowledge about local market or a particular technology.

5. An alternative to setting up production facilities abroad is to <u>license</u> a local firm which will manufacture the company's products. The investment outlay for licensing is very minimal, but the firm may be faced with difficulties in the following areas:

   a. Maintenance of product quality standards.

   b. Control over exports by foreign licensees.

F. The Global Manager

1. In order to remain competitive internationally, management must be able to adjust to change volatility at an ever faster rate.

2. While the risk is high, the capacity to manage it and profit from it is greater.

3. The global manager is required to:

    a. Understand political and economic differences.

    b. Search for the most cost effective mix of supplies, components, transport and funds.

    c. Be constantly aware that choices may change.

III. Multinational Financial Management: Theory and Practice

A. The distinguishing characteristic of the multinational corporation is its ability to move money and profits among its various affiliates through an internal transfer mechanism, such as transfer pricing, intracorporate loans, dividend payments, leading and lagging intracorporate payments, etc.

B. Financial transactions within the multinational corporation result from the internal transfer of goods, services, technology, and capital.

    1. Mode of Transfer.

        a. Funds can be sent from one affiliate to another by adjusting transfer pricing on intracorporate sales and purchases of goods and services.

        b. Investment flows can be sent overseas as <u>debt</u> with the choice of interest rate, currency denomination, and repayment schedule, or as <u>equity</u>, with the return coming in the form of dividends.

    2. Timing Flexibility.

        a. Although financial claims are flexible when first established, some require a fixed payment schedule.

        b. Accelerating or delaying payments (leading and lagging) is most often applied to interaffiliate trade credit.

        c. The timing of fee and royalty payments may be modified when all parties to the agreement are related.

3. Value

    a. Multinational corporations can reduce their global tax payments by shifting profits from high-tax to lower tax nations.

    b. By transferring funds among its several units, the multinational corporation may be able to circumvent currency controls and other regulations, and may, therefore, tap previously inaccessible investment and financing opportunities.

B. Functions of Financial Management

    1. The two basic functions of the financial manager consist of:

        a. Raising funds at the most favorable terms - <u>financing decision</u>.

        b. Allocating funds most efficiently - <u>investment decision</u>.

    2. The goal of the international financial manager, therefore, is to make investment and financing decisions that will maximize the value of the firm to its shareholders.

C. The financial manager of a multinational corporation is faced with a number of unique variables that have no domestic counterpart. These include:

    1. Exchange and inflation risks.

    2. International differences in tax rates.

    3. Multiple money markets often with limited access.

    4. Currency controls.

    5. Political risk, such as expropriation.

D. By having operations in different countries, the multinational corporation is able to take advantage of some unique opportunities, such as:

    1. Accessing segmented capital markets to lower its overall cost of capital.

    2. Shifting profits to lower its taxes.

    3. Taking advantage of international diversification to reduce the riskiness of its earnings.

E.   Relationship to Domestic Financial Management

1.   The major thrust of international financial management has been to apply the major methodologies and the logic of financial economics to the study of key international financial decisions.

2.   The critical problem areas include:

a.   Foreign exchange risk management.

b.   Foreign investment analysis.

c.   Working capital management.

d.   Tax management.

e.   Evaluation and control.

3.   Three concepts arising in financial economics are of particular importance in developing a theoretical foundation for international corporate finance:

a.   Arbitrage has traditionally been defined as the purchase of securities or commodities on one market for immediate resale on another in order to profit from a price discrepancy. In recent years, however, the term arbitrage has been used to describe a wider range of activities.

(1) Tax arbitrage - profiting from different tax rates.

(2) Risk arbitrage or speculation - profiting from differences in risk-adjusted returns on different securities. The arbitrage process results in equity of risk-adjusted returns unless market imperfections hinder this adjustment process.

b.   Market Efficiency means that new information is readily incorporated in the prices of traded securities. Three levels of market efficiency:

(1) Weak form.

(2) Semi-strong form.

(3) Strong form.

c. <u>Capital</u> <u>Asset</u> <u>Pricing</u> refers to the way in which securities are valued in line with their anticipated risks and returns. The two theories which price risk in the capital markets are the capital asset pricing model (CAPM) and the arbitrage pricing theory (APT). Both these theories assume that the total variability of an asset's return can be attributed to two sources:

(1) Systematic or nondiversifiable risk.

(2) Unsystematic or diversifiable risk.

F. In order to increase the value of the firm, purely financial measures or accounting manipulations are unlikely to succeed unless there are capital market imperfections, primarily caused by the government, or asymmetries in tax regulations.

IV. Appendix 1A: Size and Scope of Multinational Corporations Abroad

A. U.S. Direct Investment Abroad

1. U.S. firms prefer to invest in the developed countries.

2. The rates of returns earned from investments in the LDCs are substantially lower than those earned from comparable investments in developed countries.

3. Consequently, direct investment in Latin America has declined substantially coinciding with the Latin American debt crisis and reflecting both the poorer economic prospects of these countries and the additional constraints imposed on the ability of MNCs to repatriate profits from their Latin American subsidiaries.

4. Capital expenditures by majority-owned foreign affiliates of U.S. companies have slowed substantially since the 1970s. This drop in overseas investments may be attributed to the severity of the worldwide recession in the early 1980s. New investment is primarily concentrated in Europe and Canada, with Latin America in third place.

B. Foreign Direct Investment in the U.S.

1. Foreign direct investment in the U.S. grew by 13% compared with 12% in 1985.

2. Three countries - Great Britain, Netherlands, Japan - accounted for nearly three-fourths of the increase in foreign direct investment in the U.S.

3. Returns on foreign direct investment in the U.S. are far below returns on U.S. direct investments overseas. In addition, firms appear to be willing to earn only marginal returns from their investment in the U.S. when compared to those that can be earned from Treasury bills or other riskless instruments.

C. The Net International Wealth of the U.S.

1. Capital flows consist of foreign direct investments as well as the flow of portfolio investments and bank lending overseas.

2. The net of U.S. investments abroad and foreign investment domestically makes up the net international wealth of the U.S.

3. The consequences of a reduction in a nation's net international wealth depend on the nature of the foreign capital inflows that cause the erosion.

   a. If the capital inflows finance new investments that enhance the nation's productive capacity, then they are self-financing.

   b. On the other hand, if the investment flows finance current consumption, their repayment will necessitate an eventual reduction in the nation's standard of living below where it would have been in the absence of such inflows.

KEY TERMS

Comparative Advantage
Multinational Corporation
Raw Materials Seekers
Market Seekers
Cost Minimizers
Internationalization Process
Exporting
Licensing
Overseas Production
Internal Transfer Mechanism
Leading and Lagging

Political Risks
Economic Risks
Arbitrage
Market Efficiency
Capital Asset Pricing Model
Arbitrage Pricing Theory
Systematic Risk
Unsystematic Risk
Corporate Hedging
International Diversification
Capital Market Imperfections

CONCEPTUAL QUESTIONS

QUESTION 1: What is a multinational corporation?

ANSWER: A multinational corporation may be defined in terms of its commitment to seeking out and undertaking investment, marketing, and financing opportunities on a global, not domestic, basis.

QUESTION 2: What is arbitrage?

ANSWER: Traditionally, arbitrage has been defined as the purchase of securities or commodities in one market for immediate sale in another market in order to profit from a price discrepancy. In recent years, however, the term arbitrage has been used to describe a wider range of activities. For example, tax arbitrage refers to shifting any gains or losses from one tax jurisdiction to another in order to profit from different tax rates. Risk arbitrage or speculation is that process which ensures that risk-adjusted returns on different securities are equal unless market imperfections hinder this adjustment process. In fact, it is through arbitrage transactions that the market is efficient.

QUESTION 3: Under what circumstances can a financial executive of a multinational corporation increase the value of the firm to its shareholders?

ANSWER: The value of the firm is more likely increased in the international environment if the financial manager encounters product and market imperfections, which are primarily caused by the government, and/or asymmetries in tax regulations. In addition, the greater complexity of international operations is likely to increase the payoffs from a knowledgeable and sophisticated approach to internationalizing the traditional areas of financial management.

SELECTED QUESTIONS FROM THE TEXT

QUESTION 4: How does the internal financial transfer system add value to the multinational firm?

ANSWER: The MNC's ability to transfer funds and profits internally enable it to potentially reduce its global tax payments, circumvent currency controls and other regulations, and tap previously inaccessible investment and financing opportunities.

QUESTION 7: In seeking to predict tomorrow's exchange rate, are you bett
off knowing today's exchange rate or the exchange rates for the past 100
days?

ANSWER: In an efficient market, which the foreign exchange market
certainly appears to be, the current price of an asset such as a currenc
fully reflects all available information, including the complete price
history. Thus knowing today's price is as informative from a forecasting
standpoint as knowing all past prices. Past prices add nothing to the
current price in terms of forecasting ability.

QUESTION 12a: How might total risk affect a firm's production costs and
its ability to sell? Give some examples of firms in financial distress
that saw their sales drop.

ANSWER: Higher total risk can lead to lower sales and higher production
costs. The inverse relation between risk and expected cash flows arises
because financial distress, which is more likely to occur for firms with
high _total_ risk, can impose costs on customers, suppliers, and employees
and thereby affect their willingness to commit themselves to relationshi
with the firm. Examples include Chrysler and Texaco which saw their sale
go down and their costs of doing business rise when they were in financi
distress.

CHAPTER 2

THE DETERMINATION OF EXCHANGE RATES

Summary: The purpose of this chapter is to provide an understanding of how exchange rates are determined in a freely floating exchange rate system. Given the current system, which is a managed float, different forms and consequences of central bank intervention in the foreign exchange market will be examined. Since an exchange rate can be considered as the relative price of two financial assets, this chapter also discusses the asset market model of currencies and the role of expectations in the determination of exchange rates.

I. Setting the Equilibrium Spot Exchange Rate

    A. In the absence of government intervention, exchange rates are determined by the free market forces of supply and demand.

    B. More specifically, exchange rates are a function of the following variables:

        1. Relative Rate of Inflation.

            a. A higher rate of inflation in country A than in country B can be expected to simultaneously increase foreign exports to country A and reduce domestic exports to country B and will lead to a depreciation of country A's currency relative to country B's.

            b. The amount of country B's currency <u>appreciation</u> is the fractional increase in the value of country A's currency, which can be shown as

$$(e_1 - e_0)/e_0$$

            where e_0 is the beginning currency value and e_1 is the ending currency value.

            c. Alternatively, country A's currency is said to have <u>depreciated</u> by the fractional decrease in the value of country B's currency or by

$$(1/e_1 - 1/e_0)/(1/e_0) = (e_0 - e_1)/e_1.$$

2. Interest Rate Differentials.

    a. A rise in the interest rate in country A relative to country B will cause investors in both nations to switch from securities denominated in country B's currency to those denominated in country A's currency.

    b. These transactions, in turn, cause a depreciation (appreciation) of country B's (A's) currency.

3. Relative Growth in National Incomes.

    a. Capital is generally attracted to a stronger economy.

    b. Consequently, the healthier the economy is, the stronger its currency is likely to be.

4. Exchange rates are also crucially affected by expectations of future exchange rate changes, which, in turn, depend on forecasts of future economic and political conditions.

II. Fundamentals of Central Bank Intervention

    A. If an exchange rate appreciates beyond that necessary to offset the inflation differential between two countries, the price of domestic goods will rise relative to prices of foreign goods. T real or inflation-adjusted exchange rate leads to an improvement in the terms of trade.

    B. If an exchange rate depreciates beyond that necessary to maintai purchasing power parity (i.e., prices of goods and services worldwide are the same), the traded-goods sector will become mor competitive, stimulating domestic employment and inducing a shif in resources from the nontraded- to the traded-goods sector in t economy. In addition, the weakening currency will cause prices for imported goods and services to increase, which, in turn, wil erode the standard of living and exacerbate domestic inflation.

    C. In order to achieve certain economic or political objectives, governments intervene in the foreign exchange market by purchasing or selling foreign exchange through their central banks.

        1. The major purpose of such foreign exchange market operations is to increase the market demand for one currency by increasing the market supply of another currency.

        2. Furthermore, the simultaneous sale of one currency and purchase of another currency will bring exchange rates into equilibrium.

D. The government can control the exchange rate directly by setting the price of its currency and then restricting access to foreign markets.

E. If the government intervenes in the foreign exchange market without having insulated its domestic money supply (that is, the government has resorted to _unsterilized intervention_), then, in addition to changes in the exchange rate, both the domestic inflation rate and the foreign inflation rate will be affected. These money supply changes will also affect the interest rates in both countries.

F. The central bank can _sterilize_ the impact of foreign exchange transactions on the domestic money supply with an offsetting sale or purchase of domestic assets.

G. _Open market operations_ can affect the equilibrium exchange rate in a manner analogous to unsterilized intervention--primarily through their impact on inflation.

III. Expectations and the Asset-Market Model of Exchange Rates

A. Foreign currency decisions depend on expectations of future exchange rate movements, which, in turn, are affected by every conceivable economic, political, and social factor.

B. The role of expectations in determining exchange rates depends on the fact that currencies are financial assets, and that an exchange rate is simply the relative price of two financial assets.

C. Based on the asset-market model of exchange rate determination, the exchange rate between two currencies represents the price that brings the relative supplies of, and demands for, assets denominated in those currencies into equilibrium.

D. The value of a currency is affected by the following relevant economic factors:

1. Its usefulness as a store of value, which is determined by its anticipated rate of inflation.

2. The demand for liquidity, which is determined by the volume of transactions in that currency.

3. The demand for assets denominated in that currency which is determined by the risk-return pattern in that nation's economy and by the wealth of its residents.

4. The risk associated with holding money, which is linked to the nature of a fiat money (money not backed by any commodity, such as gold).

E. Today there is no standard of value that investors can use to ascertain what the currency's future value might be. Instead, the value of a currency is largely determined by the central bank through its control of the money supply.

F. Thus, if the underlying domestic economic policies are highly unstable, investors are more likely to alter their beliefs about the future expected exchange rate which, in turn, results in added volatility in the value of the currency and more risk associated with holding the currency.

IV. The Equilibrium Approach to Exchange Rates

A. The real exchange rate, also known as the terms of trade, is the relative price of foreign goods in terms of domestic goods. It is measured as the nominal exchange rate adjusted for changes in the relative price level.

B. According to the disequilibrium theory of exchange rates, nominal disturbances can cause changes in real exchange rates; changes in nominal exchange rates are naturally translated into changes in real exchange rates because of slow price adjustment.

C. Based on the equilibrium approach to exchange rates, however, markets clear through price adjustments.

D. The equilibrium approach has four important implications for exchange rates.

1. Exchange rates do not cause changes in relative prices but are part of the process through which the changes occur in equilibrium.

2. The correlation between nominal and real exchange rates cannot be exploited by government policy.

3. There is no simple relation between changes in the exchange rate and changes in international competitiveness or employment.

4. There is no simple relation between the exchange rate and the balance of current account.

E. The alternative disequilibrium theories of the exchange rate, which are based on sluggish adjustment of nominal prices, have shown that nominal disturbances can cause changes in real exchange rates.

F. Thus, the implications of the disequilibrium view can be summarized as follows.

    1. The correlation between the real exchange rate and nominal exchange rate changes is exploitable by government policy.

    2. Currencies may become overvalued or undervalued relative to equilibrium.

    3. There are systematic relations between the exchange rate and the current account balance.

G. Statistical evidence indicates that:

    1. Changes in real and nominal exchange rates tend to be permanent.

    2. Changes in real and nominal exchange rates are highly correlated and have similar variances.

    3. The exchange rate is more volatile than the ratio of nominal GNP deflators.

H. The equilibrium theory has quite different policy implications than do the disequilibrium theories.

    1. By simply changing the nominal exchange rate, the real exchange rate cannot be affected.

    2. Changes in the exchange rate do not cause or reduce inflation.

    3. The choice of fixed versus flexible exchange rates is not important by itself for real exchange rates, the trade balance, and other real phenomena.

    4. The government should not impose protectionist restrictions on trade in goods or financial assets as a response to changes in exchange rates.

I. However, the equilibrium theory fails to explain the greater volatility of real exchange rates when currencies are floating than when they are fixed.

J. Its major contribution is to provide an explanation for exchange rate behavior which is consistent with the notion that markets work reasonably well if they are permitted to do so.

KEY TERMS

Devaluation

Revaluation

Depreciation

Appreciation

Exchange Rate

Real or Inflation-Adjusted Exchange Rate

Equilibrium Approach to Exchange Rates

Disequilibrium Theories to Exchange Rates

Unsterilized Intervention

Sterilized Intervention

Open Market Operation

Asset Market Model

Fiat Money System

Exchange Market Intervention

CONCEPTUAL QUESTIONS

QUESTION 1: Define the following terms: (a) devaluation, (b) revaluation, (c) depreciation, and (d) appreciation.

ANSWER: A devaluation refers to a decrease in the stated par value of a pegged currency while a revaluation refers to an increase in par value. The terms depreciation and appreciation are used to describe changes in th exchange rate under a floating rate system. An exchange rate depreciates if it loses currency value, while an exchange rate appreciates if it gains currency value.

QUESTION 2: Why do governments intervene in the foreign exchange market?

ANSWER: Governments often intervene in the currency markets to affect the exchange rate in order to achieve certain economic or political objectives Although the mechanics of such intervention vary, the general purpose of each variant is basically the same: to increase the market demand for one currency by increasing the market supply of another. Alternatively, the government can control the exchange rate directly by setting a price for its currency and then restricting access to the foreign exchange market.

SELECTED QUESTIONS FROM THE TEXT

QUESTION 4: If a foreigner purchases a U.S. government security, what happens to the supply of, and demand for, dollars?

ANSWER: In order to purchase a U.S. government security, a foreigner must first acquire dollars. This increases the demand for dollars, but has no affect on the supply of dollars.

QUESTION 7: Suppose the Fed switches to an easier monetary policy. How is this likely to affect the value of the dollar and U.S. interest rates?

ANSWER: If the Fed switches to an easier monetary policy, the value of the dollar will drop as fears of inflation rise. Short-term U.S. interest rates will initially fall but will eventually rise as investors seek to protect themselves from anticipated inflation. Long-term rates will probably rise immediately because of fears of future inflation. Over time, however, if the growth in the money supply stimulated the economy to grow more rapidly than it otherwise would, the value of the dollar could rise, and so could real interest rates.

SELECTED PROBLEMS FROM THE TEXT

QUESTION 2: Suppose the Mexican peso devalues by 75% against the dollar. What is the percentage appreciation of the dollar against the peso?

SOLUTION:

The peso is now worth 25% of its previous dollar value. This means that the dollar is now worth 4 times its previous peso value. The peso value of the dollar has, therefore, increased by 300% (the first 100% is its previous value). This can also be shown by the following calculations:

Since the Mexican peso devalues by 75% against the dollar, we have:

(a) $(e_1 - e_0)/e_0 = -0.75$
$$e_1 - e_0 = -0.75e_0$$
$$e_1 = 0.25e_0.$$

The appreciation of the dollar against the peso is shown to be:

(b) $\dfrac{(e_0 - 0.25e_0)}{0.25e_0} = \dfrac{0.75e_0}{0.25e_0} = 3$ or 300%.

QUESTION 3: Suppose the dollar appreciates by 500% against the Brazilian cruzado. How much has the cruzado devalued against the dollar?

SOLUTION:

The dollar is now worth 6 times as many cruzados as before. This means that the cruzado's dollar value is one-sixth or 16.67% of its previous value. Thus, the cruzado has devalued by 83.33%. This can be shown by the following calculations:

Since the dollar appreciated by 500% against the cruzado, we have:

(a) $(e_1 - e_0)/e_0 = 5$

$e_1 - e_0 = 5e_0$

$e_1 = 6e_0.$

The devaluation of the cruzado against the dollar is shown to be:

(b) $\dfrac{(e_0 - e_1)}{e_1} = \dfrac{e_0 - 6e_0}{6e_0} = \dfrac{-5e_0}{6e_0} = -0.8333$ or $-83.33\%.$

NEWS ITEMS

Plaza Agreement of September 1985

The Group of Five, or G-5 nations (United States, West Germany, Japan Great Britain, and France), agreed to launch a coordinated program designed to force down the dollar against other major currencies. This agreement appears to be a recent example of successful intervention that altered expectations in the foreign exchange market. Prior to the meeting at the Plaza Hotel in New York City, the dollar was depreciating, but the market seemed uncertain about the future course of U.S. monetary and fiscal policies. The dollar money supply was growing in excess of its target range, suggesting to observers that the Fed might reduce money growth.

THE INTERNATIONAL MONETARY SYSTEM

Summary: This chapter discusses the international monetary system and how the choice of a system affects currency values. It also provides a historical background of the international monetary system to enable managers to gain perspective when trying to interpret the likely consequences of new policy moves in the area of international finance.

I. Alternative Exchange Rate Systems

    A. Free Float.

        1. The market exchange rates are determined by the free play of supply and demand.

        2. The supply and demand schedules, in turn, are influenced by price level changes, interest differentials, and economic growth.

        3. In a freely floating system, market participants will adjust their current and expected future currency needs, as the economic parameters change.

        4. Thus, the exchange rate will fluctuate randomly as market participants assess and react to new information.

        5. This type of system is usually referred to as a <u>clean</u> <u>float</u>.

    B. Managed Float.

        1. Since there is greater economic uncertainty associated with a clean float, most countries actively intervene in the foreign exchange market.

        2. It is feared that a highly volatile exchange rate could imperil a nation's export industry or lead to a higher rate of inflation.

        3. Therefore, most countries with floating currencies have attempted, via central bank intervention, to smooth out exchange rate fluctuations.

        4. Such a system of managed exchange rates is also known as a <u>dirty</u> <u>float</u>.

5. Managed floats fall into three distinctive categories of central bank intervention.

    a. <u>Smoothing</u> <u>out</u> <u>daily</u> <u>fluctuations</u>. Governments following this route attempt only to preserve an orderly pattern of exchange rate changes by eliminating <u>excess</u> currency variability.

    b. <u>Leaning</u> <u>against</u> <u>the</u> <u>wind</u>. This approach is an intermedia policy designed to moderate or prevent abrupt short- and medium-term fluctuations brought about by random events whose effects are expected to be only temporary.

    c. <u>Unofficial</u> <u>pegging</u>. This strategy involves resisting fundamental upward or downward exchange rate movements fo reasons clearly unrelated to exchange market forces.

C. Target-Zone Arrangement

1. Under a target-zone system, countries adjust their national economic policies to maintain their exchange rates within a specific margin around agreed-upon, fixed central exchange rates.

2. Such a system already exists for the major European currencie participating in the <u>European</u> <u>Monetary</u> <u>System</u> (EMS).

3. Operation of the EMS began in March 1979 with its major purpo to foster monetary stability in the European Economic Community.

    a. All members of the Common Market, except Portugal, have signed the EMS Agreement; but Great Britain, Greece, and Spain have opted not to participate in the <u>joint</u> <u>float</u> th is at the heart of the system.

    b. As part of the system, the members have established the <u>European</u> <u>Currency</u> <u>Unit</u> (ECU), which is a composite curren that consists of fixed amounts of ten European currencies

    c. Each member of the joint float determines a mutually agre upon central exchange rate for its currency; each rate is denominated in currency units per ECU.

    d. These central rates attempt to establish equilibrium exchange values, but members can seek adjustments to the central rates.

    e. Central rates establish a grid of bilateral cross-exchang rates between currencies.

f. With the exception of Italy, nations participating in the joint float pledged to keep their currencies within a ±2.25% margin of the central cross-exchange rates (Italy has a ±6% margin).

D. Fixed Rate System

1. Under a fixed rate system, such as the Bretton Woods Conference, governments are committed to maintaining target exchange rates.

2. Each central bank actively buys or sells its currency in the foreign exchange market whenever its exchange rate threatens to deviate from its stated par value by more than an agreed-upon percentage.

3. Policy alternatives to a persistent balance of payments deficit:

   a. One popular means of offsetting a trade deficit is through overseas borrowing.

      (1) Short-term capital can be attracted by high interest rates. Such short-term funds, however, are highly volatile because they can be withdrawn as easily as they were brought in.

      (2) Governments often borrow long-term funds to finance payments deficits.

      (3) Generally, these are only temporary measures.

   b. Austerity brought about by reductions in government spending and in the money supply and by increases in taxes can be a permanent substitute for devaluation.

      (1) For austerity to work properly, its primary effect must be to bring about deflation. The more downward the flexibility of wages and prices, the greater the relative price change will be. As domestic prices fall (or rise less rapidly), the currency's value will be strengthened, thus lessening the need for devaluation.

      (2) A high income elasticity of imports will also help to make authority work at a lower cost in terms of lost output.

c. An alternative to austerity is the imposition of <u>wage</u> <u>and</u> <u>price</u> <u>controls</u>. This policy, however, is likely to increa pressure on the currency because it clearly indicates that the government does not possess the political will to deal with fundamental causes.

d. Many government attempt to achieve a balance of payments equilibrium by imposing <u>exchange</u> <u>controls</u>. According to this policy, nations with overvalued currencies ration foreign exchange, while countries facing revaluation, such as West Germany and Switzerland, may restrict capital inflows. In effect, government controls supersede the allocative function of the foreign exchange market.

4. In fact these controls are a major source of market imperfections, providing opportunities as well as risks for multinational corporations.

5. Some countries, such as Italy and France, have established (and abandoned) <u>two-tier</u> <u>foreign</u> <u>exchange</u> <u>markets</u>. This arrangement involves an official market (at the official rate) for current account transactions and a free market for financial (capital account) transactions.

E. The Current System of Exchange Rate Determination

1. The current monetary system is a hybrid with some currencies freely floating, major currencies floating on a managed basis, and other currencies moving in and out of various types of pegge currency relationships.

II. A Brief History of the International Monetary System

A. Gold Standard

1. Gold has been used as a medium of exchange because of its desirable properties.

a. It is durable, storable, portable, easily recognized, divisible, and easily standardized.

b. Any short-run changes in the stock of gold are limited by high production costs, thus making it costly for governments to manipulate.

c. Because gold is a commodity money, it ensures a long-run tendency toward price stability.

2. Until recently, most major currencies were on a gold standard.

    a. Each currency was valued in terms of a gold equivalent. For example, from 1821 to 1914, Great Britain maintained a fixed price of gold at £3, 17s, 10½d; the United States, over the 1834-1933 period, maintained the price of gold at $20.67 per ounce.

    b. Thus, over the period 1834-1914, the dollar 1 pound sterling exchange rate was perfectly determined.

    c. The fixed exchange rate of $4.867 per pound was referred to as the par exchange rate.

3. Since the value of gold relative to other goods and services does not change much over long periods of time, the monetary system imposed by a gold standard should ensure long-run price stability for both individual countries and groups of countries.

4. Under the classical gold standard, disturbances in the price level in one country would be wholly or partly offset by an automatic balance of payments adjustment mechanism called the price-specie-flow mechanism. This mechanism is illustrated with the following example:

    a. Given a technological advance, the productivity of the non-gold producing sector of the U.S. economy increases. This productivity, in turn, will lower the price of other goods and services relative to the price of gold, and the U.S. price level will decline (PD↓).

    b. The fall in U.S. prices will result in lower prices of U.S. exports; export prices will decline relative to import prices. Consequently, foreigners will demand more American exports (X↑) and Americans will demand fewer imports (M↓).

    c. Starting from a position of equilibrium in its international payments, the U.S. will now run a balance of payments surplus.

    d. As a result, it will experience an inflow of gold which, in turn, increases its money supply and reverse the initial decline in prices.

    e. At the same time, the other countries will experience an outflow of gold, reducing their money supplies and thus, their price levels.

f. In final equilibrium, price levels in all countries will be slightly lower than they were before due to the increases in the world wide supply of other goods and services relative to the supply of gold.

g. Exchange rates, thus, will remain fixed.

B. The Classical Gold Standard in Practice: 1821-1914

1. In 1821, England returned to the gold standard.

2. From 1821-1880, more and more countries joined the gold standard.

3. By 1880, the majority of the nations of the world were on some form of sold standard.

4. Because of the costs of maintaining a pure gold standard, most nations evolved substitutes (such as, government-issued paper money and privately produced fiduciary money for pure commodity money and attempted to shield domestic economic activity from external disturbance.

5. Many nations frequently followed policies of sterilizing gold flows; that is, governments attempted to neutralize the effects of gold flows on the domestic money supply by open-market purchases or sales of domestic securities. The result is a managed gold standard.

C. The Gold Exchange Standard: 1925-1931

1. The gold standard broke down during World War I and was succeeded by a period managed fiduciary money.

2. Under this system, also called the Gold Exchange Standard, the United States and England could hold only gold reserves, but other nations could hold both gold and dollars or pounds as reserves.

3. In 1931, England departed from gold in face of massive gold and capital flows, and the Gold Exchange Standard was finished.

D. The Bretton Woods System: 1946-1971

1. Under the Bretton Woods system initiated in 1944 and actually implemented in 1946, each government pledged to maintain a fixed or pegged exchange rate for its currency vis-a-vis the dollar or gold.

2. Since one ounce of gold was set equal to $35.00, fixing a currency's gold price was equivalent to setting its exchange rate relative to the dollar.

3. In addition, the exchange rate was allowed to fluctuate only within 1% of its stated par value.

4. Fixed exchange rates were maintained by official intervention in the foreign exchange market. This intervention took place in the form of purchases and sales of dollars by foreign central banks against their own currencies whenever the supply caused rates to deviate from the agreed-upon par value.

5. These aspects of the system had important practical implications:

   a. The stability of exchange rates removed a great deal of uncertainty from international trade and investment transactions, thus promoting their growth for the benefit of all the participants.

   b. The functioning of the system imposed a degree of discipline on the participating nation's economic policies.

   c. Because of government intervention, a country's reserves would soon become depleted and force authorities to change economic policies in order to eliminate the source of the reserve draining deficit. The reduction in the money supply and the adoption of restrictive policies would reduce the country's inflation, thus bringing it in line with the rest of the world.

   d. Changes in fixed rates were permitted only in the case of fundamental disequilibrium.

   e. The reluctance of governments to adjust currency values or to make the necessary economic adjustments to ratify the current values of their currencies led to periodic foreign exchange crisis.

   f. The maintenance of price stability under the Bretton Woods system was largely the responsibility of the United States. As long as the system remained intact, all currencies were subject to the same rate of inflation as the U.S. dollar.

   g. As long as the U.S. kept the price of gold at $35.00 per ounce, it would stabilize prices worldwide.

6. The Bretton Woods system collapsed along with the dissolution of the gold standard because the U.S. was derelict in its responsibility. There are two related reasons for the collapse of the fixed exchange rate system.

   a. Due to inflation which was caused by financing the escalating war in Vietnam, the U.S. could not maintain the price of gold at $35.00 an ounce.

   b. In addition, some countries (primarily West Germany, Japan, Switzerland) refused to accept the inflation that a fixed exchange rate with the dollar would have imposed on them. Thus, the dollar sharply depreciated relative to the currencies of the three countries.

D. The Post-Bretton Woods System: 1971-1985

   1. In December 1971, under the Smithsonian Agreement, the dollar was devalued to $38.00 an ounce of gold, and other currencies were revalued by agreed on amounts vis-a-vis the dollar.

   2. After months of such last-ditch efforts to set new fixed rates, the world officially adopted the floating rate system in 1973.

   3. October 1973 marked the beginning of successful efforts by OPEC to raise the price of oil. By 1974, oil prices had quadrupled.

   4. Nations responded in various ways to the vast shift of resources to the oil-exporting countries.

      a. The U.S. resorted to transferring resources to those hardest hit by high oil prices. To pay for this resource transfer, more money was printed instead of raising taxes. The result was high inflation, economic dislocation, a misallocation of resources, and a balance-of-payments deficit.

      b. Other nations, such as Japan, allowed the price of oil to rise to its market level. Resource transfers were paid for with taxation or additional government debt. As a result, Japan experienced a balance-of-payments surplus.

   5. These surpluses, in turn, were recycled to the debtor nations setting the stage for the international debt crisis of 1980.

6. During 1977-1978, the value of the dollar plummeted, and U.S. balance -of-payments difficulties were exacerbated as the Carter administration pursued an expansionary monetary policy that was significantly out of line with other strong currencies.

7. The turnaround came on October 6, 1979, when the Fed announced a major change in its conduct of monetary policy. From here on, it would focus its efforts on stabilizing the money supply even at the expense of greater interest rate variability.

8. The primary reason for the shift in Fed policy was to curb inflation and inflationary expectations. This shift, in fact, had its desired effect on both the rate of inflation and the value of the U.S. dollar.

9. During the 1981-1984 term of the Reagan administration, inflation declined and the dollar rebounded extraordinarily. This rebound has been attributed to vigorous economic expansion in the U.S. and to high real interest rates.

E. The Sinking Dollar: 1985-1988

1. In March 1985, the dollar hit its peak and then began a long down-hill slide.

2. This slide is largely attributed to changes in government policy and relative economic performances.

    a. Most important was the slowdown in U.S. economic growth relative to growth in the rest of the world.

    b. This factor was compounded by the effects of foreign exchange market intervention and confusing signals concerning U.S. monetary and fiscal policies.

3. By September 1985, the dollar had fallen about 15% from its March high. Later in that month, the Group of Five met to defuse protectionist measures associated with the U.S. trade deficit.

4. As a result of this policy the value of the dollar slid so fast in 1986 that other countries apparently reversed their policies.

5. By early 1987, the U.S. and its counterparts had enough. Meeting in Paris in February, the Group of Seven agreed to an ambitious plan to slow the dollar's fall.

6. While the U.S. seemed to remain committed to the Louvre
   Accord, hardly anyone else did. The failure the Louvre Acco[rd]
   provides further proof that currency manipulation is fruitle[ss]
   in a world of sovereign states.

III. European Monetary System (EMS)

   A. The EMS illustrates that the exchange rate stability afforded b[y]
      any target-zone arrangement requires a coordination of economic
      policy objectives and practices.

   B. By early 1988, the EMS realigned the values of its currencies 1[1]
      times despite heavy central bank intervention.

   C. Thus, EMS failed to provide the currency stability it promised.
      The basic reasons for the failure of the EMS include:

      1. Disagreement of economic objectives among member countries.

      2. Unwillingness of countries to permit exchange rate
         considerations to override political priorities.

   D. The experience of the EMS also demonstrates once again that
      foreign exchange market intervention not supported by a change [in]
      a nation's monetary policy, nor coordinated with the interventi[on]
      activities of other central banks, has only a limited influence
      on exchange rates.

KEY TERMS

Free or Clean Float

Managed or Dirty Float

European Monetary System (EMS)

Joint Float

European Currency Unit (ECU)

Bilateral Cross-Exchange Rates

Fixed Rate System

Income Elasticity of Imports

Two-Tier Foreign Exchange Mark[et]

Gold Standard

Par Exchange Rate

Price-Specie-Flow Mechanism

Managed Gold Standard

Pegged Exchange Rate

Plaza Agreement

Louvre Accord

CONCEPTUAL QUESTIONS

QUESTION 1: Compare and contrast the fixed rate system, the free float, and the managed float.

ANSWER: Under a fixed-rate system, governments are committed to maintaining target exchange rates. Under the free float, exchange rates are determined by the interaction of currency supplies and demands without any government intervention. Under the managed float, the government actively intervenes in the foreign exchange market in order to reduce the economic uncertainty associated with a clean float.

QUESTION 2: What is a target-zone arrangement?

ANSWER: Under a target-zone system, countries adjust their national economic policies to maintain their exchange rates within a specific margin around agreed-upon, fixed exchange rates. Such a system already exists for the major European currencies participating in the European Monetary System (EMS).

SELECTED QUESTIONS FROM THE TEXT

QUESTION 5: Is a floating rate system more inflationary than a fixed-rate system?

ANSWER: To the extent that floating exchange rates allow monetary authorities to pursue more inflationary policies, then a floating rate system can be more inflationary. However, this is an indirect effect, the direct cause of inflation being rapid money expansion. According to PPP, the direction of causation runs from price level changes to exchange rate changes, not vice versa.

QUESTION 10: Why did the Bretton Woods system break down? What lessons can economists draw from the breakdown of the Bretton Woods system?

ANSWER: Adjusting monetary growth rates is the principal way to stabilize exchange rates. For example, raising the value of the dollar relative to the yen requires tightening U.S. monetary policy relative to Japanese monetary policy. The experience of Bretton Woods and similar experiments demonstrates that conscious and explicit coordination of monetary policies among sovereign authorities is difficult. The problem stems from the inability of sovereign authorities to coordinate their monetary growth rates. An agreement to stabilize the dollar at, say, 150 yen would be relatively easy if it did not entail interdependent monetary policies, robbing the Federal Reserve, or the Bank of Japan, or both, of important degrees of monetary freedom.

Both Japan and the United States have their own targets for growth and inflation and their own independent assessment of the macroeconomic policies required to attain those targets. Except by coincidence, independent policies and preferences will not mesh at a stable exchange rate. Given clashing preferences, the only alternatives to the "chaos" of floating are:

    (1) One side persuades the other to change its policies;

    (2) One side subordinates its policies to those of the other; or

    (3) Both sides subordinate their monetary policies to an external mechanism, such as a gold standard.

Absent (3), "international monetary reform" is the search for new ways to implement (1) or (2), or some combination. We saw that Bretton Woods collapsed because the subordination it entailed was intolerable to the United State. That is, the United States refused to follow economic policies that would maintain the value of gold at $35 an ounce. The basic lesson from Bretton Woods, therefore, is that stabilizing exchange rates requires dependence and subordination, not the freedom for everybody to do their own thing. But instead of changing policies to stay with the Bretton Woods system, the major countries simply dropped the system.

QUESTION 11: What lessons can economists draw from the exchange rate experience of the European Monetary System?

ANSWER: Exchange rate stability requires that monetary policies be coordinated and geared towards maintaining exchange rate parities. The slow progress of the European community with respect to the EMS and policy coordination exemplifies the difficulties of achieving agreements on the many facets of economic policy making. Implementing target zones on a wider scale would be all the more difficult. Differences in preferences, policy objectives, and economic structures account in part for these difficulties.

    More fundamentally, however, coordination of macroeconomic policies will not necessarily benefit all participant countries equally, and those that benefit the most may not be willing to compensate those that benefit least. In the EMS, Germany is less inflation-prone than the other members and is reluctant to cooperate at the risk of increasing its inflation rate.

    Another lesson is that in target-zone arrangements such as the EMS, a disproportionately large share of the adjustment burden will fall on the "weak" currency countries. Countries with appreciating currencies, trade surpluses, and increasing reserves are less prone to adjust than countries with depreciating currencies, trade deficits, or reserve losses. The convergence of inflation rates among the EMS countries supports this view. An equal sharing of the adjustment burden implies that inflation rates among member nations would converge to the average rate.

    West Germany, however, has maintained a domestic monetary target of low or zero inflation, and often has refused to alter domestic monetary policy because of exchange rate considerations. Because of Germany's economic importance, the other member countries have had to adjust their domestic policies or their exchange rates to remain competitive in international markets. As a result, inflation rates have tended to converge toward Germany's lower rate.

NEWS ITEMS

Plaza Agreement of September 1985

The Group of Five, or G-5 nations (United States, West Germany, Japan, Great Britain, and France), agreed to launch a coordinated program designed to force down the dollar against other major currencies. This agreement appears to be a recent example of successful intervention that altered expectations in the foreign exchange market. Prior to the meeting at the Plaza Hotel in New York City, the dollar was depreciating, but the market seemed uncertain about the future course of U.S. monetary and fiscal policies. The dollar money supply was growing in excess of its target range, suggesting to observers that the Fed might reduce money growth.

Louvre Accord of February 1987

Meeting in Paris in February, the United States, Japan, West Germany, France, Great Britain, Canada, and Italy--also knows as the Group of Seven, or G-7 nations--agreed to an ambitious plan to slow the dollar's fall. The Louvre Accord called for the G-7 nations to support the falling dollar by pegging exchange rates within a narrow, undisclosed range, while they also moved to bring their economic policies into line.

THE BALANCE OF PAYMENTS AND
INTERNATIONAL ECONOMIC LINKAGES

Summary: This chapter presents the financial and real linkages between t
domestic and world economies and examines how these linkages affect
business viability. It also identifies the basic forces underlying the
flows of goods, services, and capital between countries and relates these
flows to key political, economic, and cultural factors.

I. Balance-Of-Payments Categories

    A. The BOP catalogs the flow of economic transactions between the
        residents of a given country and the residents of other countries
        during a certain period of time.

        1. These transactions include trade in goods and services,
            transfer payments, loans, and short-term and long-term
            investments. The BOP measures flows rather than stocks. Tha
            is, only changes in asset holdings and liabilities, and not
            the level of these items, are presented in this statement. I
            this sense, the BOP for a country is very similar to a
            statement of sources and uses of funds for a firm.

        2. Currency inflows are recorded as credits, and outflows are
            recorded as debits. Credits show up with a plus sign, and
            debits have a minus sign.

        3. There are three major BOP categories:

            a. Current Account, which records flows of goods, services,
                and transfers.

            b. Capital Account, which shows public and private investmen
                and lending activities.

            c. Official Reserves Account, which measures changes in
                holdings of gold and foreign currencies by official
                monetary institutions.

        4. Exports of goods and services are credits; imports of goods a
            services are debits.

        5. Interest and dividends are treated as services because they
            represent payment for the use of capital.

6. Capital inflows appear as credits because the nation is selling (exporting) to foreigners valuable assets--buildings, land, stocks, bonds, and other financial claims--and receiving cash in return (source of funds--increase in external purchasing power).

7. Capital outflows show up as debits because they represent purchases (imports) of valuable foreign assets.

8. The increase in a nation's official reserves also shows up as a debit item because the purchase of gold and other reserve assets is equivalent to importing these assets.

B. Current Account

1. The balance on current account reflects the net flow of goods, services, and unilateral transfers (gifts).

   a. It includes exports and imports of merchandise (trade balance), military transactions, and service transactions (invisibles).

   b. The service account includes investment income (interest and dividends), tourism, financial charges (banking, insurance), and transportation expenses (shipping, air travel).

   c. Unilateral transfers include pensions, remittances, and other transfers for which no specific services are rendered.

C. Capital Account

1. Capital account transactions affect a nation's wealth and net creditor position.

2. These transactions are classified as either portfolio, direct, or short-term investments.

   a. Portfolio investments are purchases of financial assets with a maturity greater than one year.

   b. Short-term investments involve securities with a maturity of less than one year.

   c. Direct investments are those where management control is exerted.

3. Government borrowing and lending is included in the balance of capital account.

D. Official Reserves Account

1. The change in official reserves measures a nation's surplus c deficit on its current and capital account transactions by netting reserve liabilities from reserve assets.

2. For example, a surplus will lead to an increase in official holdings of foreign currencies and/or gold; a deficit will normally cause a reduction in these assets.

3. International reserves consist of gold and convertible foreig exchange.

4. An increase in any of these assets constitute a use of funds.

5. A decrease in reserve assets implies a source of funds. This drop may occur, for instance, when a nation sells gold to acquire foreign currencies that it can then use to meet a deficit in its BOP.

E. Balance of Payments Measures

1. Basic Balance

   a. It focuses on transactions that are considered to be fundamental to the economic health of a currency.

   b. Thus, it includes the balance on current account and long-term capital, but it excludes such items as short-term capital flows that are heavily influenced by temporary factors--short-run monetary policy, changes in interest differentials, and anticipations of currency fluctuations.

2. Net Liquidity Balance

   a. It is used to measure the change in private domestic borrowing or lending that is required to keep payments in balance without adjusting official reserves.

   b. Non-liquid, private short-term capital flows and errors a omissions are included in the balance, while liquid asset and liabilities are excluded.

3. Official Reserve Transactions Balance

   a. It is sued to measure the adjustment required in official reserves to achieve BOp equilibrium.

   b. The assumption here is that official transactions are different from private transactions.

F. In May 1976, the U.S. Department of Commerce shifted to a new BOP format, based on a federal advisory committee's report. The new format includes only the balance on current account. All other BOP measures must be constructed by individual users.

G. The reason for this shift to a new BOP format include:

1. The usual measurement concepts no longer accurately reflect the real economic position of the U.S.

2. The increasing complexity of international financial flows, especially since the buildup of reserves by OPEC.

H. Limitations of the Accounts

1. Changes in the official reserve balance, which is supposed to be the most comprehensive measurement, may reflect investment flows as well as central bank intervention in the foreign exchange markets.

2. The basic balance, intended to serve a sa rough indicator of longer-term trends in the U.S. BOP, classifies all direct investment transactions as long-term capital flows. However, many of these flows are short-term and may be reversed. Moreover, many short-term revolving credits are more akin to long-term credits, while a long-term investment may be close to maturity and serve as a short-term vehicle.

3. The net liquidity balance, which is supposed to indicate potential pressures on the dollar, has limited usefulness because of the difficulty in separating liquid and non-liquid claims and liabilities.

    a. For example, bank loans are treated as non-liquid even though they might have to be paid off quickly.

    b. Also, the net liquidity balance was intended to provide a broad indication of pressures on the dollar by revealing pressures on U.S. primary reserve assets. With the dollar no longer convertible into these assets, this purpose and the related measure are no longer applicable.

4. The balance on current account is being retained because imports and exports can be measured fairly accurately.

I. Missing Numbers

    1. Errors and omissions

       By definition, the net change in official reserves must be equal to the overall balance (which is the sum of short-term capital account and the basic balance). Given the double-entry system of accounting in the BOP, the net of the accounts included in any balance must be equal to the net of the remaining accounts.

    2. These are transactions that have not been officially recorded.

    3. Figures that are off by $100 billion indicate that business people should exercise a degree of caution greater even than that normally employed with the products of economists.

II. The International Flow of Goods, Services, and Capital

    A. Domestic Savings and Investment and the Capital Account

       1. The national income and product accounts provide an accounting framework for recording our national product (Y) and showing how its components are affected by international transactions. It can be shown that national income is either spent on consumption (C) or savings (S).

National Income = Consumption + Savings
$$Y = C + S \tag{1}$$

       2. Similarly, national expenditure (E), which is the total amount that the nation spends on goods and services, can be divided into spending on consumption and spending on domestic real investment (I_d). Real investment refers to plant and equipment, R&D, and other expenditures designed to increase the nation's productive capacity.

National Spending = Consumption + Investment
$$E = C + I_d \tag{2}$$

       3. Subtracting equation (2) from equation (1) yields a new identity:

National Income - National Spending = Savings - Investment
$$Y - E = S - I_d \tag{3}$$

          a. This identity says that if a nation's income exceeds its spending, then savings will exceed domestic investment, resulting a capital surplus.

36

b. This surplus must be invested overseas (I_f). Thus,

Foreign Investment = Savings - Domestic Investment
$$I_f = S - I_d$$

c. Net foreign investment equals the nation's net public and private capital outflows plus the increase in official reserves.

d. The net private and public capital outflows equal the capital account deficit, while the net increase in official reserves equals the balance on official reserves account.

e. In a freely floating exchange rate system, excess savings will equal the capital account deficit, and a national savings deficit will equal the capital account surplus. This borrowing finances the excess of national spending over national income.

B. The Link Between the Current and Capital Accounts

1. Beginning with national product, if spending on domestic goods and services (D) is subtracted, the remaining goods and services must equal exports (X), or

$$Y - D = X.$$

2. Similarly, if spending on domestic goods and services is subtracted from total expenditures, the remaining spending must be on imports (M), or

$$E - D = M.$$

3. Combining these two identities leads to another national income identity:

National Income - National Spending = Exports - Imports
$$Y - E = X - M \qquad (4)$$

4. Equation (4) states that the current account surplus ($X - M > 0$) arises when national output exceeds domestic expenditures; similarly, a current account deficit ($X - M < 0$) is due to domestic expenditures exceeding domestic output.

5. Combining equation (4) with equation (3) yields a new identity:

Savings - Investment = Exports - Imports
$$S - I_d = X - M \qquad (5)$$

6. According to equation (5), if a nation's savings exceed its investment, then that nation will run a current account surplus.

7. Furthermore, if $S - I_d = I_f$, then

   Net Foreign Investment = Exports - Imports
   $$I_f = X - M \qquad ($$

8. Equation (6) states that the balance on the current account must equal the net capital outflow; that is, any foreign exchange earned by selling abroad (X) must either be spent on imports or exchanged for claims against foreigners. The net amount of those IOUs equals the nation's capital outflow.

   a. If the current account is in surplus, then the nation must be a net exporter of capital.

   b. Similarly, if the current account is in deficit, then the nation must be a net capital importer.

9. Another interpretation of equation (6) is that the excess of goods and services brought over goods and services produced domestically must be acquired through foreign trade and must be financed through an equal amount of borrowing from abroad (the capital account surplus and/or official reserves deficit).

10. Rearranging equation (6) yields a new identity:

    $$X - M - I_f = 0 \qquad (7$$

11. Equation (7) states that in a freely floating system, the current account balance and the capital account balance must exactly offset each other. With government intervention in the foreign exchange market, the sum of the current account balance plus the capital account balance plus the balance on official reserves account must be zero.

12. Thus, a nation cannot reduce its current account deficit or increase its current account surplus unless two conditions are met:

    a. Raise national product relative to national spending, and

    b. Increase savings relative to domestic investment.

C. Government Budget Deficits and Current Account Deficits

1. If government spending and taxation is separated from the private sectors, the effect of a government deficit on the current account deficit can be seen.

2. National spending (E) can be divided into household spending plus private investment (I_d) plus government spending (G). Household spending, in turn, equals national income (Y) less the sum of private savings (S) and taxes (T). Combining these terms yields the following identity:

National = Household + Private + Government
Spending   Spending   Investment   Spending

$$E = Y - (S + T) + I_d + G \qquad (8)$$

3. Rearranging equation (8) yields a new expression for excess spending:

National - National = (Investment - Savings) + Government
Spending   Product   Budget Deficit

$$E - Y = (I_d - S) + (G - T) \qquad (9)$$

4. Equation (9) states that excess national spending is composed of two parts:

   a. The excess of private domestic investment over private savings ($I_d - S$).

   b. The total government (federal, state, local) deficit (G - T).

5. Since $E - Y = I_f$, equation (9) also states that the nation's excess spending equals its net borrowing from abroad.

6. Rearranging and combining equation (3) and equation (9) provides a new accounting identity:

Current-Account Balance = Savings Surplus - Government Budget
                                                Deficit

$$X - M = (S - I_d) - (G - T) \qquad (10)$$

7. Equation (10) reveals that a nation's current account balance is identically equal to its private savings-investment balance less the government budget deficit.

   a. According to this identity, a national running current account deficit is not saving enough to finance its private investment and government budget deficit.

        b.   Conversely, a nation running a current account surplus is
            saving more than is needed to finance its private investme
            and government deficit.

8.   In general, a current account deficit represents a decision to
     consume, both publicly and privately, and to invest more than
     the nation is currently producing.

9.   The important implication is that steps taken to correct the
     current account deficit can only be effective if they also
     change private savings, private investment, and/or the
     government deficit. Policies or events that fail to affect bc
     sides of the relationship set forth in equation (9) will not
     alter the current account deficit.

III. Coping With The Current Account Deficit

A.   Currency Depreciation

1.   According to the disequilibrium theories of the exchange
     rate, sluggish adjustment of nominal prices is the key to
     effectively devalue a country's currency.

2.   By contrast, the equilibrium theory of the exchange rate
     predicts that there is no simple relation between the
     exchange rate and the current account balance.

        a.   Trade deficits do not cause currency depreciation, nor
            does currency depreciation by itself help reduce a trad
            deficit.

        b.   In strict economic terms, the equilibrium theory say th
            a nation cannot change its terms of trade by changing t
            unit of account.

3.   Currency devaluation will only work if some mechanism is in
     place that leads to a rise in savings, a cut in investments
     or a reduction in the government budget deficit. Otherwise
     any rise in exports is offset by the adverse effects of
     higher-priced imports.

B.   Protectionism

1.   Another response to a current account deficit is the
     imposition of tariffs, quotas, or other forms of restraint
     against foreign imports.

a. A _tariff_ is essentially a tax that is imposed on a foreign product sold in a country. Its purpose is to increase the price of the product thereby discouraging its purchase and encouraging the purchase of a substitute, domestically produced product.

b. A _quota_ specifies the quantity of particular products that can be imported to a country, typically an amount that is considerably less than the amount currently being imported. By restricting the supply relative to the demand, the quota caused the price of foreign products to rise.

c. In both cases, the results are ultimately a rise in the price of products consumers buy, an erosion of purchasing power, and a collective decline in the standard of living.

2. These results present a powerful argument against selective trade restrictions as a means of correcting a nation's trade imbalance. In fact, such restrictions do not work.

a. That is, either other imports rise or exports fall.

b. This conclusion follows from the basic national income accounting identity set forth in equation (5):

$$S - I_d = X - M.$$

c. Equation (5) says that a $1.00 reduction in imports will lead to a $1.00 decrease in exports unless savings or investment behavior changes.

3. The mechanism that brings about this result depends upon the basic market forces that shape the supply and demand for currencies in the foreign exchange market.

C. One approach that will eliminate a current account deficit is to forbid foreigners from owning domestic assets.

1. By ending foreign capital inflows, the available supply of capital is reduced which, in turn, raises real domestic interest rates.

2. Higher interest rates will stimulate savings and cause domestic investment to fall.

3. The outcome will be a lance between savings/investment and elimination of excess domestic spending that caused the current account deficit in the first place.

4. Although such an approach would work, it is considered to result in slower economic growth and, thus, too high a pric to pay to eliminate a current account deficit.

D. One rational for attempting to eliminate a current account deficit is that such a deficit leads to unemployment. The reas for this rationale is based on the notion that imported goods a services are substitutes for domestic goods and services and, hence, costing domestic jobs. Thus, if imports are reduced, domestic production and employment would be raised.

1. If a country buys fewer foreign goods and services, it will also demand less foreign exchange.

2. This result, in turn, will raise the value of the domestic currency, thereby reducing exports and encouraging the purchase of other imports.

3. Jobs are saved in some industries, but other jobs are lost the decline in exports and rise in other imports.

4. As a result, the net impact of a trade deficit or surplus o jobs should be nil.

E. Whether a current account deficit or surplus is viewed as a problem or a solution to a problem depends on the national preferences, to which trade flows have adjusted in a timely manner.

F. The long-term consequences of running a current account deficit can be summarized as follows:

1. If the current account deficit and resulting capital accoun surplus finances productive investment, then the nation is better off, the returns from these added investments will service the foreign debts and leave something extra.

2. Conversely, a capital account surplus that finances consumption will increase the nation's well-being today at the expense of its future well-being.

IV. Appendix 4A: The Economic and Political Consequences of Devaluation

A. There are three basic theories of the effects of devaluation on nation's economy and of the mechanism by which it eliminates payments deficits: The elasticities approach, the absorption approach, and the monetary approach.

B. Elasticities Approach

   1. The elasticities approach focuses on the effects that relative
       price changes, brought about by devaluation, have on
       consumption and production.

   2. Devaluation will increase the local (domestic) currency prices
       of traded goods (exports, imports, and import-competing goods)
       relative to non-traded goods and services. This increase
       causes consumers to substitute non-traded goods for traded
       goods, particularly imports; and it releases some output for
       exports. At the same time, the higher profitability of the
       export and import-competing sectors of the economy (due to
       higher prices) will draw more resources into those industries.

   3. According to the elasticities approach, devaluation will
       improve a nation's balance of trade if the <u>Marshall-Lerner</u>
       condition is met, that is if . . .

                        If the elasticity of
                        demand for imports plus
                        the foreign elasticity of
                        demand for the nation's
                        exports exceeds unity.

   4. The Marshall-Lerner condition says that the change in the
       quantity of imports and exports demanded must be sufficiently
       great to offset, following devaluation, the lower foreign
       currency price of a nation's exports. This offset can occur
       through a large reduction in imports, a significant expansion
       of exports, or (as is normally the case) through a combination
       of both.

C. Absorption Approach

   1. The absorption approach shifts attention from individual
       sectors to the overall economy.

   2. According to this approach, any improvement in the balance of
       current account must cause an increase in the difference
       between total output (Y) and total domestic expenditures (E).
       This conclusion follows from the national income accounting
       identity, as shown in equation (4):

$$E + X = Y + M. \tag{1A}$$

   3. Equation (1A) states that total "absorption" of goods and
       services must equal the aggregate amount of goods and services
       available.

4. If equation (1A) is rearranged to yield the identity shown i equation (2A),

$$X - M = Y - A,$$ (2.

then it can be seen that:

a. A trade surplus $(X - M > 0)$ arises when national output greater than domestic expenditures $(Y - A > 0)$.

b. A trade deficit $(X - M < 0)$ is due to domestic expenditures exceeding domestic output $(Y - A < 0)$.

5. When underemployed resources exit, output can increase withou causing inflation if there are no bottlenecks in the economy. Therefore, devaluation is likely to be most successful if unemployment and excess capacity are present. Devaluation ca then correct a trade deficit by expanding national output, with at least some of the additional output going to increase exports and import substitutes.

6. With full employment, domestic expenditures must be reduced. Otherwise, devaluation will not succeed even if the trade elasticities meet the Marshall-Lerner condition.

D. Monetary Approach

1. The monetary approach concentrates on the demand for money balances.

2. An excess demand for goods and services (a trade deficit) reflects an excess supply of money.

3. The monetary approach emphasizes the analytical equivalence between a devaluation and a reduction in the real value of th money supply. Devaluation reduces the real value of the mone supply because of price increases for traded goods and services.

4. In this view, a devaluation works by causing the public to reduce its spending in order to restore the real value of its money balances and other financial assets. This reduction in expenditures will improve the BOP.

5. However, if the monetary authorities expand the domestic mone supply following a devaluation, the favorable effects of the devaluation will be undermined.

E. The three approaches should be viewed as complementary to each other rather than as competitive.

F. Furthermore, all three of the approaches imply distributional effects of a devaluation due to the change in relative prices between traded and non-traded goods.

1. With underemployment of resources initially, real national income should rise, although factors of production used in the traded goods sector may benefit at the expense of other factors. Furthermore, consumers will face higher prices for traded goods.

2. If the economy is at full employment before devaluation, then the nation's real consumption should decline.

3. Under either situation, groups such as strong labor unions or oligopolistic industries that benefited from the disequilibrium set of prices may attempt to maintain their real incomes by raising wages or prices (inflation).

4. These attempts can succeed and improve the balance of trade only if the rest of society is willing to accept a lower share of real income. Otherwise, the initial disequilibrium will be restored, and will be necessary to either devalue again or reduce aggregate demand through deflationary policies.

KEY TERMS

Balance of Payments
Current Account
Capital Account
Official Reserves Account
Basic Balance
Net Liquidity Balance
Official Reserves Transactions Balance
Errors and Omissions
Current Account Surplus
Current Account Deficit
National Income or National Product
National Expenditures
Real Investment
Capital Surplus
Foreign Investment

Imports
Exports
Current Account Surplus
Current Account Deficit
Net Foreign Investment
Net Exporter
Net Capital Importer
Government Budget Deficit
Currency Depreciation
Tariff
Quota
Elasticities Approach
Marshall-Lerner Condition
Absorption Approach
Monetary Approach
Distributional Effects

CONCEPTUAL QUESTIONS

QUESTION 1:   What is the capital account generally made up of?

ANSWER: The capital account records all public and private capital investments between countries including:
(1)   portfolio investments which are purchases of financial assets with a maturity greater than one year;
(2)   short-term investments which involve securities with a maturity of less than one year;
(3)   direct investments which exert management control.
Government borrowing and lending is included in the balance on capital account.

QUESTION 2:   What is meant by a current account deficit/current account surplus?

ANSWER: A current account deficit arises when domestic expenditures excee domestic output; similarly, a current account surplus arises when nationa' output exceeds domestic expenditures.

SELECTED QUESTIONS FROM THE TEXT

QUESTION 1:   In a freely floating exchange rate system, if the current account is running a deficit, what are the consequences for the nation's balance on capital account and its overall balance of payments?

ANSWER: In a freely floating exchange rate system, the nation's balance c payments must always be zero.   Consequently, if the current account is running a deficit, the capital account must be running a surplus of the same size.   Overall, international payments will still be in balance.

QUESTION 5:   How does a trade deficit affect the current-account balance?

ANSWER: There is no necessary relation between a trade account deficit an the balance on current account.   This is because the current account includes both the trade account and the service account.   The current account could show a deficit, a surplus, or a zero balance, depending on what happens to the balance on the service account.

QUESTION 9:   What happens to Mexico's ability to repay its foreign loans i the United States restricts imports of Mexican agricultural produce?

ANSWER: A repayment of Mexico's foreign loans is equivalent to an export of capital from Mexico.   In order for Mexico to run a capital account deficit, it must run a current account surplus.   Anything that reduces Mexico's ability to export, also reduces its ability to repay its debts. In effect, keeping out Mexican goods while demanding repayment is equivalent to firing a worker and then demanding that he repay all the money he has borrowed from the company.   Without a job, he cannot repay th money.

PROBLEM 1: The following transactions (expressed in $ billions) take place during a year. Calculate the U.S. merchandise trade, current account, capital account, and unofficial balances.

    a. The United States exports $300 of goods and receives payment in the form of foreign demand deposits abroad.

    b. The United States imports $225 of goods and pays for them by drawing down its foreign demand deposits.

    c. The United States pays $15 to foreigners in dividends drawn on U.S. demand deposits here.

    d. American tourists spend $30 overseas, using traveler's checks drawn on U.S. banks here.

    e. Americans buy foreign stocks with $60, using foreign demand deposits held abroad.

    f. The U.S. government sell $45 in gold for foreign demand deposits abroad.

    g. In a currency support operation, the U.S. government uses its foreign demand deposits to purchase $8 from private foreigners in the United States.

SOLUTION:

    U.S. balance of payments accounts:

Exports	Imports
a. merchandise: $300 in goods	b. $225 in goods and services
c. $15 payment of dividends	d. $30 in tourist services

Balance on current account: + $30

Capital Outflows	Capital Inflows
a. $300 increase in foreign demand deposits	b. $225 decrease in foreign demand deposits
e. $60 increase in U.S. holdings of foreign stocks	c. $15 increase in foreign-owned U.S. demand deposits
g. $8 decrease in foreign-owned demand deposits	e. $60 decrease in foreign demand deposits
	d. $30 increase in foreign-owned traveler checks drawn on U.S. banks

Balance on capital account: - $38

Reserve Inflows	Reserve Outflows
f. $45 in gold sales	f. $45 increase in foreign demand deposits
	g. $8 decrease in foreign demand deposits

Balance on official reserves: + $8

CHAPTER 5

THE FOREIGN EXCHANGE MARKET

Summary: The primary function of the foreign exchange markets is to facilitate international trade and investments. Thus, it is important to understand the operation and mechanism of these markets in order to make sound decisions in international financial management. In this chapter, the organization, institutional characteristics and mechanics of the spot and forward exchange markets, as well as currency futures and options markets, are examined.

I. Organization of the Foreign Exchange Market

   A. The foreign exchange market permits the transfer of purchasing power by trading one currency for another.

   B. Most currency transactions are channeled through the worldwide interbank market, the wholesale market in which major banks trade with each other.

   C. In the spot market, currencies are traded for immediate delivery, which usually takes place within two business days after the transaction has been concluded.

   D. In the forward market, contracts are made to buy and sell foreign currencies for future delivery.

   E. The foreign exchange market is not a physical market. It is a network of banks, foreign exchange brokers, and dealers whose function it is to bring buyers and sellers of foreign currencies together.

   F. The major participants in the foreign exchange market are the large commercial banks; foreign exchange brokers in the inter-bank market; commercial customers, primarily multinational corporations; and central banks.

   G. Only the head offices or regional offices of the major commercial banks are actually the market makers.

   H. With a worldwide volume of foreign exchange transactions ranging up to $1 trillion daily or $250 trillion annually, the foreign exchange market is by far the largest financial market in the world.

II. The Spot Market

A. Spot Quotations

1. In almost all major newspapers, up to four different quotes o prices of the currencies most actively traded are displayed. These include the spot price and the 30-day, 90-day, and 180-day forward prices.

2. Quotes which are for trades among dealers in the interbank market are expressed either in:

   a. American <u>terms</u>, i.e., the amount of U.S. dollars it will take to buy one unit of foreign currency (e.g., $0.56/DM).

   b. European <u>terms</u>, i.e., the amount of foreign currency it will take to buy one unit of the U.S. dollar (e.g., DM 1.80/$).

3. With the exception of the U.K. and Irish exchange rates, all foreign currencies are expressed in <u>American terms</u>.

4. When dealing with nonbank customers, banks in most countries use a system of <u>direct quotation</u>. That is, the price of a foreign currency is expressed in terms of the home currency. For example, in West Germany the U.S. dollar would be quoted at DM 1.80.

5. An exception to this rule is Great Britain which quotes the value of the British pound in terms of the foreign currency (e.g., £1 = $1.8470). This method of <u>indirect quotation</u> is also used in the U.S. for domestic purposes and for the Canadian dollar.

6. Foreign exchange rates are always quoted in pairs because a dealer usually does not know whether a potential customer is buying or selling foreign currency in the market.

   a. The first rate is the buy, or bid, price.

   b. The second rate is the sell, or ask or offer, rate.

   c. In practice, dealers will only quote the last two digits of the decimal of a foreign currency.

7. The profit banks realize from their currency transactions result from the <u>spread</u> between the bid and ask prices of the currencies.

8. The cross-rate for a currency other than the dollar is the exchange rate between two given currencies. For example, if the German mark is quoted in U.S. dollars as $0.50/DM and the British pound is quoted in U.S. dollars as $1.80/£, then the cross-rate is

$$\frac{DM}{£} = \frac{DM}{\$} \times \frac{\$}{£}$$

$$\frac{DM}{£} = (1/\$0.50) \times (\$1.80)$$

$$\frac{DM}{£} = 3.60$$

or £1 = DM 3.60

9. A discrepancy in quotes in different money centers provides an opportunity for somebody to earn a profit by buying a currency at a low price in one market and selling it at a higher price in another market. Such arbitrage transactions will keep exchange rates approximately the same in the various markets.

10. Transactions triggered by inconsistencies between exchange rates in different money centers will put pressures on the market for a change in the quote.

11. The spread between the buying and selling rates for a currency is based on the breadth and depth of the market for that currency as well as on the currency's volatility.

12. Because the exchange rates quoted in the financial press are not those that individuals or firms would get at a local bank, it may be advantageous to shop around at several banks for quotes before a transaction is made.

13. Exchange gains and losses are primarily caused by the immediate adjustment of quotes as traders receive and interpret new economic and political information.

14. With increasing uncertainty about exchange rate movements, traders want to be compensated for the added risk they are taking. This is reflected in a wider bid-ask spread.

B. The Mechanics of Spot Transactions

1. In a spot transaction, the trader will forward a dealing slip containing all the relevant information to the settlement section of his/her bank.

2. That same day, a contract note will be sent to the importer.

3. The contract note includes:

    a. The amount of foreign currency.

    b. The dollar equivalent at the agreed rate.

    c. Confirmation of the payment instructions.

4. The settlement section, in turn, will cable the bank's correspondent or branch in the foreign country, requesting transfer of the amount of foreign currency to the account specified by the importer.

5. On the value date, the U.S. bank will debit the importer's account, and the exporter will have his or her account credited by the correspondent in the foreign country.

III. The Forward Market

A. A forward contract between a bank and a customer calls for delivery, at a fixed future date, of a specified amount of one currency against dollar payment, with the exchange rate fixed at the time the contract is entered into.

B. An importer, who is required to make payment at some future agreed date, can cover his position against unfavorable exchange rate movements in the forward market.

C. If the importer does not currently own the foreign currency, he can offset this short position by going long in the forward market, that is, by buying the foreign currency for future delivery.

D. The gains and losses from short and long forward positions are related to the difference between the contracted forward price and the spot price of the underlying currency at the time the contract matures.

E. There are three points worth noting.

    1. The gain or loss on a forward contract is unrelated to the current spot price.

    2. The forward contract gain or loss exactly offsets the change in the dollar cost of foreign goods that is associated with movements in the value of the foreign currency.

    3. The forward contract is a contractual agreement which must be carried out by both parties.

F. Forward Market Participants

1. The <u>arbitrageur</u> seeks risk-free profits by taking advantage
    of differences in interest rates among countries. They use
    forward contracts to dominate the exchange risk involved in
    transferring funds from one nation to another.

2. The <u>trader</u> uses a forward contract to eliminate or cover the
    risk of loss on export or import orders denominated in
    foreign currencies. A forward covering transaction relates
    to a specific payment to be made or receipt expected at a
    specific future point in time.

3. The <u>hedger</u>, usually a multinational corporation, engages in
    forward contracts to protect the home currency value of
    various foreign currency denominated assets and liabilities
    on its balance sheets which are not to be realized over the
    life of the contracts.

4. While arbitragers, traders, and hedgers seek to reduce their
    exchange risk by locking in the exchange rate on future trade
    or financial operations, <u>speculators</u> actively expose
    themselves to currency risk by buying or selling foreign
    currencies forward in order to profit from exchange rate
    fluctuations. Their degree of participation is not a
    function of their business transactions in foreign
    currencies; instead, it is based on prevailing forward rates
    and their expectations for spot exchange rates in the future.

G. Forward Quotations

1. Commercial customers are usually quoted the actual price,
    otherwise known as the <u>outright quote</u>.

2. In the interbank market, however, dealers quote the forward
    rate only as a discount from, or premium on, the spot rate.
    This forward differential is known as the <u>swap rate</u>.

3. A foreign currency is at a <u>forward discount</u> if the forward
    rate expressed in dollars is less than the spot rate.

4. A <u>forward premium</u> exists if the forward rate is greater than
    the spot rate.

5. Alternatively, the forward discount or premium may be
    expressed as an annualized percentage deviation from the spot
    rate. The percentage discount or premium is computed with
    the following formula:

$$\begin{array}{c} \text{Forward} \\ \text{premium (+)} \\ \text{or} \\ \text{discount (-)} \end{array} = \frac{\text{Forward} - \text{Spot}}{\text{Spot}} \times \frac{12}{\text{Forward contract}}$$

6. A swap rate can be converted into an outright rate by adding the premium to, or subtracting the discount from, the spot rate.

7. Although a swap rate does not carry a plus or minus sign, an experienced dealer will immediately know whether the forward rate is at a discount or premium.

8. Even without that knowledge, the outright rate can be easily determined because:

   a. The buying rate must always be lower than the selling price.

   b. The margin for forward rates is greater than for spot rates.

9. Thus, if the first forward quote (the bid or buying rate) is smaller than the second forward quote (the offer or selling price), the quotes are added to the spot rate. Conversely, if the bid rate is greater than the offer price, the quotes are subtracted from the spot rate.

10. Spreads in the forward market are a function of both the breadth of the market (or volume of transactions) in a given currency and the risk associated with forward contracts.

    a. The greater uncertainty about future rates will be reflected in the forward market.

    b. Uncertainty will also increase with lengthening maturities if forward rates.

    c. Greater unpredictability of future spot rate may reduce market participants, leaving the dealer with greater risk in taking even a temporary position in the forward market.

11. Forward cross rates are calculated in much the same way as spot cross rates.

H. Forward Contract Maturities

   1. The rates quoted on the forward market are normally for 1-month, 2-month, 3-month, 6-month, or 12-month delivery.

2. Contracts between a bank and its customers, however, may not coincide with these maturities. As a result, the rate for each contract is determined individually, although the forward market rates provide the basis of quotes to customers.

3. For currencies most actively traded, such as the British pound or German mark, forward contracts with maturities greater than one year can usually be arranged.

I. Forward Options Contract

1. If a buyer or seller of a currency knows only the approximate date that the currency will be needed or received, he or she may enter into a forward option contract.

2. A forward option contract calls for delivery at the beginning of the month, the middle of the month, or the end of the month. However, more specific dates can be arranged on an individual basis.

3. With an option contract, the bank agrees to make payment or take delivery of the currency at any time during the option period at a set price.

4. An option contract, however, is more expensive than an ordinary forward contract because the bank is not certain when the option will be exercised and tries to cover itself by quoting the most costly of the beginning-of-period and end-of-period rates.

J. Bank Policy on Speculation

1. Clearly, there is greater risk for a bank in its forward transactions than in spot contracts because of the more remote payment date and greater chance of unfavorable currency fluctuations.

2. There are two types of risk:

   a. The risk of price fluctuations which banks lay off by taking an offsetting transaction.

   b. The risk that the contract will not be carried out.

3. If a bank believes that currency speculation is involved, it might require a customer to put up a margin of 10% of the forward contract to protect itself incase of default.

IV. Futures Contracts

    A. In 1972, the Chicago Mercantile Exchange opened its International Monetary Market (IMM) to currency speculators and hedgers.

    B. Trade takes place in currency futures, which are contracts for specific quantities of given currencies; the exchange rate is fixed at the time the contract is entered into, and the maturity date is set by the Board of Directors of the IMM.

    C. Futures contracts are currently available for the British pound, Canadian dollar, German mark, Swiss franc, French franc, Japanese yen, Australian dollar, and European Currency Unit. Contracts in the Dutch guilder and Mexican peso have been dropped.

    D. Contract sizes are standardized according to the amount of foreign currency--e.g., £50,000, Can $100,000, SFr 125,000.

    E. Characteristics of currency futures trading:

        1. Leverage is high.

        2. Margin requirement average less than 4% of the value of the futures contract.

        3. Commissions are relatively low. For example, on the value of a sterling contract the cost is less than 0.05%.

        4. The low cost, along with the high degree of leverage, has provided a major inducement for speculators to participate in the market.

    F. Volume in the currency futures market is still small compared to the exchange market; but it is growing rapidly.

    G. The success of the IMM led to the opening of the London International Financial Futures Exchange (LIFFE) where currency futures are traded in sterling, German mark, Swiss franc, and yen. Contract sizes are identical to those traded at the IMM.

    H. Basic differences between forward and futures contracts

        1. Regulation

            a. The IMM is regulated by the Commodity Futures Trading Commission.

            b. The forward market is self-regulated.

2. Price Fluctuations

    a. Forward contracts have no daily limits on price fluctuations.

    b. The IMM imposes a daily limit on price fluctuations.

3. Frequency of Delivery

    a. More than 90% of all forward contracts are settled by actual delivery.

    b. By contrast, less than 10% of the IMM futures contracts are settled by delivery.

4. Size of Contract

Forward contracts are individually tailored and tend to be much larger than the standardized contracts on the futures market.

5. Delivery Date

    a. Banks offer forward contracts for delivery on any date.

    b. IMM futures contracts are available for delivery at only four specified times a year: the third Wednesday of March, June, September, or December.

6. Settlements

    a. Settlement of a forward contract occurs on the date agreed upon between the bank and its customer.

    b. Futures contracts are settled on a daily basis via the exchange's clearing house; profits and losses are paid over every day at the end of trading, a practice called <u>market</u> <u>to</u> <u>market</u>.

7. Quotes

    a. Forward prices generally are quoted in European terms (units of local currency per U.S. dollar).

    b. Futures contracts are quoted in American terms (dollars per one unit of foreign currency).

I. Advantages and Disadvantages of Futures Contracts and Futures Trading

    1. With only a few standardized contracts traded, the trading volume in available contracts is higher. This situation mean superior liquidity, smaller price fluctuation, and lower transaction costs in the futures market.

    2. The organization of futures trading with a <u>clearing</u> <u>house</u> reduces the default risk.

    3. The smaller size of a futures contract and the freedom to liquidate the contract at any time before its maturity, attract many users to the currency futures market.

    4. On the other hand, the limited number of currencies traded, the limited delivery dates, and the rigid contractual amount of currencies to be delivered are disadvantages of the futur contract to many commercial users.

J. Arbitrageurs play an important role on the IMM. They translate IMM futures rates into interbank forward rates and, by realizing profit opportunities, keep IMM futures rates in line with bank forward rates.

V. Currency Options

A. While forward or futures contracts protect the holder against the risk of adverse movements in exchange rates, they eliminate the possibility of gaining a windfall profit from favorable movements

B. This consideration has apparently led some commercial banks to offer currency options to their customers.

C. Exchange-traded currency options were first offered by the Philadelphia Stock Exchange in December 1983.

D. A currency option is a financial instrument which gives the holde the right, not the obligation, to buy (call) or sell (put) a give amount of a foreign currency at a set price per unit for a specified time period.

E. Because the option not to buy or sell has value, the buyer must pay the seller of the option some <u>premium</u> for this privilege.

F. <u>Call</u> options give the customer the right to buy, and <u>put</u> options give the right to sell the contracted currency at the expiration date.

G. An _American_ option can be exercised at any time up to the expiration date; a _European_ option can only be exercised at maturity.

H. The _exercise_ _price_ or _strike_ _price_ is the specified exchange rate at which the option can be exercised. A strike price can be set:

1. _In-the-money_, which is a price that when immediately exercised at the current exchange rate would cause a gain.

2. _Out-of-the-money_, which is a price that when immediately exercised at the current exchange rate would cause a loss.

3. _At-the-money_, which is the same as the spot exchange rate.

I. The holder of a call option will gain only when the spot rate exceeds the prearranged exercise price. This is most likely to occur if the underlying exchange rate is highly volatile; the higher the variability, the greater the probability that the currency will rise substantially above the exercise price, thereby producing a large profit.

K. The profit from selling a call option is the mirror image of the profit from buying a call option.

L. Similarly, the holder of a put option will gain only if the currency has fallen below the exercise price by more than the price of the put.

M. A _straddle_ involves the simultaneous purchase of a put and a call at the same exercise price. According to this strategy, the buyer of the straddle will profit from currency volatility; the seller of the straddle accepts that risk for a fixed amount. Thus, the price of a straddle is based on the market's estimation of a currency's volatility--the more volatile the currency, the higher the price of a straddle.

N. Currency options are used primarily by:

1. Financial firms holding large investments offshore where sizable unrealized gains had occurred because of exchange rate changes, and where these gains were thought likely to be partially or fully reversed.

2. Firms having currency inflows or outflows that are possible but not certain to occur.

O. Option Pricing and Valuation

1. Theoretically, the value of an option consists of the intrinsic value and the time value.

2. The _intrinsic value_ of the option is the amount by which the option is in-the-money (S - E), where S is the current spot price and E is the exercise price. It equals the immediate exercise value of the option.

   a. The further into the money an option is, the more valuable it is.

   b. An out-of-the-money option has no intrinsic value.

   c. Generally, an option will sell for at least its intrinsic value.

3. Any excess of the option value over its intrinsic value is called the _time value_ of the contract.

   a. The more time that is left until maturity, the higher the time value tends to be.

   b. As the option approaches its maturity, the time value declines to zero.

4. The value of an American option always exceeds its intrinsic value because the time value is always positive up to the expiration date.

5. Given that European options can only be exercised at the maturity date, its value may not increase with increasing time left to maturity.

6. Before expiration, an out-of-the-money option has only time value, but an in-the-money option has both time value and intrinsic value. At expiration, an option can only have intrinsic value.

7. The time value of a currency option reflects the probability that its intrinsic value will increase before expiration; this probability depends, among other things, on the volatility of the exchange rate.

   a. An increase in currency volatility increases the chance of an extremely high or low exchange rate at the time the option expires.

b. The chance of a very high exchange rate benefits the call owner.

c. The chance of a very low exchange rate is irrelevant; the option will be worthless for any exchange rate less than the striking price.

d. Inasmuch as the effect of increased volatility is beneficial, the value of the call option is higher. Put options similarly benefit from increased volatility in the exchange rate.

8. Since the option is a claim on a specified amount of an asset over a period of time into the future, that claim must have a return in line with market interest rates on comparable instruments. Thus, a rise in the interest rate will cause call option values to rise and put option values to fall.

9. The pricing of currency options, however, requires consideration of both domestic and foreign interest rates. A foreign currency is normally at a forward premium or discount vis-a-vis the domestic currency which is determined by relative interest rates. Thus, for foreign currency options, call values rise and put values fall when the domestic interest rate increases and the foreign interest rate decreases.

10. The more valuable put or call options are, the higher option premiums tend to be. Hence, options become more expensive when exchange rate volatility rises. Similarly, when the interest rate differential between the home country and the foreign country increases, call options become more expensive, and put options less expensive.

P. Market Structure

1. Options are purchased and traded either on an organized exchange (such as the PHLX) or in the over-the-counter (OTC) market.

2. Exchange-traded options have the following characteristics:

a. Standardized contracts with pre-determined exercise prices.

b. Standard maturities (one, three, six, nine, and twelve months).

c. Fixed maturities (March, June, September, and December).

d. Limited amount of currencies (German mark, British pound Canadian dollar, French franc, Swiss franc, Japanese yen, and ECU).

e. Standard contracts are half the size of the IMM futures contracts.

3. Other organized exchanges are located in Amsterdam (EOE), Chicago (CME), and Montreal (MSE).

4. In January 1984, the IMM introduced options on currency futur contracts.

a. Options on currency futures are available for the German mark, British pound, Japanese yen, Swiss franc, and Canadian dollar.

b. Trading involves purchases and sales of puts and calls or contract calling for delivery of a standard IMM contract the currency rather than the currency itself.

c. When exercised, the holder receives a short or long position in the currency futures contract that expires or week after the expiration of the options contract.

d. Once the option contract is exercised and the futures contract delivered, the holder may sell the contract on t IMM at a price that provides the holder with exactly the same profit as the holder would have realized with a straight currency option.

5. OTC option specifications are generally negotiated as the amount, exercise price and rights, underlying instrument, and expiration date.

a. OTC currency options are traded to varying degrees by commercial and investment banks in virtually all financia centers.

b. The average maturity of OTC options ranges from two to si months, and few options are written for more than one yea

c. American options are most common, but European options ar popular in Switzerland and Germany.

6. The OTC options market consists of two sections:

a. A _retail_ market which is composed of nonbank customers wh purchase from banks what amounts to customized insurance against adverse exchange rate movements.

b. A <u>wholesale</u> market among commercial banks, investment banks, and specialized trading firms.

7. The structure of the currency options market is distinctly <u>asymmetrical</u> when compared with the ordinary market for spot and forward foreign exchange; that is, a balance between customers purchasing or selling currency does not exist.

Q. The choice of whether to employ listed or OTC options depends on both cost and flexibility.

1. OTC options are easier to manage because they can be tailored to the specific needs of the customer in terms of strike price, maturity, expiration date and currency amount. By contrast, listed options have preset strike prices, standard maturities, fixed expiration dates, and set lot sizes.

2. On the other hand, listed options are regarded as less expensive than OTC options.

3. Listed options are generally more tradeable than OTC options.

R. Reading Futures and Options Prices

1. Futures and exchange-listed options prices appear daily int he financial press.

2. Futures prices on the IMM are listed for five currencies, with three or four contracts quoted for each currency. Included are the opening and lost settlement prices, the change from the previous day, and the number of contracts outstanding (open interest).

3. The price data on Chicago Mercantile Exchange (IMM) options are provided ont he same futures contracts.

4. Note the difference between futures options and currency options.

a. A futures call option gives the holder the right to buy the relevant futures contract, which is settled at maturity.

b. The Philadelphia call options contract is an option to buy foreign exchange spot, which is settled when the option is exercised; the buyer receives foreign currency immediately.

c. Price quotes usually reflect this difference.

KEY TERMS

Spot Market
European Terms
American Terms
Direct Quotation
Indirect Quotation
Bid Price
Ask Price
Cross Rate
Arbitrage
Bid-Ask Spread
Forward Market
Arbitrageur
Trader
Hedger
Speculator
Outright Quote
Swap Rate
Forward Premium
Forward Discount
Forward Option Contract
Futures Contract
Intrinsic Value
Time Value

Chicago Mercantile Exchange (CME)
International Monetary Market (IMM)
London International Financial Exchange (LIFFE)
Currency Options
Philadelphia Stock Exchange (PHLX)
European Options Exchange (EOE)
Montreal Stock Exchange (MSE)
Premium
Call Option
Put Option
American Option
European Option
Exercise Price
Strike Price
In-The-Money
Out-Of-The-Money
At-The-Money
Straddle
Options On Currency Futures

CONCEPTUAL QUESTIONS

QUESTION 1: How can a forward contract be used by an importer?

ANSWER: An importer, who is required to make payment in a foreign currency at some future agreed date, can cover his position against unfavorable exchange rate movements in the forward market.

SELECTED QUESTIONS FROM THE TEXT

QUESTION 2: Suppose a currency increases in volatility. What is likely happen to its bid-ask spread? Why?

ANSWER: As a currency's volatility increases, it becomes riskier for traders to take positions in that currency. To compensate for the added risks, traders quote wider bid-ask spreads.

QUESTION 3: Who are the principal users of the forward market? What are their motives?

ANSWER: The principal users of the forward market are currency arbitragers, hedgers, importers and exporters, and speculators. Arbitragers wish to earn risk-free profits; hedgers, importers and exporters want to protect the home currency values of various foreign currency-denominated assets and liabilities; and speculators actively expose themselves to exchange risk to benefit from expected movements in exchange rates.

QUESTION 5: What is the major difference between a spot transaction and a forward transaction?

ANSWER: A spot transaction requires immediate delivery (within two business days after the transaction) of a currency at the prevailing spot exchange rate, while a forward transaction requires delivery of a currency at a specified future date with the exchange rate fixed at the time the forward contract is entered into.

PROBLEMS

PROBLEM 1: Suppose that the spot rate of the Danish krona is $0.1740 and the 90-day forward rate of the Danish krona is $0.1744. What is the swap rate on the Danish krona?

SOLUTION:

Since the forward rate is greater than the spot rate, the Danish krona is at a premium of 4 points.

SELECTED PROBLEMS FROM THE TEXT

PROBLEM 1: The $/DM exchange rate is DM 1 = $0.35, and the DM/FF exchange rate is FF 1 = DM 0.31. What is the FF/$ exchange rate?

SOLUTION:

Since $\frac{\$}{DM} = 0.35$ and $\frac{DM}{FF} = 0.31$, then

$\frac{\$}{FF} = \frac{\$}{DM} \times \frac{DM}{FF} = 0.35 \times 0.31 = 0.1085$ or $0.1085/FF.

PROBLEM 2: Suppose the following direct quotes are received for spot and 30-day Swiss francs in New York: 0.6963-68 4-6. What is the outright 30-day forward quote for the Swiss franc?

SOLUTION:

Since the first forward quote is smaller than the second forward quote, there is a premium and the points are added to the spot quote which yields an outright 30-day forward quote of 0.6967-0.6974.

PROBLEM 5: The spot and 90-day forward rates for the pound are $1.1376 and $1.1350, respectively. What is the forward premium or discount on the pound?

SOLUTION:

The forward premium (+) or discount (-) on the British pound is

$$[(f_1 - e_0)/e_0] \times (360/n)$$

$$[(1.1350 - 1.1376)/1.1376] \times 4$$

$$- 0.91\%,$$

i.e., a forward discount of 0.91%.

PROBLEM 8: Assuming no transaction costs, suppose £1 = $2.4110 in New York, $1 = FF 3.997 in Paris, and FF1 = £0.1088 in London. How could you take profitable advantage of these rates?

SOLUTION:

Sell pounds in New York for $2.4110. Sell the dollars in Paris for FF3.997, and sell the French francs in London for £0.1088. This yields 2.4110 x 3.997 x .1088 pounds or £1.0485 per pound initially traded.

PARITY CONDITIONS IN INTERNATIONAL FINANCE

Summary: In this chapter the usefulness of a number of different models and methodologies in profitably forecasting currency changes under both fixed and flexible exchange rate systems is examined. Assuming that prediction is aided by understanding, this chapter presents different theories of spot and forward exchange rate determination along with the empirical evidence on their explanatory power.

I. Arbitrage and the Law of One Price

    A. The <u>law</u> <u>of</u> <u>one</u> <u>price</u> indicates that exchange-adjusted prices of identical tradeable goods and financial assets must be within transactions costs of equality worldwide.

    B. This idea is enforced by international arbitragers who follow the profit-guaranteeing dictum of "buy low, sell high" and prevent all but trivial deviations from equality.

    C. There are five key theoretical economic relationships which result from arbitrage activities:

        1. Purchasing power parity (PPP)

        2. Fisher effect (FE)

        3. International Fisher effect (IFE)

        4. Interest rate parity (IRP)

        5. Forward rates as unbiased predictors of futures spot rates (UFR).

    D. This framework emphasizes the links that exist among prices, spot exchange rates, interest rates, and forward exchange rates.

    E. <u>Purchasing</u> <u>power</u> <u>parity</u> and the <u>Fisher</u> <u>effect</u> are based on the notion that money is neutral. That is, a change in the quantity of money should not affect the rate at which domestic goods are exchanged for foreign goods or the rate at which goods today are exchanged for goods in the future.

        1. The international analogue to inflation is home currency depreciation relative to foreign currencies.

           a.   Inflation involves a change in the exchange rate between the home currency and domestic goods.

           b.   Home currency depreciation, in turn, results in a change the exchange rate between the home currency and foreign goods.

     2.   If the law of one price is enforced by international arbitra, then the exchange rate between the home currency and domesti goods must equal the exchange rate between the home currency and foreign goods. In other words, the foreign exchange rat must change by (approximately) the difference between the domestic and foreign rates of inflation. This relationship the <u>purchasing power parity</u>.

F.   The <u>nominal interest rate</u>, which is the price quoted on lending borrowing transactions, determines the exchange rate between current and future dollars.

G.   According to the <u>Fisher</u> and <u>International Fisher effects</u>, howeve it is the exchange rate between current and future purchasing power, as measured by the <u>real interest rate</u>, that really matter

     1.   If the exchange rate between current and future goods--the r interest rate--varies across countries, arbitrage between domestic and foreign capital markets, in the form of international capital flows, should occur.

     2.   These flows will tend to equalize real interest rates across countries.

II. Purchasing Power Parity

A.   Purchasing power parity is often used to forecast future exchan, rates, for purposes ranging from deciding on the currency denomination of long-term debt issues to determining in which countries to build plants.

B.   The effectiveness of using PPP in this manner depends on the extent to which PPP can signal profitable international arbitra, opportunities.

C.   In the <u>absolute version</u> of PPP the equilibrium exchange rate between domestic and foreign currencies equals the ratio betwee, domestic and foreign price levels shown as

$$e_0 \; = \; \frac{P_h}{P_f}$$

or

$$P_h = e_0 P_f$$

where: e_0 = current equilibrium exchange rate
P_h = home currency price level
P_f = foreign price level.

Thus, a unit of home currency (HC) should have the same purchasing power worldwide.

1. This theory is based on the assumption that free trade will equalize the price of any good in all countries (the law of one price).

2. However, this theory ignores the effects on free trade of transportation costs, tariffs, quotas and other restrictions, and product differentiation.

D. The _relative_ _version_ modifies this parity condition by stating that in comparison to a period when equilibrium rates prevailed, changes in the ratio of domestic and foreign prices would indicate the necessary adjustment in the exchange rate between any pair of currencies. This relationship can be shown as:

$$\frac{e_t}{e_0} = \frac{P_h(t) / P_h(0)}{P_f(t) / P_f(0)}$$

where: e_t = home currency value of one unit of foreign currency at time t
e_0 = base period exchange rate
$P_h(t)$ = domestic price level at time t
$P_h(0)$ = base period equilibrium domestic price level
$P_f(t)$ = foreign price level at time t
$P_f(0)$ = base period equilibrium foreign price level.

1. This equation can be stated in terms of relative inflation rates. If $i_{h,t}$ and $i_{f,t}$ are the (anticipated) price level increases (rates of inflation) between time 0 and time t for the home country and the foreign country, respectively, then it can be shown that

$$\frac{P_h(t)}{P_h(0)} = 1 + i_{h,t}$$

and

$$\frac{P_f(t)}{P_f(0)} = 1 + i_{f,t}$$

equals

$$\frac{e_t}{e_0} = \frac{1 + i_{h,t}}{1 + i_{f,t}} \, .$$

2. The relative (anticipated) exchange rate change between 0 and t, should equal the relative price level change from 0 to t:

$$\frac{e_t - e_0}{e_0} = \frac{i_{h,t} - i_{f,t}}{1 + i_{f,t}}$$

3. A simplified version of this formula is

$$(e_t - e_0) \, / \, e_0 = i_{h,t} - i_{f,t}$$

That is, the inflation differential between 0 and t should equal the exchange differential for that same time period.

4. As with the absolute version of PPP, this relative version relies on arbitrage in the goods market to bring about those currency changes that are necessary to return to equilibrium.

E. Just as the price of goods in one year cannot be meaningfully compared to the price of goods in another year without adjusting for interim inflation, so exchange rate changes may indicate nothing more than the reality that countries have different inflation rates.

1. If this is the case, then exchange rate movements just cancel out changes in the foreign price level relative to the domestic price level.

2. These offsetting movements should have no effects on the relative competitive positions of domestic firms and their foreign competition.

3. Thus, changes in nominal rates may be of little significance in determining the true effects of currency changes on a firm and a nation.

4. In terms of currency changes affecting relative competitiveness, the focus must be on changes in the real purchasing power of one currency relative to another.

   a. The _real_ exchange rate is the _nominal_, or actual, exchange rate adjusted for changes in the relative purchasing power of each currency since some base period.

b. The real exchange rate in period t is given as

$$e'_t = e_t \frac{(1 + i_{f,t})}{(1 + i_{h,t})}$$

c. If purchasing power parity holds exactly, that is, if

$$e_t = e_0 \frac{(1 + i_{f,t})}{(1 + i_{h,t})},$$

then e'_t equals e_t. That is, if changes in the nominal exchange rate are fully offset by changes in the relative price levels between the two countries, then the real exchange rate remains unchanged. Alternatively, a change in the real exchange rate is equivalent to a deviation from PPP.

d. If the real exchange rate remains constant, currency gains or losses from nominal exchange rate changes will generally be offset over time by the effects of differences in relative rates of inflation, thereby reducing the net impact of nominal devaluations and revaluations. Deviations from PPP, however, will lead to real exchange gains and losses.

F. Changes in expected, as well as actual, inflation will cause changes in the exchange rate.

1. An increase in a currency's expected rate of inflation, all other things equal, makes that currency more expensive to hold over time and less in demand at the same price.

2. The value of higher-inflation currencies will tend to be depressed relative to the value of lower-inflation currencies, all other things equal.

G. Since the relative version of PPP is not affected as severely by the various trade distortions as is absolute PPP, most empirical tests have focused on it.

1. Henry Gailliot (1971) tested PPP for the U.S. and seven other industrial countries (Canada, Great Britain, France, West Germany, Italy, Japan, Switzerland) between 1900 and 1967.

2. Hali Edison (1987) took an even longer time period--1890 to 1978--to study the behavior of the dollar/pound exchange rate. His data show that despite large deviations from PPP over lengthy periods of time, the British pound exhibited a strong tendency to return to its PPP value.

3. The general conclusion from the studies by Gailliot and othe
    is that the theory holds up well in the long-run but not as
    well over shorter time periods.

4. But evidence is accumulating that PPP is not just a long-run
    theory. Studies by Richard Rogalski and Joseph Vinso (1977)
    and by Richard Roll (1979) clearly indicate that PPP is also
    valid in the short-run.

5. The most common interpretations for the failure of PPP to ho
    include that:

    a. Goods prices are sticky, leading to short-term violation
        of the law of one price. Adjustment to PPP eventually
        occurs, but it does so with a lag.

    b. Tests to support PPP in the short run ignore the problem
        caused by the combination of differently constructed pri
        indices and relative price changes.

6. Change in relative prices of various goods and services will
    cause differently constructed indices to deviate from each
    other, falsely signalling deviations from PPP.

    a. Kravis (1975) and others have demonstrated empirically
        that deviations from PPP are for smaller when using the
        same weights than when using different weights in
        calculating the U.S. and foreign price indices.

    b. Furthermore, price indices heavily weighted with non-
        traded goods and services will provide misleading
        information about a nation's international
        competitiveness.

    c. Bradford Cornell (1979) preserved a related point: Sinc
        the exchange rate is determined by the prices of a
        relatively small subset of internationally traded goods,
        its variance will exceed the variance of a broader index
        or portfolio of prices used to measure inflation. Thus,
        the exchange rate will fluctuate around the more stable
        inflation differential trend line, resulting in apparent
        deviations from PPP.

H. If nominal currency changes result in deviations from PPP,
    however, these deviations do not indicate that a currency is
    overvalued or undervalued.

I. Deviations from PPP either signal slow adjustment to equilibrium
    or that PPP is a poor proxy for the true equilibrium exchange
    rate.

III. The Fisher Effect

A. The Fisher Effect states that the nominal interest rate, r, is made up of two components:

   1. The real required rate of return, a.

   2. An inflation premium equal to the expected amount of inflation i. Thus,

$$r = a + i .$$

B. The generalized version of the Fisher effect asserts that real returns are equalized across countries through arbitrage.

   1. If expected real returns were higher in currency A than in currency B, capital would flow from currency B to currency A. This process of arbitrage would continue, in the absence of government intervention, until expected real returns were equalized.

   2. The assumption of real returns being equalized will most likely hold when using Eurocurrency rates to measure the nominal home and foreign currency rates, $r_{h,t}$ and $r_{f,t}$, respectively.

   3. In equilibrium, with no government interference, it should follow that

$$\frac{1 + r_{h,t}}{1 + r_{f,t}} = \frac{1 + i_{h,t}}{1 + i_{f,t}}$$

   which can be rewritten as

$$r_{h,t} - r_{f,t} = i_{h,t} - i_{f,t}$$

   This equation states that the nominal interest differential should (nearly) equal the anticipated inflation differential.

C. The historical evidence is consistent with the hypothesis that most of the variation in nominal interest rates can be attributed to changing inflationary expectations.

D. The proposition that inflation-adjusted returns are equal between countries has not been tested directly.

   1. In an increasingly internationalized capital market, the existence of real interest differentials will not prevail for long.

2. The only way to reintroduce interest rate differentials in this closely integrated would economy is for countries to pursue sharply differing tax policies, impose regulatory barriers to the free flow of capital, or consciously to prevent varying risks for would-be investors.

3. In many developing countries, however, currency control and other government policies impose political risk on foreign investors. The combination of such government policies and high political risk is likely to cause real interest rates i these countries to exceed real interest rates in the developed countries.

IV. The International Fisher Effect

A. PPP implies that exchange rates will move to offset changes in inflation rate differentials.

B. Thus, a rise in the U.S. inflation rate relative to those of other countries will be associated with a fall in the value of the dollar. It will also be associated with a rise in the U.S. interest rate relative to foreign interest rates.

C. These two conditions are incorporated in the <u>International Fisher effect</u>:

$$\frac{1 + r_h}{1 + r_f} = \frac{e_t}{e_o}$$

or

$$\frac{r_{h,t} - r_{f,t}}{1 + r_{f,t}} = \frac{e_t - e_o}{e_o}.$$

D. The International Fisher effect states that arbitrage between financial markets should ensure that the interest differential between any two countries is an unbiased predictor of the future change in the spot rate of exchange.

1. Thus, currencies with low interest rates are expected to revalue relative to currencies with high interest rates.

2. This condition does not mean that the interest differential is an accurate predictor; it just means that prediction errors tend to cancel out over time.

E. The ability of interest differentials to properly anticipate currency changes is supported by several empirical studies, which indicate the long-run tendency for these differentials to offset exchange rate changes. Thus, at any given time, currencies with high nominal interest rates can be expected to depreciate relative to currencies with low interest rates.

F. Changes in nominal interest rate differentials have been dominated, at times, by changes in the real interest rate differentials; at other times, they have been dominated by changes in relative inflation expectations. As a result, there is no stable, predictable relationship between changes in the nominal interest rate differential and exchange rate changes.

V. Interest Rate Parity Theory

A. The movement of short-term funds between two currencies to take advantage of interest rate differentials is a major determinant of the spread between forward and spot rates. In fact, the forward discount or premium is closely related to the interest rate differential between two currencies.

B. In an efficient market with zero transaction costs, the interest differential should be (approximately) equal to the forward differential.

   1. The currency of the country with the lower interest rate should be at a forward premium in terms of the currency of the higher interest rate country.

   2. If the interest differential equals the forward differential, then the forward rate is said to be at interest parity, and equilibrium should prevail in the money markets.

   3. If the interest differential does not equal the forward differential, then arbitrage profit opportunities exist in the money markets.

C. Covered interest arbitrage consists of a short-term investment in a foreign currency which is covered by a forward contract to sell that currency at the same time as the investment matures.

   1. As the foreign currency is bought spot and sold forward, the spot rate will increase and the forward rate will decrease.

   2. Simultaneously, as money flows from the lower interest rate country A, interest rates there will tend to increase; at the same time, the inflow of funds to the higher interest rate country B will depress interest rates there.

3.   This process will continue until interest rate parity is achieved, unless there is government interference in the form of capital controls.

4.   In the Eurocurrency markets, which are markets for funds owned outside their countries of origin, interest rate parity does prevail.

D.   The covered interest arbitrage relationship can be stated as follows:

$$\frac{1 + r_{h,t}}{1 + r_{f,t}} = \frac{f_t}{e_0}$$

where f_t is the t-period forward rate and the remaining symbols are defined as before.

E.   Interest rate parity is often approximated using the equation

$$r_{h,t} - r_{f,t} = \frac{f_t - e_0}{e_0}.$$

F.   Interest rate parity is one of the best documented relationships in international finance.

1.   In the Eurocurrency markets, the forward rate is calculated from the interest differential between two currencies using the no-arbitrage condition.

2.   Deviations from interest rate parity do occur between national capital markets, however, due to capital controls, the imposition of taxes on interest payments to foreigners, and transaction costs.

VI. The Relationship Between the Forward Rate and the Future Spot Rate

A.   Under a system of freely floating exchange rates, both the spot rate and the forward rate are influenced heavily by current expectations of future events and that both rates move in tandem, with the link between them based on interest differentials. Any new information, such as a change in interest rate differentials, is reflected almost immediately in both spot and forward rates.

B.   When the forward differential equals the expected change in the exchange rate, equilibrium is achieved, and the forward rate is said to be an unbiased predictor of the future spot rate.

C. A formal statement of the unbiased nature of the forward rate is

$$f_t = e_t$$

where: f_t = t-period forward rate
e_t = t-period expected future exchange rate.

D. Market efficiency requires that people process information and form reasonable expectations; it does not require that $f_t = e_t$.

1. Market efficiency allows for the possibility that risk-averse investors will demand a risk premium on forward contracts.

2. Since currency risk is largely diversifiable, investors will not be willing to pay a risk premium for holding a forward contract; the forward rate and expected future spot rate will be approximately equal.

E. Early studies have shown that forward rates are unbiased predictors of future spot rates. More recently studies using more sophisticated econometric techniques argue that the forward rate is a biased predictor, probably because of a risk premium. However, the premium appears to change signs and averages near zero.

F. While forward rates may be treated as unbiased predictors of future spot rates during floating rate periods, there is evidence of biasness in forward rates under the Bretton Woods fixed-rate system. This evidence suggests the possibility of earning arbitrage profits through forward market speculation when exchange rates are fixed.

VII. Inflation Risk, and its Impact on Financial Markets

A. Given the Fisher effect both borrowers and lenders factor expected inflation into the nominal interest rate.

B. Inflation risk is defined as the possibility that actual inflation could turn out to be higher or lower than expected.

C. Since both lenders and borrowers are affected by high and variable rates of inflation, they demand to be compensated for bearing inflation risk.

D. Thus, an inflation risk premium, p, and be added to the basic Fisher equation.

$$r = a + i + ai + p .$$

E. Inflation risk is most devastating on long-term, fixed-rate
    bonds.

    1. The longer the maturity of a bond, the greater the impact o
        the present value of that bond associated with a given
        change in the rate of inflation.

    2. A change in the rate of inflation is equivalent to a change
        in the rate at which future cash flows are discounted back
        the present.

F. Since the problem of inflation risk increases with the maturity
    of a bond, the presence of volatile inflation will make corpora
    borrowers less willing to issue, and investors less willing to
    buy long-term, fixed-rate debt.

    1. The use of long-term, fixed-rate financing will decline.

    2. The reliance on debt with shorter maturities, floating-rate
        bonds, and indexed bonds will increase.

    3. The international evidence clearly supports this conjecture

        a. In highly inflationary countries (such as Argentina,
            Brazil, Israel, and Mexico) long-term, fixed-rate
            financing is no longer available. Instead, long-term
            financing is done with floating rate bonds or indexed
            bonds.

        b. Similarly, in the U.S. during the late 1970s and early
            1980s, when inflation risk was at its peak, 30-year
            conventional fixed-rate mortgages were being replaced
            with so-called adjustable-rate mortgages.

KEY TERMS

Competitive Markets
Law of one price
Purchasing Power Parity
Nominal Interest Rate
Fisher Effect
International Fisher Effect
Absolute PPP
Relative PPP
Real Exchange Rates
Fisher Effect

International Fisher Effect
Interest Rate Parity
Covered Interest Arbitrage
Eurocurrency Market
Currency Swap
Inflation Risk
Floating Rate Bonds
Indexed Bonds
Adjustable Rate Mortgage

CONCEPTUAL QUESTIONS

QUESTION 1:   Compare and contrast the purchasing power parity, the international Fisher effect, and the interest rate parity.

ANSWER: Purchasing power parity shows that the inflation differential of two countries will be reflected in the expected change in the spot rate over time.   The international Fisher effects shows that the interest rate differential of two countries will be reflected in the expected change in the spot rate over time.   And the interest rate parity theory states that the interest rate differential of two countries will be reflected in the forward premium or discount.

SELECTED QUESTIONS FROM THE TEXT

QUESTION 2:   What are some reasons for deviations from purchasing power parity?

ANSWER: Purchasing power parity might not hold because:
  (a) The price indices used to measure PPP may use different weights or different goods and services.
  (b) Some of the goods and services used in the indices are not traded, and hence there could be price discrepancies between countries.
  (c) Arbitrage may be too costly, because of tariffs and other trade barriers and high transportation costs, or too risky, because prices could change between the time in which an item is bought in one country and resold in another.
  (d) Relative price changes could lead to exchange rate changes even in the absence of an inflation differential.
  (e) Government intervention could lead to a disequilibrium exchange rate.

QUESTION 6:   What factors might lead to persistent-covered interest arbitrage opportunities among countries?

ANSWER: The principal reason would be the existence of political risk, particularly the fear that at some point the government would impose exchange controls, not allowing capital to be removed.   Another possible factor is differential tax laws which could lead to similar after-tax returns, even if before-tax returns differ.

QUESTION 12:   The interest rate in England is 12% while in Switzerland it is 5%.   What are possible reasons for this interest rate differential? What is the most likely reason?

ANSWER: Although there are several possible explanations for higher interest rates, the most likely explanation is that inflation is expected to be higher in England than in Switzerland.

QUESTION 16: To an efficient market, what pattern should the time series of the real exchange rate follow?

ANSWER: According to the efficient markets version of PPP, the real exchange rate should follow a random walk through time. Otherwise, there will be profitable arbitrage opportunities.

SELECTED PROBLEMS FROM THE TEXT

PROBLEM 5: Assume the interest rate is 16% on pound sterling and 7% on Deutsche marks. If the Deutsche mark is selling at a one-year forward premium of 9% against the pound, is there an arbitrage opportunity?

SOLUTION:

In order for there to be no arbitrage opportunity, the return on investing in sterling, 16%, must equal the sterling return on investing in DM,

$$.07 + .09 + 0.7 \times .09 = .1663.$$

According to these numbers, there is an arbitrage incentive of 0.63% (16% - 16.63%) for investing in the DM. The inexact version of the IRPT is wrong when it says that the return on investing in the DM is 16%.

PROBLEM 6: In July, the one-year interest rate is 4% on Swiss francs and 13% on U.S. dollars. (a) If the current exchange rate is $0.63:SFr, what is the expected future exchange rate in one year? (b) Suppose a change in expectations regarding future U.S. inflation causes the expected future spot rate to rise to $0.70:SFr. What should happen to the U.S. interest rate?

SOLUTION:

a. According to the international Fisher effect, the spot exchange rate expected in one year equals

$$.63 \times 1.13/1.04 = \$.6845.$$

b. If r_{us} is the unknown U.S. interest rate, and assuming that the Swiss interest rate stayed at 4% (because there has been no change in expectations of Swiss inflation), then according to the IFE,

$$.70/.63 = (1+r_{us})/1.04 \text{ or } r_{us} = 15.56\%.$$

PROBLEM 9: If expected inflation is 100%, and the real required return is 5%, what will the nominal interest rate be according to the Fisher effect?

SOLUTION:

According to the Fisher effect, the relationship between the nominal interest rate, r, the real interest rate a, and the expected inflation rate, i, is

$$1 + r = (1 + a)(1 + i).$$

Substituting in the numbers in the problem yields

$$1 + r = 1.05 \times 2 = 2.1$$

$$\text{or } r = 110\%.$$

PROBLEM 11: If the Swiss franc is $0.40 on the spot market, and the 180-day forward rate is $0.42, what is the expected inflation rate in the United States over the next six months annualized? The anticipated annualized inflation rate in Switzerland is 2%.

SOLUTION:

If i_{us} and i_{sw} are, respectively, the expected U.S. and Swiss rates of inflation and r_{us} and r_{sw} are the associated U.S. and Swiss nominal interest rates, then the Fisher effect says that

$$(1 + i_{us})/(1 + i_{sw}) = (1 + r_{us})/(1 + r_{sw}).$$

According to interest rate parity,

$$(1 + r_{us})/(1 + r_{sw}) = f_1/e_0$$

where f_1 and e_0 are the forward and spot values of the Swiss franc. Combining these two equations yields

$$(1 + i_{us})/(1 + i_{sw}) = f_1/e_0.$$

Substituting in the numbers and recalling that everything must be converted to a semi-annual basis, we have

$$(1 + .5i_{us})/1.01 = .42/.40$$

$$\text{or } .5i_{us} = 1.0605.$$

The solution is $i_{us} = 12.1\%$.

PROBLEM 12:   The interest rate in the United States is 10%; in Japan the comparable rate is 7%.   The spot rate for the yen is $0.003800.   If interest rate parity holds, what is the 90-day forward rate?

SOLUTION:

According to the IRPT, the 90-day forward rate on the yen should equal

$$\$.003800[(1 + .10/4)/(1 + .07/4)] = \$.003828.$$

CHAPTER 7

FORECASTING EXCHANGE RATE CHANGES

Summary: In this chapter the usefulness of a variety of forecasting models and techniques is evaluated. Also, the politics of currency devaluation and revaluation are examined because government interference in the foreign exchange markets is potentially of great importance in forecasting exchange rate changes.

I. Forecasting Floating Exchange Rates

    A. In a world of fixed exchange rates as well as managed exchange rates the government will intervene.

        1. Government objectives are clear in a foxed rate system.

        2. In the present managed float, however, government interference is less obvious for a number of reasons:

            a. Some countries do not intervene at all.

            b. Others intervene on both sides of the market.

            c. And still others attempt to impede or hasten exchange rate changes.

        3. This situation, in turn, points out a persistent problem for forecasters in a system of managed floating.

            a. In a fixed-rate system, the government's exchange rate target is publicly known, namely the official rate.

            b. In a managed float, however, there is no certainty regarding the desired currency level. In fact, government officials often confuse the issue in order to reduce speculative attacks by increasing the uncertainty facing currency traders.

            c. At times, intervention policy seems to be determined by a random process.

    B. Most analysts in the area of currency prediction have attempted to find some key indicators of when a currency is in trouble. Some of these indicators are balance-of-payments deficits or surpluses, levels of gold and hard currency reserves, external borrowings, and comparative rates of inflation. While this approach may have been appropriate in a period of essentially fixed exchange rates with massive government intervention, it is of little use in a world of floating exchange rates.

C. To successfully forecast floating currencies, it is necessary to determine the future values of key economic parameters and establish the relationship between them and future exchange rates.

1. The difficulty in forecasting exchange rates, however, is consistent with accumulating empirical evidence that the foreign exchange market is efficient.

2. The implication of market efficiency is that price changes follow a random walk. That is, price changes from one period to the next are independent of past price changes and are no more predictable than is new information.

D. Currency forecasting can lead to consistent profits only if the forecaster meets at least one of the following four criteria. The forecaster:

(1) Has exclusive use of a superior forecasting model.

(2) Has consistent access to information before the other investors.

(3) Exploits small, temporary deviations from equilibrium.

(4) Can predict the nature of government intervention in the foreign exchange market.

A fifth possible criterion is luck which, by its very nature, is a random variable and is impossible to induce on a consistent basis.

1. Governments that maintain fixed exchange rates have removed some of the requirements for luck when it comes to successful forecasting.

2. When it comes to forecasting in a floating-rate system, however, the forecaster has the choice of using market-based forecasts or model-based forecasts, neither of which provides guarantee of success.

E. Market-based forecasts of exchange rate changes can be derived from current spot and forward rates. In other words,

$$f_1 = e_1$$

where f_1 is the forward rate for one period from new and e_1 is the expected future spot rate.

1. Various empirical studies of forward and spot rates have shown that the forward rate is a poor predictor of the future spot exchange rate.

    a. It is probably a poor predictor because spot rates move quickly to the value warranted by the market's expectations of future policies.

    b. Most variation in exchange rates is due to new and, therefore, unpredictable information.

2. Nonetheless, currencies selling at forward discounts tend to depreciate over time, and those selling a forward premiums tend to appreciate. In the long-run, relative inflation rates, which largely determine expectations of currency movements, apparently dominate variation in other factors.

3. The absence of longer-term forward contracts (more than one year) necessitates the use of interest rate differentials for exchange rate predictions beyond one year. These implicit forecasts are imbedded in the term structure of Euro-currency interest rates.

4. The market's expected spot rate in n years can be found by assuming that in equilibrium, investors demand equal returns on domestic and foreign securities.

$$e_n = e_0 \frac{(1 + R\$_s)^n}{(1 + R^n_f)^n}$$

    where: e_n = expected spot rate in year n
            e_0 = current spot rate
            $R\$_s$ = current n-year dollar Euro-deposit rate
            R^n_f = current n-year foreign currency Euro-deposit rate

5. When using market-based forecasts, it should be remembered that the empirical evidence indicates only that forward rates and interest differentials are unbiased predictors of future currency changes; there is little reason to believe that they are accurate estimators.

F. The two principal model-based approaches to currency prediction are known as technical analysis and fundamental analysis.

    1. Fundamental analysis relies on examining macroeconomic variables and policies that are likely to influence a currency's prospects. The variables examined include relative inflation and interest rates, national income growth, and changes in money supplies.

a. Most analysts treat currency values as determined by demand-and-supply flows in the foreign exchange currency determination, also called the <u>traditional flow model</u>, th analysis of the different economic variables centers on their impact on the balance-of-payments (BOP).

   (1) Forecasters attempt to anticipate the direction and magnitude of imbalances that may occur in each of the various accounts in the BOP and in the overall balanc

   (2) If the overall balance can be successfully estimated, then the forecaster can determine the demand and supp of a currency as well as its future value.

   (3) Factors affecting trade flows include relative inflation rates, growth rates of national income, and real interest rates.

b. According to the <u>asset market model</u>, an exchange rate is simply the relative price of two assets and is determined in the same way as are the prices of other financial assets, such as bonds, stocks, and real estate. The asse market model predicts that:

   (1) The value of a currency depends on the current expectation of all future variables that help determi the value of these services.

   (2) A healthy, growing economy should result in a stronge currency.

   (3) There should be no determinate relationship between exchange rates and movements in either the trade or t current-account balance.

c. Because currencies are assets, the modern theory of asset price determination in efficient markets has an important implication for those interested in assessing currency values:

   (1) Exchange rates will fluctuate randomly as market participants assess and then react to new information.

   (2) As a result, exchange rate movements are unpredictable other wise, it would be possible to earn arbitrage profits.

d. The simplest form of fundamental analysis involves the use of purchasing power parity (PPP).

(1) The usefulness of PPP as a currency forecasting technique depends on whether a lag exists between price level changes and currency value changes. The greater the lag, the greater the ability to forecast currency movements.

(2) If exchange rates adjust immediately to price level changes, then PPP will be worthless for currency predictions.

e. There is an inherent conflict between the efficient markets concept and any lagged adjustment to PPP.

(1) Based on sophisticated statistical approaches, Rogalski and Vinso (1977) concluded that in a world of freely floating exchange rates, currency values reacted immediately, or nearly so, to change sin inflation.

(2) In a later study, Roll (1979) examined the possibility that PPP might not hold in periods characterized by fixed or managed floating exchange rates. The results of his study indicate that prices adjust rapidly to a long-run parity relationship.

2. Technical analysis focuses exclusively on past price and volume movements, while totally ignoring economic and political factors to forecast currency changes. Success depends on whether technical analysts can discover price trends that are forecastable, which will only be possible if price patterns repeat themselves. There are two primary methods of technical analysis: charting and trend analysis.

a. Chartists examine bar charts or use more sophisticated computer-based extrapolation techniques to find recurring price patterns and then issue buy and sell recommendations if prices deviate from their past pattern.

b. Trend analysis seeks to identify price treads by applying various mathematical computations. The object here is to determine whether particular price trends will continue or shift direction.

3. The possibility that fundamental analysis can be used to profitably forecast future exchange rates is inconsistent with the semi-strong form of market efficiency, which states that current exchange rates reflect all publicly available information.

4. The possibility that technical analysis discovers price trend or patterns that repeat themselves is inconsistent with the weak form of market efficiency, which states that the present price incorporates all relevant information contained in past prices.

5. Any currency forecasting model should be able to consistently outperform the market's estimate of currency changes.

6. To determine whether currency forecasts are worth their costs the performance must be evaluated on the basis of accuracy and correctness.

   a. The <u>accuracy</u> measure focuses on the deviations between the actual and the forecasted exchange rates.

   b. The <u>correctness</u> measure examines whether or not the forecast predicts the right direction of the change in exchange rates.

7. The relative predictive ability of the forecasting services can be evaluated by using the following decision rule:

   (1) if $f_1 > e_1$ sell forward

   (2) if $f_1 < e_1$ buy forward

   where: f_1 = forward rate
   e_1 = forecasted spot rate.

   a. This decision rule states that if the forecasted rate fall below the forward rate, the currency should be sold forward; if the forecasted rate falls above the forward rate, the currency should be bought forward.

   b. Where e_1 is the actual spot rate being forecasted, the percentage profit (loss) realized from this strategy is

      (1) $100[(f_1 - e_1)/e_1]$ when $f_1 > e_1$, and

      (2) $100[(e_1 - f_1)/e_1]$ when $f_1 < e_1$

   c. Levich (1980) investigated 14 forecast advisory services and found that the profits associated with using several of these forecasts seem too good to be explained by chance.

   d. Later studies by Bilson, Dooley, and Schaefer (1981) and Goodman (1981) support this conclusion.

   e. These studies all strongly suggest a favorable risk-return tradeoff from using currency forecasting services.

8. The above mentioned decision rule is basically geared toward evaluating forecasting models whose outputs is to be used in planning forward market hedging activities. These forecasts could also be employed in:

    a. Evaluating investment opportunities, or

    b. Developing marketing strategies.

9. When trying to make profitable hedging decisions, it is not necessary that the forecast to be acted on is accurate, what is essential is that one of the following four relationships between the forecasted rates (e_1), the forward rate (f_1), and the actual future spot rate (e_1) hold:

    (1) $e_1 \; < \; e_1 \; < \; f_1$

    (2) $e_1 \; < \; e_1 \; < \; f_1$

    (3) $e_1 \; > \; e_1 \; > \; f_1$

    (4) $e_1 \; > \; e_1 \; > \; f_1$.

10. While empirical studies suggest that forecasting services can enable users to earn a profit, it may just provide compensation for the additional risks of currency speculation. Moreover, currency forecasting models which worked well in the past may not work well in the future if there are structural changes in government monetary, fiscal, or intervention policies or in the asset-demand preferences of individuals.

G. Even if the forward rate or PPP rate are highly inaccurate predictors of future spot rates, whether or not they are unbiased, we should be able to construct a new, <u>composite forecast</u> that is superior than any individual forecast.

1. A composite forecast ($\hat{e}_t$) can be constructed of the form:

$$\hat{e}_t \; = \; w_1 \, \hat{e}_{t,1} \; + \; w_2 \, \hat{e}_{t,2}$$

    where: $\hat{e}_{t,n}$ = forecast of the spot rate at time $t = 1,\ldots,n$.
    w_n = weights selected by linear regression analysis to maximize the forecasting efficiency of the composite forecast.

2. Bilson (1981) and Levich (1981) present strong evidence that such composite forecasts are generally more accurate and more reliable than the best individual forecasts.

H. Currency forecasting services typically provide forecasts of nominal exchange rates. These forecasts may be of value for deciding whether or not to buy or sell currencies forward. But i is changes in the real exchange rate that have the most severe competitive consequences for companies operating in the international environment.

1. In a floating exchange rate system, real exchange rates follo a random walk, which, in turn, has two important implications

   a. The best forecast of the future real exchange rate is today's spot exchange rate.

   b. The expected change in the real exchange rate is zero.

   c. Thus, any changes in real exchange rates are unexpected. And it is these unexpected real exchange rate changes that are the primary cause of exchange risk.

   d. The way to deal with exchange risk is to forecast the changes in the operating cash flows associated with unexpected real exchange rate changes and then structure corporate operations and corporate liabilities to offset these cash flow effects.

2. In a fixed exchange rate system, changes in nominal exchange rates will result in real exchange rate changes as well.

   a. Thus, nominal and real exchange rate forecasting are likel to be synonymous.

   b. The forecasting emphasis, therefore, should be on nominal exchange rate changes.

II. Exchange Rate Forecasting in a Fixed-Rate System

A. In a world of fixed exchange rates, the forecaster has to focus o the ability of the authorities to hold to their announced commitment.

B. This forecasting involves a five-step procedure:

1. Calculating an equilibrium exchange rate based on a variety o economic factors, such as relative inflation and interest rates.

2. Forecasting the balance-of-payments, taking into account its likely balance of trade, other current-account items that may be significant, and capital flows.

3. Combining the output from step (2) with an estimate of the central bank's level of owned and borrowed reserves.

4. Predicting which of the rather limited policy options the government will choose. These options include:

   a. Devaluation.

   b. Currency controls.

   c. Deflation.

   d. Borrowing abroad.

5. Examining the implications for future exchange rate changes based on the government policy options selected.

C. While in the long run, relative rates of inflation and other economic forces determine the currency adjustment required, in the short run, a government can sustain a persistent balance-of-payments disequilibrium for several years.

1. The timing of implementing government policies is a political decision.

2. Predicting a government's likely response involves an assessment of:

   a. The key political decision makers.

   b. Their often conflicting economic goals.

   c. The economic consequences of a currency change on these goals.

   d. The ruling party's ideology.

   e. Internal and external political pressures.

   f. The existence of any special events, such as upcoming elections.

3. The decision on what amount of pressure to apply on a currency to adjust is also political.

D. The basic forecasting methodology in a fixed-rate system involves the following steps:

1. Ascertaining the pressure on a currency to devalue or revalue.

2. Determining how long the nation's political leaders can, and
    will, persist with this particular level of disequilibrium.

E. Currency forecasting in a fixed-rate system can be quite
    profitable for two reasons:

    1. Forecasting is made easier because the direction, and often
        the magnitude, of any potential currency change is generally
        known in advance.

    2. Betting against the willing loser can earn consistent profit
        because down-side risk is minimal: Either the exchange rate
        will move in the generally expected direction, or the
        government will manage to maintain the fixed rate; there are
        few surprises.

F. Aliber (1979) estimated that between 1967 and 1973, in which the
    Bretton Woods system was in place, speculators in foreign exchan
    were able to earn about $12 billion at the expense of central
    banks.

G. As a general rule, when forecasting in a fixed-rate system,
    resources should be concentrated on the governmental decision-
    making structure because the decision to revalue or devalue at a
    given time is clearly political.

III. Forecasting Controlled Exchange Rates

    A. Currency forecasting is more difficult in a world in which the
        widespread existence of exchange controls as well as
        restrictions on imports and capital flows often hide the true
        pressures on a currency to devalue.

    B. In such situations, forward markets and capital markets are
        invariably nonexistent or subject to such stringent controls
        that interest and forward differentials are of little practical
        use in providing market based forecasts of exchange rate change

    C. An alternative to conducting an exhaustive economic analysis of
        the various components of the balance of payments is to use
        black-market exchange rates as useful indicators of devaluation
        pressure on a country's currency.

        1. Black-market exchange rates for a number of countries are
            published regularly.

        2. Black markets for foreign exchange are likely to develop
            whenever exchange controls cause a divergence between the
            equilibrium exchange rate and the official exchange rate.

3. The black-market rate depends on the difference between the official and equilibrium exchange rates as well as the penalties for illegal transactions.

    a. This rate is therefore not influenced by exactly the same set of supply-and-demand forces that influence the free market rate.

    b. Thus, it cannot be regarded in itself as indicative of the true equilibrium rate that would prevail in the absence of controls.

4. Economists assume that for an overvalued currency, the hypothetical equilibrium rate lies somewhere between the official rate and the black-market rate.

5. The usefulness of the black-market rate is that it is a good indicator of where the official rate is likely to go if the monetary authorities give in to market pressure.

6. Empirical evidence has shown that the changes in the black-market rate are closely associated with changes in both the hypothetical equilibrium rate and the official rate. In particular, the black-market rate seems to be most accurate in forecasting the official rate one month ahead and is progressively less accurate in forecasting the future rate for longer time periods.

KEY TERMS

Market-Based Forecasts
Model-Based Forecasts
Technical Analysis
Fundamental Analysis
Traditional Flow Model
Asset Market Model
Charting

Trend Analysis
Semi-Strong Form Market
  Efficiency
Weak-Form Market Efficiency
Composite Forecasts
Exchange Risk
Political Analysis
Black-Market Exchange Rate

CONCEPTUAL QUESTIONS

QUESTION 1: Explain the market-based technique for forecasting exchange rates.

ANSWER: The market determines the spot rates and forward rates which can be used to forecast exchange rates. When using market-based forecasts, it should be remembered that the empirical evidence indicates only that forward rates and interest differentials are unbiased predictors of future currency changes; there is little evidence to believe that they are accurate predictors.

QUESTION 2:   How can exchange rates be forecasted in a fixed-rate system

ANSWER: In a world of fixed exchange rates, the forecaster has to focus
the ability of the authorities to hold to their announced commitment.   Th
forecasting involves a five-step procedure:

1. Calculating an equilibrium exchange rate based on a variety of
    economic factors, such as relative inflation and interest rates
2. Forecasting the balance-of-payments, taking into account its
    likely balance of trade, other current-account items that may h
    significant, and capital flows.
3. Combining the output from step (2) with an estimate of the
    central bank's level of owned and borrowed reserves.
4. Predicting which of the rather limited policy options the
    government will choose. These options include devaluation,
    currency controls, deflation, and borrowing abroad.
5. Examining the implications for future exchange rate changes
    based on the government policy options selected.

QUESTION 3:   What is a black-market exchange rate?

ANSWER: A black market for foreign exchange is likely to develop wheneve
exchange controls cause a divergence between the equilibrium exchange rat
and the official exchange rate.   The black-market rate is that rate which
depends on the difference between the official and equilibrium exchange
rates as well as on the penalties for illegal transactions.   This rate is
not influenced by exactly the same set of supply-and-demand forces that
influence the free market rate.   Thus, it cannot be regarded in itself as
indicative of the true equilibrium exchange rate that would prevail in th
absence of currency controls.

SELECTED PROBLEMS FROM THE TEXT

PROBLEM 1:   Chase Econometrics has just published projected inflation ra
for the United States and West Germany for the next five years.   U.S.
inflation is expected to be at 10% per year; West German inflation is
expected to be at 4% per year.   If the current exchange rates is DM 1 +
$0.50, what should the exchange rates for the next five years be?

SOLUTION:

According to PPP, the exchange rate for the DM at the end of year
should equal

$$.5(1.10/1.04)^t.$$

Hence, projected exchange rates for the next 5 years are

.5288, .5594, .5916, .6258, .6619.

PROBLEM 3:   Suppose today's spot exchange rates is \$0.51:DM 1.   The 6-month
interest rates on dollars and DM are 13% and 6%, respectively.   The 6-month
forward rate is \$0.5170:DM 1.   A foreign exchange advisory service has
predicted that the DM will appreciate to
40.54:DM 1 within six months.

    a.   How would you use forward contracts to profit in the above
        situation?

    b.   How would you use money market instruments (borrowing and
        lending) to profit?

    c.   Which alternative (forward contracts or money market instruments)
        would you prefer?   Why?

SOLUTION:

    a.   The forecast suggests that the DM will appreciate above the
        forward rate.   To profit, buy DM forward.

    b.   To profit via the money market, borrow dollars at 6.5%, buy DM
        spot, and lend the DM at 3% (interest rates are halved to
        reflect the 6-month time period).   If your expectations are
        correct, your dollar return on DM will be

$$1.03(.54)/.5 - 1 = 11.24\%.$$

        Subtracting the 6.5% cost of borrowing dollars yields 4.74%.

    c.   The numbers are selected so the interest parity relationship
        holds.   Thus, there is no difference in profit or risks between
        the two alternatives.   Clearly, there would be a disequilibrium
        situation if one alternative were preferred.   People would shift
        to the preferred alternative until prices adjusted to the point
        at which IRPT held and equilibrium was restored.

PROBLEM 5:   Suppose 3-year deposit rates on Eurodollars and Eurofrancs
(Swiss) are 12% and 7%, respectively.   If the current spot rate for the
Swiss franc is \$0.3985, what is the spot rate implied by these interest
rates for the franc three years from now?

SOLUTION:

    If r_{us} and r_{sw} are the associated Eurodollar and Eurofranc nominal
    interest rates, then the international Fisher effect says that

$$e_t/e_0 = (1 + r_{us})^t/(1 + r_{sw})^t$$

    where e_t is the period t expected spot rate and e_0 is the current
    spot rate (Sfr1 = \$e).   Substituting in the numbers given in the
    problem yields

$$e_3 = \$.3985 \times (1.12/1.07)^3 = \$.4570.$$

Mexican Peso Devaluation on November 18, 1987

Expectations of continued high inflation and a more pessimistic vi
of Mexico's economic prospects following the October 1987 market crash
aroused fears of peso devaluation. The resulting capital flight forced 1
hand of Mexico's central bank. It withdrew support from the peso on
November 18, 1987, and the peso immediately tumbled 31% against the dolla
The peso's free fall further undermined confidence in the Mexican
government and made the drain on reserves even worse than it was before 1
government moved to staunch it.

CHAPTER 8

MEASURING ACCOUNTING EXPOSURE

Summary: This chapter presents alternative currency translation methods, focusing on <u>Statements</u> <u>of</u> <u>Financial</u> <u>Accounting</u> <u>Standards</u> No. 8 (the past translation method) and No. 52 (the current translation method). The chapter also discusses the differences between accounting requirements and economic reality, making recommendations to accountants and financial executives on how to adjust reporting standards in order to reconcile those differences.

I. Alternative Currency Translation Methods

   A. The financial statements of a MNC's overseas subsidiaries must be translated from local currency to home currency prior to consolidation with the parent's financial statements.

   B. If currency values change, foreign exchange translation gains or losses may result.

      1. Assets and liabilities that are translated at the <u>current</u> exchange rate are considered <u>exposed</u>.

      2. Those translated at a historical rate will maintain their historic rate will maintain their historic home currency values and thus are regarded as not exposed.

   C. <u>Translation</u> <u>exposure</u> is simply the difference between exposed assets and exposed liabilities.

   D. Controversies among accountants center on the following issues:

      1. The identification of which assets and liabilities are exposed.

      2. The timing of recognizing accounting-derived exchange gains and losses.

   E. Four principal translation methods are used by MNCs around the world:

      1. Current/Noncurrent Method

         a. Current assets and liabilities are translated into home currency at the current rate.

       b.   Noncurrent assets and liabilities are translated at a _historical_ rate; that is, at the rate in effect at the t: the asset was acquired or the liability incurred.

       c.   Income statement items are translated at the average exchange rate of the period, except for those revenues ar expenses associated with noncurrent assets or liabilities

2.   Monetary/Nonmonetary Method

       a.   Monetary items, such as cash, accounts payables and receivables, and long-term debt, are translated at the current rate.

       b.   Nonmonetary balance sheet items, such as inventory, fixec assets, and long-term investments, are translated at historical rates.

       c.   The income statement is translated at the average exchang rate during the period, except for revenue and expense items related to nonmonetary assets and liabilities.

3.   Temporal Method

       a.   This currency translation method is a modified version of the monetary/nonmonetary method.

       b.   The only difference is that inventory, which is normally translated at the historical rate, could also be translat at the current rate if the inventory is shown on the balance sheet at market values.

       c.   The choice of exchange rate for translation is based on t type of asset or liability in the monetary/nonmonetary method; in the temporal method, it is based on the underlying approach to evaluating cost.

       d.   Income statement items are normally translated at an average weight for the reporting period. However, cost o goods sold and depreciation and amortization charges associated with balance sheet items carried at past price are translated at historical rates.

4.   Current-Rate Method

       a.   All balance sheet and income statement items are translat at the current rate.

      b.   Under this method, if a firm's foreign currency denominated assets exceed its foreign currency denominated liabilities, a devaluation must result in a loss and a revaluation in a gain.

      c.   One variation is to translate all assets and liabilities except not fixed assets at the current rate.

II. Statement of Financial Accounting Standards No. 8 (FASB-8)

  A. FASB-8 established uniform standards for the translation into dollars of foreign currency-denominated financial statements and transactions of U.S.-based multinational corporations.

  B. FASB-8, which was based on the temporal method, became effective on January 1, 1976.

  C. Its main purpose was its consistency with generally accepted accounting practice (GAAP) that requires balance sheet items to be valued or translated according to their underlying measurement basis, i.e., current or historical.

  D. A major source of corporate dissatisfaction with FASB-8 was the ruling that all reserves for currency losses be disallowed.

      1. Before FASB-8, firms established reserves and could defer unrealized translation gains and losses by charging them against the reserves, thus cushioning the impact of sharp changes in currency values on reported earnings.

      2. Under FASB-8, currency fluctuations had far greater impacts on the profit-loss statements than did the sales and profit margins of multinational corporations' product lines.

III. Statement of Financial Accounting Standards No. 52 (FASB-52)

  A. Widespread dissatisfaction by corporate executives over FASB-8 led to a new translation standard: FASB-52.

  B. According to FASB-52, which is effective for fiscal years on, or after, December 15, 1981, firm's must use the current rate method to translate foreign currency-denominated assets and liabilities into dollars.

  C. All foreign currency revenue and expense items on the income statement must be translated at either the exchange rate in effect on the date those items are recognized or at an appropriately weighted average exchange rate for the period.

D. The most important difference between FASB-8 and FASB-52 is tha
    most FASB-52 translation gains and losses are accumulated in a
    separate equity account on the parent's balance sheet, thus
    bypassing the income statement. This account is call the
    accumulated translation adjustment.

E. Furthermore, FASB-52 differentiates for the first time between
    the functional currency and the reporting currency. This
    distinction forms the basis for determining which translation
    gains and losses are to be excluded from income.

    1. The functional currency of an affiliate is the currency of
        the primary economic environment in which the affiliate
        generates and expenses cash.

    2. In the case of a hyperinflation country, which is defined a;
        one having cumulative inflation of approximately 100% or mo
        over a three-year period, the functional currency must be t
        dollar.

    3. The reporting currency is the currency in which the parent
        firm prepares its own financial statements.

F. FASB-52 requires that the financial statements of a foreign
    subsidiary first be stated in the functional currency and then
    translated at the current exchange rate at each balance sheet
    date.

G. Transaction gains and losses that result from adjusting assets
    and liabilities denominated in a currency other than the
    functional currency, or from settling such items, generally mus
    appear on the affiliate's income statement.

H. The only exception to this requirement include:

    1. Gains and losses attributable to a foreign currency
        transaction that is designated as an economic hedge of a ne
        investment in a foreign subsidiary which must be included i
        the accumulated translation adjustment (CTA) account.

    2. Gains and losses attributable to intercompany foreign
        currency transactions that are of a long-term investment
        nature which must be included in the CTA account.

    3. Gains and losses attributable to foreign currency
        transactions that hedge identifiable foreign currency
        commitments which are to be deferred and included in the
        measurement on the basis of the related foreign transaction

I.   The requirements regarding translation of transactions apply both to:

    1.   Transactions entered into by a U.S. company and denominated in a currency other than the U.S. dollar.

    2.   Transactions entered into by a foreign affiliate of a U.S. company and denominated in a currency other than its functional currency.

J.   If the functional currency is the dollar, then the foreign unit's local currency financial statements must be remeasured in dollars. In this case, the temporal method, as previously required by FASB-8, is applied with translation gains and losses included in the income statement.

IV. Accounting Practice and Economic Reality

A.   In developing an effective strategy for managing currency risk, management must first determine what is at risk. This determination requires an appropriate definition of foreign exchange risk.

B.   There is a major discrepancy between accounting practice and economic reality in terms of measuring exposure.

    1.   Accounting measures of exposure focus on the effect of currency changes on previous decisions of the firm, as reflected in the balance sheet values of assets acquired and liabilities incurred in the past.

    2.   Economic exposure is defined as the extent to which the value of the firm, as measured by the present value of its expected future cash flows, will change when exchange rates change.

C.   In theory, at least, there should be no discrepancy between accounting and economic values. All assets and liabilities should be priced according to the present values of their expected future cash inflows and outflows.

D.   The problem is that information derived from a historical-cost accounting system cannot truly account for the economic effects of a devaluation or revaluation on the value of a firm.

V. Recommendations for Accountants and International Financial Executives

A.   Since the real effect of currency changes is on a firm's future cash flows, information based on retrospective accounting techniques may bear no relationship to a firm's actual operating results.

B. The distortions associated with measures of accounting exposure d
    not mean that accounting statements are irrelevant; clearly these
    statements serve a useful purpose and are necessary for
    consolidating the results of a worldwide network of operating
    units. The danger is that the results will be misinterpreted by
    stockholders, bankers, security analysts, and the board of
    directors.

C. In fact, financial managers generally are aware of the misleading
    nature of many of these results. Yet, they undertake cosmetic
    exchange risk management actions because they are concerned about
    those who will not understand the real, as opposed to the
    accounting, effects of currency changes.

D. A 1978 study sponsored by the Financial Accounting Standards Boar
    has shown that investors are concerned that emphasis on accountin
    exposure, in fact, causes financial managers to take incorrect or
    incomplete actions in managing economic exposure.

E. According to Evans, Folks, and Yelling (1978), FASB-8 affected
    investment policies to the extent that 29% of the respondent
    companies reframed from making investments, that were otherwise
    acceptable, because of the potential impact of translation gains
    and losses.

F. The existence of sophisticated traders should preclude a firm's
    ability to change its market value purely by manipulating
    accounting data.

G. Moreover, in an efficient market, translation gains or losses wil
    be placed in a proper perspective by investors and, therefore,
    should not affect the stock price of a MNC.

H. The adoption of FASB-52 has helped increase insight, into the
    effects of currency changes on foreign operations. Consequently,
    an increasing number of MNCs are now placing greater emphasis on
    management of longer term economic exposure.

KEY TERMS

Exposure
Accounting Exposure
Translation Exposure
Current/Noncurrent Method
Monetary/Nonmonetary Method
Temporal Method
Current-Rate Method
Historical Rate

FASB-8
FASB-52
Cumulative Translation
    Adjustment Account
Functional Currency
Reporting Currency
Hyperinflation
Economic Exposure

CONCEPTUAL QUESTIONS

QUESTION 1: What is the major difference between FASB-8 and FASB-52:

ANSWER: Under FASB-8 translation gains and losses are funneled through the income statement, thereby affecting the accounting profits of the firm. The translation gains and losses under FASB-52 are recorded in a separate equity account, called the "cumulative translation adjustment account," thus bypassing the income statement.

QUESTION 2: Compare and contrast the functional currency and the reporting currency of an affiliate.

ANSWER: The functional currency of an affiliate is the currency of the primary economic environment in which the affiliate generates and expends cash. The reporting currency is the currency in which the parent firm prepares its own financial statements.

QUESTION 3: What is economic exposure?

ANSWER: Economic exposure is defined as the extent to which the value of the firm as, measured by the present value of its expected future cash flows, will change when exchange rates change.

SELECTED PROBLEMS FROM THE TEXT

PROBLEM 1: Suppose an American firm has a French subsidiary. On January 1, the subsidiary's balance sheet showed current assets of FF 1 million, current liabilities of FF 300,000; total assets of FF 2.5 million; and total liabilities of FF 900,000. On December 31, the subsidiary's balance sheet in francs was unchanged from the figures given above, but the franc had declined in value from $0.1270 at the start of the year to $0.1180 at the end of the year. Under FASB-52, what is the translation amount to be shown on the parent company's equity account for the year if the franc is the functional currency? How would your answer change if the dollar were the functional currency?

SOLUTION:

According to FASB-52, balance sheets must be translated using the current rate method; that is, all assets and all liabilities must be translated at the current rate.

Exposed Assets:

Current assets	FF 1,000,000	
Fixed assets	1,500,000	
Total exposed assets		FF 2,500,(

Exposed Liabilities

Current liabilities	FF 300,000	
Long-term liabilities	600,000	
Total exposed liabilities		900,(

Net Exposed Assets   FF 1,600,(

At the original rate of $.1270, the value of the franc net exposure w

$$FF\ 1,600,000 \times .1270 = \$203,200.$$

By the end of the year, this net exposure equals

$$FF\ 1,600,000 \times \$.1180 = \$188,800.$$

This involves a translation loss of $14,400 ($203,200 - $188,800).

Assuming that the current assets are all monetary or that inventory carried at market value, the firm's exposure if the dollar is the functional currency would be current assets minus current liabilities or

$$FF\ 1,000,000 - FF\ 900,000 = FF\ 100,000.$$

In this case, the firm would have a translation loss equal to

$$100,000 \times (.1270 - .1180) = \$900.$$

This loss would have to be included in the income statement.

PROBLEM 2:   Suppose that at the start and at the end of the year your subsidiary in England had current assets of £1 million, fixed assets of £2 million, and current liabilities of £1 million.   There are no long-term liabilities.   If the pound depreciated during that year from $1.50 to $1.30, what is the FASB-52 translation gain (loss) to be included in the parent company's equity account?

SOLUTION:

Under FASB-52 the English affiliate has net pound exposure equal to:

Exposed Assets

Current assets	£1.0 million	
Fixed assets	2.0 million	
Total exposed assets		£3.0 million

Exposed Liabilities

Current liabilities	£1.0 million	
Total exposed liabilities		£1.0 million

Net Exposed Assets	£2.0 million

At the original exchange rate of $1.50, the value of this net exposure is $3 million.

By the end of the year, this net pound exposure is worth only

$$2 \text{ million x } \$1.30 = \$2.6 \text{ million.}$$

The net result is a translation loss equal to the difference between the beginning and end-of-year values or $400,000.

MEASURING ECONOMIC EXPOSURE

Summary: In this chapter it is attempted to develop an appropriate definition of foreign exchange risk. The nature and origins of exchange risk are discussed, and a theory of the economic consequences of currency changes on the value of the firm is presented. This chapter also illustrates how economic exposure can be measured and provides an operational measure of exchange risk.

I. Foreign Exchange Risk and Economic Exposure

    A. The most critical aspect of foreign exchange risk management is t incorporate expectations about exchange rate changes into all bas corporate decision affecting cash flow and financial structure.

    B. Management can choose between:

        1. Self-insuring the risks of unanticipated currency fluctuations.

        2. Laying these risks off in the financial markets.

    C. In making this decision, the firm must know what is at risk.

        1. Those who use an accounting definition--whether FASB-8 or FASB-52 or some other translation method--divide the assets and liabilities into those accounts that will be exposed to exchange rate changes and those that remain unexposed.

        2. Economic theory focuses on the impact of an exchange rate change on future cash flows; that is, economic exposure is based on the extent to which the value of the firm--measured the present value of the expected future cash flows--will change when exchange rates change.

        3. Exchange risk, in turn, is defined as the variability in the firm's value that is caused by uncertain exchange rate change Thus, exchange risk is viewed as the possibility that currenc fluctuations can alter the expected amounts or variability of the firm's future cash flows.

    D. The definitions of economic exposure and exchange risk, which are based on market value, assume that the goal of financial managemer is to maximize the value of the firm.

1. While some managers will prefer to pursue other objectives, many multinational financial managers probably consider the reduction of the variability of translated earnings as the principal function of exchange risk management.

2. Market efficiency is closely associated with value maximization. If the capital markets did not rationally price the firm's securities, it would be difficult to convince managers to design a foreign exchange strategy that could be expected to maximize shareholders' wealth.

E. In order to determine a firm's true economic exposure, it is necessary to explicitly recognize the implications of two equilibrium relationships, and deviations from the, for the estimation and valuation of future cash flows.

1. According to the theory of purchasing power parity, changes in the ratio of domestic to foreign prices will cause offsetting changes in the exchange rate so as to maintain the relative purchasing powers of the currencies involved.

2. The international Fisher effect states that returns on assets being held and the costs of liabilities incurred should implicitly incorporate anticipated currency changes.

II. The Economic Consequences of Exchange Rate Changes

A. Economic exposure to exchange risk can be separated into two components: transaction exposure and real operating exposure.

1. Transaction exposure is the possibility of incurring exchange gains or losses, upon settlement at a future date, on transactions already entered into and denominated in a foreign currency.

2. Real operating exposure arises because currency fluctuations combined with price changes can alter company's future revenues and expenses.

B. Thus, a company faces real operating exposure from the time it invests in servicing a market subject to foreign competition or in sourcing goods or inputs abroad. Transaction exposure arises later on, and only if the company's commitments lead it to engage in foreign-currency-denominated sales or purchases.

C. Measuring economic exposure is difficult because it is impossible to assess the effects of an exchange rate change without simultaneously considering the impact on cash flows of the underlying relative rates of inflation associated with each currency. Specifically,

$$e_t^{\wedge} = e_t \frac{(1 + i_{f,t})}{(1 + i_{h,t})}$$

where: $e_t^{\wedge}$ = real exchange rate at time t

e_t = nominal exchange rate at time t

$i_{f,t}$ = amount of foreign inflation between times 0 and t

$i_{h,t}$ = amount of domestic inflation between times 0 and t

This equation states that the real exchange rate is equal to the nominal exchange rate adjusted for changes in the relative purchasing power of each currency since some base period.

1. Real exchange rate and exchange risk.

   a. A dramatic change in the nominal exchange rate accompanie by an <u>equal</u> change in the price level should have no effects on the relative competitive positions of domestic firms and their foreign competitors and, therefore, will not alter the <u>real</u> cash flows.

   b. If the real exchange rate changes, it will cause relative price changes which, in turn, cause exchange risk.

2. Inflation and exchange risk.

   a. If the law of one price holds and if there is no variatic in the relative prices of goods or services, then the rat of change in the exchange rate must equal the difference between the inflation rates in the two countries.

   b. Without relative price changes, the MNC faces no real operating exchange risk.

   c. Without any fixed contractual agreement in foreign currency terms, the firm's foreign cash flows will vary with the foreign rate of inflation.

   d. Since the exchange rate is also determined by the inflation rate differential between the two countries, th movement of the exchange rate exactly cancels the change in the foreign price level, leaving home currency cash flows in affected.

   e. With fixed contractual agreements in terms of foreign currencies and assuming further that the real exchange rate remains constant, the risk introduced by entering into fixed contracts is not exchange risk, but inflation risk.

f. According to the international Fisher effect, gains or losses on Contractual cash flows in hard currencies (those likely to appreciate) will be offset by low interest rates, and those in soft currencies (those likely to depreciate) by higher interest rates. Thus, at any point in time, currency gains or losses are to be expected from foreign-currency-denominated contractual cash flows.

3. Relative price changes and exchange risk.

   a. For real operating exposure to exist, exchange rate changes must cause relative price changes within and among countries.

   b. A change in the real exchange rate should lead to changes in the price of imports relative to the price of goods from domestic sources, thus benefiting some sectors in the economy and adversely affecting others.

   c. Real long-run exchange risk is largely the risk associated with relative price changes that are brought about by real exchange rate changes.

4. The economic impact of a currency change on a firm depends on whether the exchange rate change is fully offset by the difference in inflation rates or whether the real exchange rate and, therefore, relative prices change. It is these relative price changes that determine a firm's long-run exposure.

D. Transaction exposure arises out of the various types of transactions that require settlement in a foreign currency, examples are cross-border trade, borrowing and lending in foreign currencies, and local purchasing and sales activities of foreign subsidiaries.

   1. The transaction exposure report contains:

      a. Items already on a firm's balance sheet, such as loans and receivables, which capture some of the transactions.

      b. A number of off-balance sheet items which include future sales and purchases, lease payments, forward contracts, loan repayments, and other contractual or anticipated foreign currency receipts and disbursements.

   2. The flow-of-funds report is constructed by forecasting revenues as well as expenses (interest, royalties, management fees, dividends, and purchases) the company expects to incur, broken down by currency.

3. By consolidating the reports of all its affiliates with the parent company's operations, the firm can come up with a worldwide flow-of-funds report by currency.

E. Often an attempt to cover a firm's accounting exposure can actually increase its economic exposure.

F. To measure the likely exchange gains or losses to a currency change requires reference to the accompanying inflation rate. Otherwise, results will be misleading.

G. A change in the real exchange rate will affect a number of aspec of a firm's operations.

1. With respect to a home currency (dollar) appreciation, the k issue for a domestic firm is its degree of <u>pricing flexibility</u>, which depends largely on the price elasticity c demand.

   a. The <u>less</u> price-elastic the demand, the greater the price flexibility a company has in responding to currency changes.

   b. Price elasticity, in turn, depends on the degree of competition and the location of key competition.

   c. The <u>more</u> differentiated a company's products, the less competition it faces and the greater is its ability to maintain its domestic currency prices both at home and abroad.

   d. If most competition are located in the home country, the all will face the same change in their cost structure fr home currency appreciation, and all can raise their foreign currency prices without putting any of them at a competitive disadvantage relative to their domestic competitors.

   e. Conversely, the <u>less</u> differentiated a company's products are and the more internationally diversified its competitors, the <u>greater</u> the price elasticity of demand for its products and the <u>less</u> its pricing flexibility. These companies face the greatest amount of exchange ris]

2. With respect to a local currency depreciation, the foreign operations of a MNC will be affected in the following way:

   a. Local Demand. A devaluation will reduce import competition. With strong import competition, local currency prices will increase, although not to the full extent of the devaluation. However, with import weak or nonexistent import competition, local prices will increase little, if at all, because prices would have already been raised as much as possible.

   b. Foreign Demand. Foreign prices, expressed in the home currency, should remain the same or decrease, depending on the degree of competition from other exporters. The extent of foreign price changes depends on the price elasticity of foreign demand.

   c. Cost of Local Input. Local currency costs will rise, although not to the full extent of the devaluation. The increase is positively associated with the import content of local inputs as well as with the availability of these inputs.

   d. Costs of Imported Inputs. The costs of imported inputs in terms of the home currency should remain the same or decrease somewhat. The decrease will depend on the elasticity of demand for these imported goods as well as on the size of the local market relative to the world market.

   e. Depreciation. The cash flow associated with the depreciation tax shield can have a substantial net present value, particularly for a capital-intensive corporation. Unless indexation of fixed assets is permitted, the dollar value of the local-currency-denominated tax shield will unambiguously decline by the percentage of nominal devaluation.

   f. Working Capital. The impact of a minimal currency change on working capital can be analyzed in two ways.

      (1) From a traditional view, the firm will show a loss (gain) on its net local currency monetary assets (liabilities) if a devaluation occurs.

(2) If the firm is considered to be an ongoing entity, a minimum level of working capital is required as plant and equipment. Thus, in terms of the present value o cash flows associated with the net investment in working capital, the real loss (gain) on working capital is equal to the net increase (decrease) in th dollar value of working capital required following a devaluation.

4. To measure the firm's true economic exposure, it is important to consider the sector of the economy in which a firm operates, the sources of the firm's inputs, and the fluctuations in the real exchange rate.

5. From this analysis it is not surprising to find that domestic facilities which supply foreign markets normally entail much greater exchange risk than do foreign facilities supplying local markets. The reason is that material and labor used in a domestic plant are paid for in the home currency while the products are sold in a foreign currency.

6. A firm or its affiliate producing solely for the domestic market and using only domestic sources of inputs can be strongly affected by currency changes, even though its accounting exposure is zero.

III. An Operational Measure of Exchange Risk

A. The exchange risk faced by a parent or one of its foreign affiliate can be defined as the extent to which variations in the dollar value of the unit's cash flow are correlated with variations in the nominal exchange rate.

B. This definition, in turn, can be used to determine a firm's true economic exposure and its susceptibility to exchange risk.

C. A simple way to implement this definition is to regress actual cash flows from post periods, converted into their dollar values, on the average exchange rate during the corresponding period. Specifically, this involves running the regression

$$CF_t = X + \beta\ EXCH_t + u_t$$

where: CF_t = dollar value of total affiliate (parent) cash flows in period t;

$EXCH_t$ = average nominal exchange rate during period t;

u = random error term with mean equal to zero.

D. The output from such a regression includes three key parameters:

   1. The foreign exchange beta (β) coefficient, which measures the sensitivity of dollar cash flows to exchange rate changes.

   2. The t-statistic, which measures the statistical significance of the beta coefficient.

   3. The R^2, which measures the fraction of cash flow variability explained by variation in the exchange rate.

E. The validity of this approach is clearly dependent on the sensitivity of future cash flows to exchange rate changes being similar to their historical sensitivity. In the absence of additional information, this assumption may be reasonable. But a firm may have reason to modify the implementation of this model because of some other important variables, such as exposed currency tax shields or contractual cash flows resulting in transaction exposure.

F. The impact of fluctuating currency values is to affect the variability or riskiness of the firm's corporate earnings and, in turn, its ability to raise funds at a reasonable cost. However, a firm's actual exchange risk can be determined only by examining the impact of variations in nominal exchange rates on variations in the firm's worldwide consolidated cash flows.

G. There are several reasons to believe that the real impact of nominal currency fluctuations will be less severe than is generally supposed.

   1. The offsetting effects of inflation.

   2. Business conditions and currency changes are not perfectly correlated.

   3. Most MNCs have cash inflows and cash outflows in a variety of different currencies, which are imperfectly, and even negatively, correlated. Thus, international currency diversification could reduce the total variability of dollar cash flows.

H. The shareholder can most likely reduce his or her risk without sacrificing return by holding a well-diversified portfolio of stocks and other financial assets. Hence, currency risk will probably be unsystematic in nature for which an efficient capital market does not provide a premium.

KEY TERMS

Economic Exposure
Exchange Risk
Transaction Exposure
Real Operating Exposure
Inflation Risk
Contractual Cash Flows
Hard Currencies
Soft Currencies

Exposure Report
Fund-Flow Report
Transaction Exposure Report
Pricing Flexibility
Price Elasticity of Demand
Currency of Denomination
Currency of Determination

CONCEPTUAL QUESTIONS

QUESTION 1: Define the two components of economic exposure, and explain when each exposure arises to the firm.

ANSWER: The two components of economic risk are transaction exposure and real operating exposure. Transaction exposure is defined as the possibility of incurring exchange gains or losses on transactions already entered into and denominated in a foreign currency. Real operating exposure is defined as the impact of currency fluctuations, together with price changes, on the company's future revenues and costs.

   A firm faces operating exposure the moment it invests in servicing a market subject to foreign competition or in sourcing goods or inputs abroad. Transaction exposure arises later on, and only if the company's commitments lead it to engage in foreign-denominated sales or purchases.

SELECTED QUESTIONS FROM THE TEXT

QUESTION 1a: Define exposure, differentiating between accounting and economic eaxposure. What role does inflation play?

ANSWER: Accounting exposure results when exchange rate changes alter the home currency value of foreign currency-denominated assets and liabilities. The big debate in the accounting profession centers on which foreign currency-denominated assets should be translated at the current rate (these assets and liabilities are exposed because their home currency values change in line with the exchange rate) and which assets and liabilities should be translated at the historical rate (the rate in effect at the time the asset was acquired or the liability incurred). These latter assets and liabilities are regarded as not being exposed because they maintain their home currency values regardless of what happens to the exchange rate. By contrast, economic exposure measures the extent to which a given currency change affects the value of the firm. Nominal exchange rate changes affect the home currency value of the transaction exposure component of economic exposure because these cash flows are fixed. But only real exchange rate changes--inflation-adjusted exchange rate changes--affect the firm's future sales revenues and costs, its operating cash flows.

QUESTION 1b: What is exchange risk as compared to exposure?

ANSWER: Exchange risk involves the extent to which uncertain exchange rate changes lead to uncertain fluctuations in the value of the firm. If the firm has no exposure, it has no exchange risk.

QUESTION 3: Suppose the Brazilian rate of inflation is about 180%, and the South Korean inflation rate is about 20%. The Brazilian cruzado's value is adjusted every week so as to maintain PPP, whereas the Korean won's value is fixed for months and sometimes years at a time. Which investment is likely to face the most exchange risk?

   a. A Brazilian shoe factory that exports shoes to the United States and is financed with dollars.
   b. A Brazilian textile plant whose output is sold in Brazil and is financed with cruzados.
   c. A South Korean shoe factory that exports shoes to the United States and is financed with dollars.
   d. A South Korean textile plant whose output is sold in South Korea and financed with won.

ANSWER: If PPP holds exactly in Brazil, then the Brazilian shoe exporter financing with dollars faces no exchange risk. The Brazilian textile manufacturer financed with cruzeiros faces a great deal of inflation risk, but not exchange risk. In the case of South Korea, by fixing the nominal value of the won, the government is implicitly allowing the real value of the won to fluctuate in line with the difference between South Korean and U.S. inflation rates. The South Korean shoe exporter thus faces exchange risk relating to the changing real value of the won. The South Korean textile manufacturer faces inflation risk but not exchange risk, unless it faces competition from foreign imports.

QUESTION 4: Under what circumstances is economic exposure likely to exist?

ANSWER: There are at least three situations in which economic exposure may exist:
   (1) The firm has entered into sales or purchase contracts denominated in a foreign currency.
   (2) The real exchange rate changes and the firm is selling or buying abroad or it faces domestic competition from imports.
   (3) A firm is operating in a foreign country whose government taxes nominal rather than real income.

PROBLEMS

PROBLEM 1:   Consider a Brazilian firm with fixed-rate debt in cruzados which faces the same risk as a subsidiary of an American firm with cruzado debt.   If the rate of inflation declines, what happens to the real interest costs and the real cash flows of both companies?

SOLUTION: In both cases, the real interest cost of the debt rises and the real cash flows decline.

PROBLEM 2:   Consider a period in which the U.S. dollar fell about 9% against most foreign currencies.   How will this affect the share prices of companies involved in international business and why?

SOLUTION: When the home currency devalues, the share price of these companies will rise because investors see the prospect of a cheaper dollar as good for profits.

SELECTED PROBLEMS FROM THE TEXT

PROBLEM 6:   On January 1,   the U.S. dollar-Japanese yen exchange rate is $ = ¥250.   During the year, U.S. inflation is 4% and Japanese inflation is 2%.   On December 31, the exchange rate is $1 = ¥235.   What are the likely competitive effects of this exchange rate change on Caterpillar Tractor, the American earth-moving manufacturer, whose thoughest competitor is Japan's Komatsu?

SOLUTION: The real value of the yen changed from $.006667 (1/150) at the start of the year to $.007265 (1/135 x 1.04/1.02) at the end of the year, an increase of 8.97%.   Caterpillar Tractor should benefit from this increase in the real value of the yen since Komatsu does most of its manufacturing in Japan.   The inflation-adjusted dollar cost of Japanese-supplied components and labor will rise in line with the increase in the real value of the yen.   Komatsu's raw materials and energy prices should not rise in dollar terms because these resources are imported.

PROBLEM 14:   Cooper Industries is a maker of compressors, pneumatic tools and electrical equipment.   It does not face much foreign competition in th United States, and export account for only 7% of its sales.   Does it face exchange risk?

SOLUTION: As a supplier to industrial customers who compete against imports and that sell overseas, Cooper Industries benefits from a weaker dollar and is hurt by a stronger dollar.   Customer sales rise with a weak dollar and fall with a strong dollar and these changes translate into more or less sales for Cooper.

PROBLEM 17:   Black & Decker Manufacturing Co. of Towson, Maryland, has roughly 45% of its assets and 40% of its sales overseas.   How does a soaring dollar affect its profitability, both at home and abroad?

SOLUTION: Black & Decker has a rough balance between foreign sales and costs.   Thus, as the dollar appreciates, both its sales revenue and its costs decline approximately in line with each other.   This means that its profits will decline roughly in line with the rise of the dollar.   (If both revenues and costs fall, say, 10%, then profit must also fall by10%.) Dollar depreciation leads to corresponding increases in dollar revenues and costs.   The bottom line is that B&D's profits fall as the dollar rises and rise as the dollar falls.   If B&D didn't produce overseas, but instead exported from its U.S. plants, then currency changes would lead to much greater swings in its profits.   Note that B&D's domestic profitability is also affected by currency changes since it faces competition in the United States from foreign companies such as Japan's Makita.

MANAGING ACCOUNTING EXPOSURE

Summary: Since the advent of the floating rate system in 1973, many financial managers have been subjected to increased volatility of exchan rates and, thus, considerably larger losses than ever before. A variety financial instruments have provided the financial risk manager with mean to reduce the risks from foreign currency exposure. This chapter discus the <u>hedging</u> <u>techniques</u> used by firms to manage their accounting exposure including both transaction and translation exposure.

I. Managing Transaction Exposure

    A. A transaction exposure arises whenever a company is committed to foreign-currency-denominated transaction.

    B. To protect future currency cash inflows and cash outflows from adverse changes in the exchange rate, a MNC can enter into a transaction that exactly offsets or counterbalances the cash flo from the transaction. This action taken centers around the conc of <u>hedging</u>.

    C. Hedging operations used by MNCs include the forward market hedge the financial market hedge, price adjustment clauses, currency options, risk shifting, risk sharing, currency selection, and exposure netting.

    D. Eliminating transaction exposure does not mean however, that all foreign exchange risk is eliminated. The residual exposure in t form of longer-term operating exposure still remains.

    E. Forward Market Hedge

        1. The forward market hedge consists of offsetting a receivable payable denominated in a foreign currency with a forward contract to sell or buy that currency with a delivery date s so that it will coincide with the date of the anticipated receipt or payment of the foreign currency.

        2. The cost of the forward cover is usually measured as its annualized forward discount or premium:

$$\frac{(e_0 - f_1)}{e_0} \times \frac{360}{n}$$

3. A more correct approach to measuring the true annualized dollar cost of a forward cover is given as

$$\frac{(e_1 - f_1)}{e_0} \times \frac{360}{n}$$

in which case a comparison is made between f_1, the dollars per unit of foreign currency received with hedging, and e_1, the future spot rate on the date of settlement. That is, the real cost of hedging is an opportunity cost.

F. Money Market Hedge

1. A money market hedge involves reversing a receivable or payable denominated in a foreign currency by creating a matching payable or receivable in that same foreign currency through borrowing and lending in the money markets.

2. The gain or loss on the money market hedge is the difference between the cost of repaying the liability incurred and the funds of the investment made.

3. In effect, the simultaneous borrowing and lending transactions associated with a financial hedge allow a firm to create a "homemade" forward contract.

4. The effective rate on this forward contract will equal the actual forward rate if interest rate parity holds. Otherwise, a covered interest arbitrage would exist.

G. Risk Shifting

1. Firm's engaged in international trade typically attempt to invoice exports in strong currencies and imports in weak currencies.

2. While this strategy does not eliminate currency risk, it simply shifts that risk to the other side of the international transaction.

3. A firm implementing this policy may lose valuable sales if the contract terms are limited to the home currency.

4. Flexibility in the choice of currencies for sales as well as for purchases should give a firm added bargaining power to extract price concessions or enable it to maintain or expand its sales. The increased profit generated from the added sales can more than offset the potential exchange losses involved.

H. Pricing Decisions

   1. On credit sales overseas, the foreign currency price is
      converted to the dollar price by using the forward rate.

      a. Thus, if the dollar price is high enough, the exporter
         should make the sale.

      b. Similarly, if the dollar price of the foreign currency-
         denominated import is low enough, the importer should make
         the purchase.

   2. If a sequence of payments is received at several points in
      time, the foreign currency price should be a weighted average
      of the forward rates for delivery on those dates.

I. Exposure Netting

   1. Hedging against exposure to exchange rate changes can be
      achieved by selecting currencies so as to minimize net
      exposure.

   2. Exposure netting involves offsetting exposures in one currency
      with exposures in the same or another currency so that any
      gains (losses) in one exposure is exactly offset by the losses
      (gains) in the other exposure.

   3. In essence, the MNC is constructing a currency exposure
      portfolio in which the total variability of the portfolio is
      less than the sum of the individual variabilities of each
      currency exposure.

   4. There are three possibilities to exposure netting.

      a. A firm can offset a long position in a currency with a
         short position in that same currency.

      b. If two currencies are positively correlated, then the firm
         can offset a long position in one currency with a short
         position in the other.

      c. If two currencies are negatively correlated, the short or
         long positions can be used to offset each other.

J. Risk Transformation

   1. Some companies switch their foreign-currency-denominated
      contracts from one currency to another, in which case inflation
      risk is substituted for currency risk.

2. Thus, the choice of hedging or not hedging depends on which is the bigger risk.

   a. For countries with moderate inflation, the risk to be hedged is currency risk.

   b. But for countries with <u>hyperinflation</u>, currency risk will be less of a concern than inflation risk.

3. Similarly, hedging one end of a transaction without hedging the other end can result in more risk than not hedging at all.

K. Currency Risk Sharing

   1. Instead of a traditional hedge, companies may agree to share the currency risk associated with a transaction denominated in a foreign currency.

   2. In this situation, a customized hedge contract can be built into the transaction, so that each party to the contract can share equally in the currency risk. For example, the <u>base price</u> would be set at a fixed amount, but the parties would share the currency risk beyond a <u>neutral zone</u>, which represents the agreed upon currency range in which risk is not shared.

   3. Currency risk sharing is typically used by companies involved in long-term export/import contracts for the following reasons:

      a. It reduces both the frequency of contract revisions and the impact of currency fluctuations on profits.

      b. It helps avoid adjusting prices continuously as exchange rates change or holding the price constant so that one party has a price fixed in its home currency while the other party either realizes a windfall profit or suffers a drastic loss in profit margin or market share.

   4. Srinivasulu and Massura (1987) recommend that prospective parties to a risk-sharing agreement consider ten points when negotiating the contract.

      a. <u>Base price of the product</u> which is typically set in the exporter's currency. All future adjustments are made relative to this base price.

      b. <u>Base exchange rate</u> which can be set equal to the exchange rate prevailing at the time the contract is negotiated or when the first delivery actually takes place.

c. Frequency of revision which is chosen by the firms.

d. Method of determining actual revised exchange rates. The exchange rate selected can be the average of closing pric on all business days during a quarter, the final closing price for the quarter, the average of the previous quarter's exchange rate and the final closing price, or some other variation. It is also necessary to specify whether the bid, ask, or mid-rate is to be used.

e. Method of adjustment. Exchange rate changes in any quart could be reflected in the rate used in the next quarter, prices could be adjusted retroactively for the past quarter, based on actual exchange rates during the quarte

f. Selection of a neutral zone. The neutral zone can be specified in absolute or percentage terms.

g. Fraction of risk shared by each party which can be equal unequal.

h. Price reopener which is a provision giving either party t option to reopen the contract if the exchange rate moves beyond a much broader band.

i. Invoice currency is the currency in which the contract is actually settled each period. This currency can be eithe the exporter's or the importer's currency.

j. Adjustment of other contract terms. The contract may contain other provisions, such as adjustment of the base price to reflect inflation and productivity gains.

L. Currency Options

1. At times MNCs are engaged in business transactions that are possible but not certain to occur.

2. For example, submitting a competitive bid will leave the firm partially exposed to currency risk.

3. Hedging this currency exposure with a forward contract will be impracticable. The reason is simply that a forward hedge represents a commitment to deliver a specified amount of a foreign currency at a specified date for a fixed price.

4. Instead, the company can hedge its currency exposure with a foreign currency option, which gives the holder the right, but not the obligation, to buy (call option) or sell (put option) specified amount of a foreign currency at a predetermined pric during a stipulated period of time:

122

a. In essence, buying or selling a currency option is like in during one's position against adverse movements in the foreign currency.

b. The option premium is the price paid for the risk involved.

c. Any losses realized from adverse exchange rate movements are limited to the price of the premium.

d. The profits earned from participating in any favorable exchange rate movements are unlimited.

5. In contrast, the holder of a forward contract shares equally in any gains or losses in the underlying transaction.

6. Financial managers, whose objective it is to reduce currency risk, should follow the general rules suggested when choosing between currency options and forward contracts for hedging purposes:

a. When the quantity of a foreign currency cash outflow is known, buy the currency forward; when the quantity is unknown, buy a call option on the currency.

b. When the quantity of a foreign currency cash inflow is known, sell the currency forward; when the quantity is unknown, buy a put option on the currency.

c. When the quantity of a foreign currency cash flow is partially known and partially unknown, use a forward contract to hedge the known portion and an option to hedge the maximum value of the uncertain remainder.

II. Managing Translation Exposure

A. The basic hedging strategies for managing translation exposure involve increasing assets denominated in hard currency (likely to appreciate) and decreasing assets denominated in soft currency (likely to depreciate). While simultaneously decreasing liabilities denominated in hard currency and increasing liabilities denominated in soft currency.

B. Most hedging techniques reduce local currency assets or increase local currency liabilities, thereby generating local currency cash. In order to reduce accounting exposure, these funds must be converted into assets denominated in hard currency. This conversion can be accomplished, directly or indirectly, by using various funds adjustment techniques.

1. Funds adjustment involves altering either the amounts or th
    currencies (or both) of the planned cash flows of the paren
    and/or its subsidiary to reduce the firm's local currency
    accounting exposure.

2. _Direct_ _funds_ _adjustment_ methods include:

    a. Purchasing imports denominated in hard currency.

    b. Investing in securities denominated in hard currency.

    c. Repaying post borrowings denominated in hard currency.

3. _Indirect_ _funds_ _adjustment_ techniques include:

    a. Adjusting transfer prices on the sale of goods between
        affiliates.

    b. Speeding up or leading the payment of dividends, fees, a
        royalties.

    c. Adjusting the leads and lags of intersubsidiary accounts
        which involves speeding up the payment of intersubsidiar
        accounts payable and delaying the collection of
        intersubsidiary accounts receivable.

4. In addition, local currency loans can be used to substitute
    for home currency funds that the parent company would
    otherwise have provided.

5. Some of these hedging techniques may require considerable le
    time (e.g., transfer pricing) and cannot be easily reversed
    once implemented. In addition, methods such as transfer
    price, fees and royalties, and dividend flow adjustments are
    part of corporate policy and are not usually under the
    control of the treasurer.

6. The net cost of shifting funds is the cost of the source of
    funds minus the profit generated from the use of the funds,
    with both adjusted for expected exchange rate changes. If
    this cost is negative, it is profitable on an expected value
    basis to undertake the transaction.

C. A forward market hedge can reduce a firm's translation exposure
    creating an offsetting asset or liability in the foreign currency

D. Selecting currencies for invoicing imports and exports, swaps, a
    transfer pricing are three techniques that are less frequently
    used by MNCs, possibly caused by the constraints on the use of
    these techniques.

E. Exposure netting is an additional exchange management technique that is available to MNCs with positions in more than one foreign currency or with offsetting positions in the same currency.

F. While the forward market hedge is the most popular hedging technique, there are many countries for which leading and lagging of payables and receivables and local currency borrowing are the most important techniques because a formal market for local currency forward contracts is not available.

G. Selecting a funds-adjustment strategy involves evaluating each possible technique separately. If the level of forward contracts entered into is unrestricted, the following two-stage analysis can be used. This methodology allows the optimal level of forward transactions to be determined apart from the selection of what funds-adjustment technique to use.

   1. Compute the profit associated with each funds-adjustment technique on a covered after-tax basis. In those cost formulas which require use of the expected future exchange rate, insert the forward rate as a proxy for the future exchange rate.

   2. Select an optimal level of forward transactions based on the firm's initial exposure, adjusted for the impact on the exposure of decisions made in stage one. If a forward market is nonexistent, or if access to it is limited, the firm must determine both the techniques to use and their appropriate level. A comparison of the net cost of a funds-adjustment technique with the anticipated currency depreciation will indicate whether the expected value of hedging is positive.

H. Any financing decision will affect a firm's exposure to currency changes. Thus, hedging and financing decisions are said to be interrelated.

   1. In financing inventories, accounts receivables, or any other assets, the firm can borrow either dollars, or some other foreign currency, or the local currency. For example, the expansion of the Euro-currency markets has increased the range of borrowing opportunities for the multinational firm.

   2. In addition, tax considerations and currency changes can affect the cost of loans denominated in various currencies. In fact, allowing for taxes may indicate that a dollar loan provides protection in the event of a local currency devaluation.

III. Designing a Hedging Strategy

    A. The hedging strategies selected by a firm are largely determine by its objectives.

        1. The basic purpose of hedging is to reduce exchange risk, i.e., the variability of those cash flow elements which are affected by currency fluctuations.

        2. In operational terms, hedging to reduce the variance of cas flows translates into the following exposure management goa to arrange a firm's financing affairs in such a way that no matter how the exchange rate may move in the future, the affects on dollar returns are minimized.

        3. Instead of following a universally subscribed objective, ma firms follow a selective hedging policy designed to protect against anticipated currency changes.

        4. But if financial markets are efficient firms cannot hedge against expected exchange rate changes. Interest rates, forward rates, and sales-contract prices should already reflect currency changes that are anticipated, thereby offsetting the loss-reducing benefits of hedging with highe costs. Thus, a firm can protect itself only against unexpected currency changes.

        5. A MNC can benefit from the various hedging techniques only it is able to estimate the probability and timing of a devaluation with greater accuracy than the general market. However, attempting to profit from foreign exchange forecasting is speculating rather than hedging. A hedger i advised to assume that the market knows as much as he or sh does.

        6. In the event of financial market imperfections and/or tax asymmetries, however, it is possible for a company to benef from its hedging activities. Such financial market imperfections are created by the local government or the individual investors in that market.

    B. The amount of Hedging that is necessary to protect a given currency position is crucially dependent on the tax laws involved.

        1. Foreign subsidiaries can incur exchange losses in any of th following areas:

a. Forward contract.

b. Foreign currency loans.

c. Export/import transactions.

d. Translation of foreign-currency-denominated assets and liabilities.

2. If a parent company's primary concern is with the accounting exposure, it must carefully assess the tax consequences of exchange gains or losses for its subsidiaries, because those gains or losses will be reflected in the firm's consolidated financial statements.

3. It is important to recognize that there are significant differences between countries in the tax treatment of foreign exchange gains and losses. For example:

a. Some nations, such as Australia, recognize the gains and losses from foreign currency translation for tax purposes while others, such as the U.S., does not recognize a translation gain or loss until the subsidiary is liquidated.

b. Still others, including West Germany and Sweden, allow unrealized losses to be tax-deductible and do not tax unrealized gains.

c. In Italy, unrealized gains are taxed and translation losses are tax-deductible.

4. It is also important to know how these tax differences will impact on the amount of hedging that is needed to cover a position on an after-tax basis as well as on the location and cost of the hedging to be done.

C. In the area of management of foreign exchange, there are good arguments both for and against centralization.

1. The arguments for centralization of foreign exchange risk management include the firm's ability:

a. To take advantage of all its possibilities to trade-off positive and negative currency exposure positions by consolidating exposure worldwide.

b. To take advantage, through exposure netting, of the portfolio effect.

        c.   To reduce the among of hedging required to achieve a given level of safety.

        d.   To take advantage of the before-tax hedging cost variations that are likely to exist among subsidiaries because of market imperfections.

    2.   The arguments against centralization of foreign exchange r management include:

        a.   Loss of local knowledge.

        b.   Lack of incentive for the local managers to take advantage of a particular situation that only they may familiar with.

        c.   Allowing local units to manage their own exposures by engaging in forward contracts with a central unit at negotiated rates. The central unit, in turn, may or m not lay off these contracts in the market place.

IV. Appendix 10 A: An Insurance Approach to Financial Hedging

    A.   Any realistic hedging strategy must take into account the existence of risk aversion.

    B.   The theoretically superior approach to account for this risk aversion is to make decisions on the basis of expected utility, taking into account the covariances between asset returns and t effects of currency change on the firm's systematic risk.

    C.   A different approach requires estimates of the minimum and maximum values of future exchange rates along with the maximum loss the firm is willing to accept. Based on these parameters, the firm can then decide on a maximum exposure to take and hedg the rest.

        1.   In general, if a company has a net exposure of E units of a foreign currency that can change from its spot exchange rat of e_o to a minimum value of e_m or a maximum value of e_M wi

$$e_m < e_o < e_M ,$$

then the firm's maximum possible exchange loss is

$$(e_o - e_m) E .$$

By varying E, the firm can limit its maximum loss to any se dollar amount L, which can be done by setting

$$E = L / (e_o - e_m) .$$

2. There are two possible approaches to take account of the probabilities associated with the various potential losses.

   a. One approach is to limit the <u>expected</u>, rather than the actual, loss. If b is the expected depreciation, then the expected exchange loss is bE. By varying E, a firm's expected loss can be constrained to any desired level.

   b. The other approach directly considers the various probabilities by suing chance-constraints, which limit the probability of losing more than L dollars in any one time period to a probability of a% or less. This approach is useful if a company feels it is highly desirable to limit losses to a certain level, but it is also mindful of the costs involved.

3. To be able to make rational decisions, the manager should be presented with various threshold probabilities (a%) and maximum permissible loss levels (L) so as to ponder expected corporate savings from relaxing these exposure constraints. These savings equal the difference between the expected savings in hedging costs and the expected devaluation losses associated with an increase in exposure.

4. There is a strong possibility that this method is of no value to the firm.

   a. If forward contracts are available and the market is efficient, the expected savings from relaxing these constraints should be approximately zero.

   b. However, if forward contracts are not available or are restricted in their use, then expected exchange risk management costs may be a function of the levels of the threshold probability, a%, and the maximum permissible loss level, L.

   c. As a% is lowered or as L is decreased, more expensive hedging techniques will probably have to be employed because there are likely to be limits on the use of any particular hedging method.

D. When several currencies are involved, the portfolio approach to hedging is used which recognizes that the net gain or loss on the entire currency portfolio is more important than the gain or loss on any individual currency.

   1. The risk associated with a particular currency exposure portfolio depends on the correlations between the currencies.

2. The correlations based on long-term data appear to be less
    positive or more negative than the shorter-run correlations
    as was shown in a study by Shapiro and Rutenberg (1976).

3. Thus, the more diversified the currency portfolio of a MNC,
    the fewer long-term fluctuations there should be in the dol
    value of its foreign cash balances.

4. In the absence of knowledge about future value of currency
    correlations, it is possible to obtain crude bounds on
    possible exchange losses by studying extreme situations.

5. With exposure in numerous (n) currencies, the maximum possi
    exchange loss can be found by calculating, the maximum
    possible exchange loss in each currency and summing. Setti
    probabilistic limits on total losses can be achieved by
    varying exposure in selected currencies.

6. By selectively hedging its accounting exposure, a firm can
    limit its fluctuations in its current reported comings due
    exchange rate changes.

KEY TERMS

Hedging
Forward Market Hedge
Money Market Hedge
Risk Shifting
Pricing Decision
Exposure Netting
Multi-currency Exposure Netting
Risk Transformation
Currency Risk Sharing
Neutral Zone
Management

Foreign Currency Option's Hed
Put Option
Call Option
Hard Currency
Soft Currency
Funds Adjustment
Market Imperfections
Tax Asymmetries
Centralized Exposure Manageme
Decentralized Exposure

CONCEPTUAL QUESTIONS

QUESTION 1: In what situation is a call option a valuable hedging tool?

ANSWER: A call option is valuable when a firm has offered to buy some
foreign asset, such as another firm, at a fixed foreign currency price b
is uncertain whether its bid will be accepted. By buying a call option
the foreign currency, the firm can lock in a maximum dollar price for it
tender offer and, at the same time, limit its downside risk to the call
premium in the event its bid is rejected.

QUESTION 2: Explain how exposure netting can be used by a firm to reduce its transaction exposure.

ANSWER: Exposure netting involves offsetting exposures in one currency with exposures in the same or another currency so that any gains (losses) in one exposure is exactly offset by the losses (gains) in the other exposure. It involves one of three possibilities:
(1) A firm can offset a long position in a currency with a short position in that same currency; (2) if two currencies are positively correlated, then the firm can offset a long position in one currency with a short position in the other; and (3) if two currencies are negatively correlated, the short or long positions can be used to offset each other.

SELECTED QUESTIONS FROM THE TEXT

QUESTION 1: A U.S. firm has fully hedged its sterling receivables and has bought credit insurance to cover the risk of default. Has this firm eliminated all risk on these receivables? Explain.

ANSWER: No. The company has converted its sterling receivables into a fixed amount of dollars to be received in the future. But because this sum of money is set in nominal terms, the firm bears exchange risk. That is, it knows how many dollars it will receive in the future but it does not know what the purchasing power of those dollars will be.

QUESTION 2: What is the basic translation hedging strategy? How does it work?

ANSWER: The basic translation hedging strategy involves increasing hard-currency assets and decreasing soft-currency assets, while simultaneously decreasing hard-currency liabilities and increasing soft-currency liabilities. The specific techniques used to hedge a particular translation exposure all involve establishing an offsetting currency position (e.g., by means of a forward contract) such that whatever is lost or gained on the original currency exposure is exactly offset by a corresponding foreign exchange gain or loss on the currency hedge.

QUESTION 8: What is the domestic counterpart to exchange risk? Explain.

ANSWER: The domestic counterpart to exchange risk is inflation risk. Exchange risk involves uncertain changes in the exchange rate between domestic currency and foreign currency (and, ultimately, between domestic currency and foreign goods and services), while inflation risk involves uncertain changes in the exchange rate between domestic currency and domestic goods and services.

PROBLEM 1: A U.S. distributor purchases goods from Germany in the amoun of DM 125 million. Payment in German marks is due in 180 days. The following market data is given:

$$\begin{array}{ll}
\text{Spot rate} & = \$0.50/\text{DM} \\
\text{Forward rate (6 months)} & = \$0.52/\text{DM} \\
\text{Interest rate (DM)} & = 8\% \text{ per year} \\
\text{Interest rate (\$)} & = 13\% \text{ per year}
\end{array}$$

Would the U.S. distributor be better off using a forward hedge or a mone market hedge?

SOLUTION:

a. The forward market hedge will fix the cost of the goods today:

DM 125 million ($0.52) = $65,000,000.

b. With a money market hedge, the firm will

(1) invest German marks in a German deposit at 8% per year whi will accumulate to DM 125 million in 180 days. The amount be invested in Germany is

DM 125,000,000/(1.04) = DM 120,192,307.70.

(2) borrow the amount of German marks today in the U.S.

DM 120,192,307.70 ($0.50) = $60,096,153.85.

(3) pay back the loan in 180 days in the amount of

$ 60,096,153.85 (1.065) = $64,002,403.85.

c. With the forward market hedge the U.S. distributor will have to pay $65,000,000 compared to the money market hedge which involv paying $64,002,403.85. Thus, it should use the money market hedge.

PROBLEM 2: A U.S. firm has negotiated a forward contract to receive 500,000 British pounds in 90 days. If the 3-month forward rate is $1.10 and the current spot rate is $1.1120, what is the real cost of hedging these receivables?

SOLUTION:

a. The U.S. dollars received in 90 days from hedging are

$$£500,000 \ (1.1015) = \$550,750.$$

b. The U.S. dollars received if unhedged are

$$£500,000 \ (1.1120) = \$556,000.$$

c. The real cost of hedging is

$$\$556,000 - \$550,750 = \$5,250.$$

SELECTED PROBLEMS FROM THE TEXT

PROBLEM 2: An importer has a payment of 8 million due in 90 days.

a. If the 90-day pound forward rate is $1.4201, what is the hedged cost of making that payment?
b. If the spot rate expected in 90 days is $1.4050, what is the expected cost of payment?
c. What factors will influence the hedging decision?

SOLUTION:

a. $8,000,000(2.4201) = \$19,360,800.$

b. $8,000,000(2.4050) = \$19,240,000.$

c. Risk is clearly one factor. Risk aversion could lead the firm to sell its receivables forward to hedge their dollar value. However, if the firm has pound liabilities, they could provide a natural hedge. Exposure netting would then reduce or eliminate the amount necessary to hedge. The existence of a cheaper hedging alternative, such as borrowing pounds and converting them to dollars for the duration of the receivables, would also make undesirable the use of a forward contract. This latter situation assumes that interest rate parity is violated. The tax treatment of foreign exchange gains and losses on forward contracts could also affect the hedging decision.

PROBLEM 5:   Suppose that the spot rate and the 90-day forward rate on the pound sterling are $1.35 and $1.30, respectively. Your company, wishing avoid foreign exchange risk, sells £500,000 forward 90 days. Assuming th the spot rate remains the same 90 days hence, your company would

    a.   receive £500,000 in 90 days.
    b.   receive more than £500,000 in 90 days.
    c.   have been better off not to have sold pounds forward.
    d.   receive nothing.

SOLUTION: Since the forward rate ($1.30) is below the actual rate ($1.35 at maturity of the forward contract, the firm would have been better off not selling pounds forward. Of course, the purpose of hedging is risk avoidance, not profit.

PROBLEM 10:   Sumitomo Chemical of Japan has one week in which to negotiate a contract to supply products to a U.S. company at a dollar price that wi remain fixed for one year. What advice would you give Sumitomo?

SOLUTION: This problem is identical to that faced by Weyerhaeuser in the example given in the text. The general rule on credit sales overseas is convert between the foreign currency price and the dollar price using the forward rate, not the spot rate. In the case of a sequence of payments to be received at several points in time, the foreign currency price should b a weighted average of the forward rates for delivery on those dates.

    Here, Sumitomo should decide on the yen price that it would set and then convert that yen price into a dollar price using the forward rate or an average of forward rates, depending on whether it will be paid all at once or in installments on several dates.

CHAPTER 11

Summary: Growing competition at home and abroad combined with the increased volatility of exchange rates has spurred many firms to focus on the economic effects of currency changes and how to cope with the associated risks. This chapter discusses the basic considerations that go into the design of a strategy for managing operating exposure. Specific details are provided on the marketing, production, and financial management strategies that are appropriate for coping with both anticipated and unanticipated real exchange rate changes.

I. An Overview of Operating Exposure Management

  A. The impact of currency-induced relative price changes on corporate revenues and costs depends on the extent of a firm's commitment to international business as well as on its degree of operational flexibility.

   1. The <u>occasional</u> <u>exporter</u>. This exporter produces primarily for the domestic market but occasionally receives an order from abroad.

       a. If the sales price is denominated in a foreign currency, the exporter's receivable is subject to exchange rate changes.

       b. On the other hand, setting the price in the home currency simply shifts the risk to the exporter's customer.

       c. To cope with the exchange risk problem, the following hedging techniques can be used.

           (1) <u>Forward market</u>. Before a forward contract is signed, the exporter should calculate the true home currency price that can be realized from a sale in either market. If P_D and P_E are the domestic and export prices, respectively, and f is the forward rate, then the exporter's decision rule should be as follows:

$$\text{if } f < \frac{P_D}{P_E} \text{ , sell in the home market.}$$

$$\text{if } f > \frac{P_D}{P_E} \text{ , sell in the foreign market.}$$

(2) <u>Money</u> <u>market</u> <u>hedge</u> which involves borrowing in the local currency and investing these funds in the home currency.

(3) The exporter could either build anticipated exchange rate changes into its quoted local currency price or not submit a bid.

2. The <u>committed</u> <u>exporter</u>. This exporter has committed substantial resources to develop and service its foreign market(s).

   a. If the foreign currency depreciates, the home currency value of the exporter's current foreign receivables are reduced. This represents a one-time loss depending on th future required level of receivables.

   b. The exporter will suffer a continuing loss on its future export revenues unless purchasing power parity holds and foreign inflation permits an increase in the export price

3. The <u>multinational</u> <u>corporation</u>. This multinational enterprise derives a substantial portion of its income from its foreign operations. It serves global market segments from production facilities that are located in many countries. Thus, it too will be affected by exchange rate changes that result in relative price changes.

4. To the extent that real exchange rate changes occur, the competitive situation for both the committed exporter and the multinational corporation are altered. In this situation, management may decide to make necessary <u>production</u> and <u>marketing</u> revisions, which can either counteract the harmful effects of, or capitalize on the opportunities presented by, currency appreciation or depreciation.

5. Managers trying to cope with actual or anticipated currency changes must first determine whether the currency change is real or nominal. If real, the permanence of change must be assessed.

II. Marketing Management of Exchange Risk

A. International marketing managers have generally ignored foreign exchange risk management. Marketing programs are almost always adjusted <u>after</u> changes in exchange rates. Yet, designing a firm' marketing strategy under conditions of home currency fluctuation presents considerable opportunity for gaining competitive leverage.

B. The task of the international marketing manager should be to
    identify the possible effects of exchange rate changes and then
    act on them by adjusting the pricing, product, credit, and market
    selection policies.

    1. Market selection and market segmentation provide the basic
        parameters within which a company may adjust its marketing mix
        over time.

        a. In the short-run neither of these two basic strategic
            choices can be altered in reaction to actual or
            anticipated currency changes. Instead, the firm must
            select certain tactical responses, such as adjustment of
            pricing, promotional, and credit policies.

        b. In the long-run, the firm will have to revise its
            marketing strategy, particularly if real exchange rate
            changes persist.

    2. Each company's product prices are set according to its own
        unique business strategy, and the impact of exchange rate
        changes must be incorporated into the pricing decision.

        a. A firm selling overseas should follow the standard
            economic proposition of setting the price that maximizes
            dollar profits. Any realized profits should be translated
            using the forward exchange rate that reflects the true
            expected dollar value of the receipts upon collection.

        b. Under conditions of a foreign currency devaluation, an
            exporter may be able to adjust product prices in the
            following ways:

            (1) At best, the exporter may be able to raise prices by
                the extent of the foreign currency devaluation.

            (2) At worst, in an extremely competitive situation, the
                exporter will be forced to absorb a reduction in home
                currency revenues equal to the percentage decline in
                the value of the local currency.

            (3) In the most likely case, foreign currency prices can
                be raised somewhat, and the exporter will make up the
                difference through a lower profit margin on its
                foreign sales.

c. In the event of a real home currency devaluation, the exporter will gain a competitive price advantage on the world market. Certainly the company does not have to reduce export prices. Instead, it has the option of increasing unit profitability (<u>price skimming</u>) or expanding its market share (<u>penetration pricing</u>).

d. Firms in international competition differ in their abili and willingness to adjust prices in response to exchange rate changes.

    (1) Some firms <u>constantly</u> adjust their prices for exchang rate changes which, in turn, requires distributors t constantly adjust their margins to confirm to the prices they pay.

    (2) Other firms feel that <u>stable</u> prices are essential in maintaining their customer base.

e. Anticipatory or proactive planning in pricing is particularly important if price controls are expected to follow a devaluation. Several options are available to a firm to counteract these expected controls.

    (1) Set prices at an artificially high level and accept the resulting loss of market share.

    (2) Raise list prices but continue selling at existing prices, thus effectively selling at a discount.

    (3) Develop new products that are only slightly altered versions of the firm's existing goods, and then sell them at a higher price.

3. <u>Promotional</u> <u>decisions</u> should explicitly incorporate exchange rates, especially for allocating budgets among countries.

a. After a domestic devaluation, the exporting firm may find that it has:

    (1) Increased the return per dollar expenditure on advertising or selling because of the product's improved price positioning.

    (2) Improved its ability to <u>push</u> the product because of the option of greater distribution margins or consume dealing.

b. A foreign currency devaluation is likely to reduce the return on marketing expenditures and may require a more fundamental shift in the firm's product policy.

4. A firm should devise its product strategy as a function of its relative exposure in different markets. Exchange rate fluctuations may affect:

   a. The timing of the introduction of new products because of distributor reluctance to accept new product-introduction risks.

   b. The product deletion decisions when products become obsolete or fall into consumer disfavor.

   c. The product line decision because of an increased ability to cover a wider spectrum of consumers in the foreign market.

   d. Product innovation financed by an expanded research-and-development budget.

III. Production Management of Exchange Risk

   A. Product sourcing and plant location are the principal variables that companies manipulate to manage competitive risks that cannot be dealt with through marketing changes alone.

      1. A well-managed firm should be searching constantly for ways to substitute between domestic and imported inputs, depending on the relative prices involved and the degree of substitution possible.

      2. For the longer term, when increasing production capacity, the firm should consider the option of designing new facilities that provide added flexibility in making substitutions among various sources of goods.

      3. Multinational corporations with worldwide production systems can allocate production among their several plants in line with the changing dollar cost of production. Management should consider the option of increasing production in a nation whose currency has devalued, and decreasing production in a country in which its currency has been revalued.

      4. A firm without foreign facilities that is exporting to a competitive market whose currency has devalued may find that sourcing components abroad is insufficient to maintain unit profitability. In this situation, the firm may have to locate new plants abroad.

5. Many U.S. companies faced with intense foreign competition made substantial efforts to improve their productivity by closing inefficient plants, automating heavily, and negotiating wage and benefit cutbacks and work rule concessions with unions. Many firms also began programs to increase productivity and improve product quality through employee motivation.

6. An increasingly attractive option is to take the exchange rate change as given and focus on the new pattern of opportunities and risks. The better prepared corporations are for constant change, the more they will come to regard exchange rate volatility as a strategic opportunity rather than risk. The emphasis, therefore, must be on developing more competitive options, streamlining their operations, and emphasizing resilience and adaptability over stability.

IV. Financial Management of Exchange Risk

A. The role of financial management, based on the definition of hedging, is to structure the firm's liabilities in such a way that during the time the strategic marketing and production adjustments are underway, the reduction in asset earnings is matched by a corresponding decrease in the cost of servicing these liabilities.

B. The implementation of a hedging policy is likely to be quite difficult, because the specific cash flow effects of a given currency change are difficult to predict. Consequently, hedging should be undertaken only when the effects of anticipated exchange rate changes are expected to be significant.

C. Where financial market imperfections are significant, a firm might consider exposing itself to more exchange risk in order to lower its expected financing costs.

KEY TERMS

Occasional Exporter
Committed Exporter
Multinational Corporation (MNC)
Market Selection
Market Segmentation
Pricing Strategy
Promotional Strategy

Product Strategy
Product Deletion Decision
Product Line Decision
Product Innovation
Product Sourcing
Plant Location
Input Mix

CONCEPTUAL QUESTIONS

QUESTION 1: Explain the two principal implications of the <u>comparative advantage</u> for exchange risk management.

ANSWER: The comparative advantage has the following two implications for exchange risk management:

1. The primary goal of exposure management to financial executives should be to arrange their firms' financial affairs in such a way as to minimize the real effects of exchange rate changes, subject to the costs of such rearrangements.

2. The major burden of exchange risk management must fall on the shoulders of marketing and production executives, because these executives deal in imperfect product and factor markets where their specialized knowledge provides them with a real advantage; that is, they should be able to consistently outperform competitors in the markets in which they operate because of their superior knowledge.

SELECTED QUESTIONS FROM THE TEXT

QUESTION 1: Why should managers focus on marketing and production strategies to cope with foreign exchange risk?

ANSWER: Unlike transaction exposure, which is amenable to financial hedging, competitive exposures--those arising from competition with firms based in other currencies--are longer-term, harder to quantify, and cannot be dealt with solely through financial hedging techniques. Rather, they require more strategic maneuvers involving changes in operating strategies. For this reason, the major burden of exchange risk management must fall on the shoulders of marketing and production executives. In addition, these executives deal in imperfect product and factor markets where their superior knowledge and specialized skills provide them with a comparative advantage in adjusting to the relative price changes caused by currency changes.

QUESTION 3: What is the role of finance in protecting against exchange risk?

ANSWER: The role of financial management is to structure the firm's liabilities in such a way that, during the time strategic operational adjustments are underway, the reduction in asset earnings is matched by a corresponding decrease in the cost of servicing these liabilities. For example, a company that has developed a sizable export market should hold a portion of its liabilities in the currency of that country. In this way, any shortfall in operating cash flows due to an exchange rate change will be offset by a reduction in the debt service expenses.

PROBLEM 6: Boeing Commercial Airplane Co. manufactures all its planes in the United States and prices them in dollars, even the 50% of its sales destined for overseas markets. Assess Boeing's currency risk. How can it cope with this risk?

SOLUTION: Boeing would have currency risk even in the absence of foreign competition since currency fluctuations will translate its dollar prices into varying amounts of foreign currency to its foreign customers. Given that foreign demand is somewhat responsive to price, and that Boeing prices in dollars, dollar appreciation will reduce foreign demand. Alternatively to maintain sales volume, Boeing will be forced to cut its dollar price. Dollar depreciation benefits Boeing since it can either raise its dollar price, while keeping its foreign currency prices constant, or keep its dollar price constant and thereby cut its foreign currency prices and boost sales overseas.

In reality, Boeing does face a major foreign competitor--Airbus Industrie, a European consortium. The existence of Airbus increases Boeing's price elasticity of demand and, hence, its exchange risk. This means that Boeing is hurt more by dollar appreciation and helped more by dollar depreciation.

PROBLEM 8: Cost Plus Imports is a West Coast chain specializing in low-cost imported goods, principally from Japan. It has to put out its semiannual catalogue with prices that are good for six months. Advise Cost Plus Imports on how it can protect itself against currency risk.

SOLUTION: A company such as Cost Plus will typically negotiate purchase contracts with the suppliers of its catalogue merchandise in advance. Cost Plus could hedge these purchases using forward contracts. A problem, though, is that if the foreign currencies devalue during the life of the catalogue, prices of substitute products for the items in the catalogue will likely come down somewhat. In this case, some customers who might have bought from Cost Plus will decide to buy the cheaper substitutes and Cost Plus will lose sales. This is particularly likely here given the nature of Cost-Plus products: low-cost goods presumably bought by a price-sensitive clientele.

The existence of quantity risk in addition to price risk suggests that Cost Plus should hedge less than 100% of its projected sales. Alternatively, Cost Plus could buy call options to cover its foreign purchases. If the foreign currencies drop below the call option price, the firm won't exercise its options; if they rise above the call price, Cost Plus will exercise them.

PROBLEM 11: In order to cut costs when the dollar was at its peak, Caterpillar shifted production of small construction equipment overseas. By contrast, Caterpillar's main competitors in that area, Deere & Co. and J.I. Case, make most of their small construction equipment in the United States. What are the most likely competitive consequences of this restructuring?

142

SOLUTION: Caterpillar now has a diversified cost structure. This means that it won't be hurt as much when the dollar rises again, but it also doesn't benefit as much when the dollar falls. Its main competitors, Deere & Co. and J.I. Case, now have a competitive advantage vis-à-vis Caterpillar by producing most of their small construction equipment in the United States.

NEWS ITEMS

Pricing Strategy of Multinational Corporations

After the 1971 currency realignment, the Wall Street Journal on December 18, 1972, reported that relatively few U.S. companies used the devaluation of the dollar to lower their prices abroad. Despite a 13.5% revaluation of the German mark against the dollar, only about one-third of American exports to West-Germany showed a decrease in their German mark prices. In the same Journal article, Honeywell was reported as saying that prices in Great Britain were "not based on devaluation but on the market place" and that price was not a major factor in selling most U.S. computers.

CHAPTER 12

SHORT-TERM FINANCING

Summary: Subsidiaries of MNCs have access to a large number of sources of financing. This chapter focuses on developing policies for borrowing from either within or without the corporation when currency risk is present and different tax rates and regulations are in effect.

I. Key Factors in Short-Term Financing Strategy

    A. The expected costs and risk of the short-term financing strategy in an international context is strongly influenced by six key factors.

        1. Differences in nominal interest rates among currencies should be matched by anticipated exchange rate changes.

        2. The risks associated with borrowing in a specific currency are related to the firm's degree of exposure in that currency.

        3. The more risk averse the firm is, the higher the price it should pay to reduce its currency exposure.

        4. Differences in the nominal interest rate among currencies should equal the annualized forward discount or premium.

        5. In comparing relative borrowing costs, these costs must be estimated on an after-tax covered basis.

        6. The borrowing decision of a firm will also be affected by the political risk present in a country.

II. Short-Term Financing Objectives

    A. There are four possible objectives which can guide a firm in deciding where and in which currencies to borrow.

        1. Minimize expected costs.

        2. Minimize risk without regard to cost.

        3. Trade off expected cost and systematic risk.

        4. Trade off expected cost and total risk.

III. Short-Term Financing Options

    A. A firm usually prefers to finance its temporary current assets with short-term sources of financing.

B. A foreign affiliate may obtain an <u>intercompany</u> <u>loan</u> provided either by the parent company or a sister affiliate.

    1. These loans may be limited in amount or duration by official exchange controls.

    2. Interest rates are generally acquired to fall within set limits.

        a. The lender's government will want the interest rate on an intercompany loan to be set as high as possible for both tax and balance-of-payments purposes.

        b. The borrower's government will want the interest rate to be low for similar reasons.

    3. The cost of an intracorporate loan is determined by the following factors:

        a. The lender's opportunity cost of funds.

        b. The interest rate set.

        c. Tax rates and regulations.

        d. The currency of denomination of the loan.

        e. Expected exchange rate changes over the term of the loan.

C. Affiliates of MNCs attempt to finance their working capital requirements locally for the purpose of both convenience and exposure management.

    1. <u>Loans</u> from commercial banks are the dominant form of short-term interest-bearing financing used worldwide.

        a. Bank loans are <u>self-liquidating</u> because they normally used to finance temporary buildups in accounts receivables and inventory.

        b. Short-term bank credits are typically unsecured promissory notes maturing in 90 days.

        c. Banks may also insert a <u>cleanup</u> <u>clause</u> requiring the firm not to incur any other debts to the bank for a period of at least 30 days during the year.

    2. Bank credit provides a highly flexible source of financing because it is readily expandable and therefore serves as a financial reserve. It can be extended in several different ways.

a. <u>Term loans</u> are straight bank loans, often unsecured, th
   are made for a fixed period of time, usually 90 days.

b. A <u>line of credit</u> is an informal agreement that permits
   the firm to borrow up to a stated maximum amount from tl
   bank.

c. An <u>overdraft</u> is a line of credit against which drafts
   (checks) can be drawn (written) up to a specified
   maximum amount.

d. A <u>revolving credit agreement</u> is similar to a line of
   credit except that the bank is legally obligated to hon
   credit up to a stated maximum amount. The firm pays
   interest on the borrowed funds plus a commitment fee on
   the unused portion of the credit line.

e. <u>Discounting</u> of trade bills is a preferred method of
   short-term financing by many European and Latin Americar
   firms. In this case, a trade bill accepted by a bank is
   sold at a discount to another bank or a money market
   dealer.

3. The interest rate on bank loans is negotiated between the
   borrower and the banker. The loan rate charged to a specifi
   customer will reflect:

   a. The customer's credit worthiness.

   b. The previous relationship with the bank.

   c. The maturity of the loan.

   d. Other factors.

4. Bank interest rates are determined in the same way as
   interest rates on financial securities:

   a. The riskfree rate plus

   b. A risk premium based on the borrower's credit risk.

5. Interest rates on loans can be paid at maturity or in
   advance. Thus, the effective interest rate will be differen
   for each payment method.

   a. The effective interest rate is estimated as

$$\frac{\text{Annual interest paid}}{\text{Funds received}}$$

b. The effective interest rate on a <u>discounted</u> loan is calculated as

$$\frac{\text{Annual interest paid}}{\text{Amount borrowed - Annual interest paid}}$$

c. The effective interest rate with a <u>compensating balance</u> requirement is determined by the following formula:

$$\frac{\text{Annual interest paid}}{\text{Usable funds}}$$

where the usable funds equal the net amount of the loan minus any compensating balance requirement in excess of the amount normally maintained on deposit.

6. An alternative to borrowing short-term from a bank is to issue <u>commercial paper</u>, which is a short-term unsecured promissory note that is usually sold by very large and financially sound corporations on a discounted basis to institutional investors and to other corporations.

   a. By going to the market directly, well-known corporations can save substantial interest costs.

   b. Commercial paper is exempt from SEC registration, thus reducing the time and expense of getting an issue ready for sale.

   c. Maturities are fairly standard across the various countries, ranging from 20-25 days in the U.S. and to over three months in the Netherlands.

   d. Noninterest costs associated with commercial paper include back-up lines of credit, fees to commercial banks, and rating service fees.

D. A non bank short-term financing instrument, resembling a commercial paper, is the <u>Euronote</u> or <u>Eurocommerical paper</u>.

   1. A Euronote is a short-term note denominated in dollars and issued by corporations and governments. The prefix "Euro" indicates that it is issued outside the country in which currency it is denominated.

   2. There are some major differences between the U.S. commercial paper and the Eurocommerical paper.

a. The average maturity on Euronotes is twice as long as the average maturity of U.S. CPs.

b. Euro CPs are actively traded in the secondary market, but most U.S. CPs are held to maturity by the original investors.

c. Holders of Euro CPs are central banks, commercial banks, and corporations; the most important holders of U.S. CPs are money market funds.

d. The distribution of U.S. issuers in the Euro CP-market is of significantly lower quality than the distribution of U.S. issuers in the U.S. CP-market.

e. Only about 45% of active Euro-CP issuers at year end 198 were rated. Credit ratings in the U.S., on the other hand, are recurrent.

IV. Estimating The Expected Cost and Risk Of Alternative Financing Option

A. In deciding on a particular financing option, a firm needs to estimate and then compare the effective after-tax dollar costs of local currency financing and dollar financing. In all situations, the cost of each source of funds must reflect the nominal interest rate, tax rate, and future exchange rate.

1. In the absence of taxes and forward contracts, calculating the effective interest rates on the loans is relatively straight-forward.

   a. The home currency cost of borrowing local currency at an interest rate of r_L and a currency change of d is equal to

   HC interest cost - exchange gain/loss

   $$r_L (1 - d) - d$$

   where $d = (e_0 - e_1)/e_0$ and e_0 and e_1 are the beginning and ending exchange rates, respectively.

2. The cost of a parent company loan to the overall corporation is determined by the following three factors:

Interest cost to parent	_	Interest income to parent	_	Interest cost to subsidiary
r_H	-	r_P	-	r_P

148

3. The breakeven rate of currency change is found by equating the dollar costs of parent and local currency financing:

$$r_H = r_L (1 - d) - d.$$

a. The borrowing decision rule can be stated as follows:

If $d < d^*$, borrow in dollars.
If $d > d^*$, borrow in the local currency

where d^* is the breakeven currency rate.

b. If forward contracts are available, then the decision rule involves comparing the covered cost of borrowing in local currency with the cost of borrowing directly.

If $D < d^*$, borrow dollars.
If $D > d^*$, borrow in local currency.

where D is the forward differential.

B. With taxes, the calculation of various loan costs is complicated.

1. The after-tax dollar cost of borrowing in the local currency for a foreign affiliate is equal to

After-tax interest expense	_	Exchange gain/loss on principal repayment

$$r_L (1 - d) (1 - t_a) - d$$

where t_a is the affiliate's tax rate.

2. The total cost of the parent company loan is the sum of the three factors in the zero tax case less the tax write-off associated with the dollar principal repayment of dt_a, or

Interest cost to parent	_	Interest income to parent	_	Interest cost to subsidiary	_	Tax gain/ loss

$$r_H (1 - t_h) - r_P (1 - t_p) + r_P (1 - t_a) - dt_a$$

or

$$r_H (1 - t_h) + r_P (t_p - t_a) - dt_a$$

where t_h is the parent company's tax rate on domestic income and t_p is the parent's effective tax rate on income from its foreign affiliate.

a. The tax rates t_a, t_h, t_p must be marginal tax rates payable in the home and host country.

b. If withholding taxes are levied on interest payments to foreign subsidiaries, t_p must be adjusted to reflect this situation.

c. Because of tax credits and tax treaties among countries, t_a and t_p are not the stated tax rates. Thus,

$$t_a \neq t_p .$$

(1) If $t_a < t_p$, then r_P will be set at the lowest permissible level by the government.

(2) If $t_a > t_p$, then r_P will be set at the highest permissible level by the government.

3. The breakeven rate of currency appreciation or depreciation can be found by equating the dollar cost of local currency and parent financing, or

$$r_H (1 - t_h) + r_P (t_p - t_a) - d t_a = r_L (1 - d) (1 - t_a) - d.$$

Solving for d yields:

$$r_L (1 - t_a) \Sigma [r_H (1 - t_h) + r_P (t_p - t_a)] (1 + r_L) (1 - t_a)$$

a. The borrowing decision rule is the same as that stated in the zero-tax case.

b. If forward contract are available, the firm can cover its local currency loan liability with a forward contract to buy local currency for dollars.

c. The covered cost of a local currency loan is equal to the after-tax cost of the uncovered local currency loan plus the after-tax cost of the forward contract.

C. Exchange risk management considerations can be integrated with the borrowing strategy. This approach involves calculating the difference in standard deviations of net profit between local currency and parent financing.

KEY TERMS

Intercompany Financing
Local Currency Financing
Bank Loans
Term Loans
Line-of-Credit
Overdraft

Revolving Credit Agreement
Discounting
Effective Interest Rate
Commercial Paper
Euronotes and Euro-Commercial
   Paper
Breakeven Analysis

CONCEPTUAL QUESTIONS

QUESTION 1: Why is it useful to perform a break-even analysis when financing in a foreign currency?

ANSWER: With the breakeven analysis, the treasurer can readily see the amount of currency appreciation or depreciation necessary to make one type of borrowing less expensive than another. The treasurer will then compare the firm's actual forecast of currency change, determined objectively or subjectively, with this benchmark.

SELECTED QUESTIONS FROM THE TEXT

QUESTION 1: How can taxes affect the choice of currency denomination for loans?

ANSWER: The currency denomination of corporate borrowings matters where tax asymmetries are present. These tax asymmetries are based on the differential treatment of foreign exchange gains and losses on either forward contracts or loan repayments, e.g., the British policy of taxing exchange gains on foreign currency borrowings but disallowing the deductibility of exchange losses on the same loans or the past U.S. policy of permitting exchange gains on forward contracts to be taxed at a lower rate than the rate at which forward contract losses are deductible. Such tax asymmetries lead to possibilities of borrowing arbitrage, even if interest rate parity holds before tax.

QUESTION 2: How can the choice of currency denomination of loans enable a firm to reduce its exchange risk?

ANSWER: The risks associated with borrowing in a specific currency are related to the firm's degree of exposure in that currency. Thus, by borrowing locally, a firm can create an offsetting liability for its exposed LC assets and thereby reduce its currency risk. On the other hand, borrowing a foreign currency in which the firm has no exposure will increase its exchange risk. What matters is the covariance between the operating and financing cash flows.

PROBLEMS

PROBLEM 1:   Assume that the nominal interest rate in Brazil is 85%.   What is the effective interest rate on a 100,000 cruzado discounted loan?

SOLUTION:

On the 100,000 cruzado loan, the bank will receive in advance 85,000 cruzados. The actual amount paid out by the bank is only 15,000 cruzados. The effective interest rate on the loan is

$$85,000/15,000 = 567\%.$$

PROBLEM 2:   A firm which currently maintains a compensating balance of $300,000 in its bank account borrows $5 million at 13% interest paid at maturity.   The compensating balance requirement is 15%.   What is the effective annual interest rate of this loan?

SOLUTION:

The compensating balance required by this loan is

$$\$5,000,000 \ (.15) = \$750,000.$$

With $300,000 already on deposit, the firm needs to keep an additional

$$\$750,000 - \$300,000 = \$450,000.$$

Thus, the $5 million loan provides only

$$\$5,000,000 - \$450,000 = \$4,550,000$$

in usable funds for an effective interest rate of

$$\$650,000/4,550,000 = 14.29\%.$$

Because of the compensating balance requirement, the effective interest rate of 14.29% is greater than the stated interest rate of 13%.

PROBLEM 1: Ford has the chance to borrow dollars at 12% or pesos at 80% for one year. The peso:dollar exchange rate is expected to move from $1 = Ps 330 currently to $1 = Ps 450 by year's end. (a) What is the expected after-tax dollar cost of borrowing dollars for one year if the Mexican corporate tax rate is 53%? (b) What is Ford's expected after-tax dollar cost of borrowing pesos for one year? (c) At what end-of-year exchange rate will the after-tax peso cost of borrowing dollars equal the after-tax peso cost of borrowing pesos?

SOLUTION:

The after-tax dollar cost of borrowing dollars overseas equals

$$r_{us} \ (1 - t) - dt,$$

where r_{us} is the dollar interest rate, t is the local tax rate, and d is the change in the dollar value of the local currency (LC). Similarly, the after-tax dollar cost of borrowing LC is

$$r_L \ (1 - d)(1 - t) - d,$$

where r_L is the LC interest rate. In the situation facing Ford, the expected devaluation of the peso over the course of the year is

$$(1/330 - 1/450)/(1/450) = 22.67\%.$$

a. The expected after-tax dollar cost of borrowing dollars for a year at 12% is

$$.12(1 - .53) - .53 \ \text{x} \ .2667 = -8.50\%.$$

b. The expected after-tax dollar cost of borrowing pesos at 80% for one year is

$$.80(1 - .2667)(1 - .53) - .2667 = 0.90\%.$$

c. The point at which the peso costs of borrowing dollars and pesos are identical is the same as the point at which their dollar costs are identical (one is just a linear multiple of the other). Using the formulas presented above, the breakeven amount of currency change d^* is found at the point at which

$$r_{us} \ (1 - t) - dt = r_L \ (1 - d)(1 - t)$$

$$\text{or} \quad d^* = (r_L - r_{us})/(1 + r_L).$$

Substituting in the numbers presented in the problem,

$$d^* = (.80 - .12)/1.80$$

$$= 37.78\%.$$

The relationship between the beginning exchange rate, e_0, and the end-of-period exchange rate, e_1, is

$$e_1 = e_0(1 - d).$$

In this case, $e_0 = 1/330$, so

$$e_1 = (1/330) \times (1 - .3778) = \$.0018855$$

or   Ps530 = \$1.

PROBLEM 2:   Suppose that a firm located in Belgium can borrow dollars at 8% or Belgium francs at 14%. (a) If the Belgian franc is expected to depreciate from BF 58 = \$1 at the beginning of the year to BF 61 = \$1 at the end of the year, what is the expected dollar cost of the Belgian franc loan? (b) If the Belgian corporate tax rate is 42%, what is the expected after-tax dollar cost of borrowing dollars, assuming the same currency change scenario? (c) Given the expected exchange rate change, which currency yields the lower expected after-tax dollar cost?

SOLUTION:

a.   The before-tax expected dollar cost of borrowing LC is

$$r_L (1 - d) - d,$$

where r_L is the LC interest rate and d is the change in the dollar value of the local currency (LC). In the situation facing the firm in Belgium, the expected devaluation of the Belgian franc over the course of the year is

$$(1/58 - 1/61)/(1/58) = 4.92\%.$$

Substituting in the numbers given in the problem, we find that the after-tax dollar cost of borrowing Belgian francs for the year is

$$.14(1 - .0492) - .0492 = 8.39\%.$$

b.   Since the after-tax dollar cost of borrowing dollars overseas equals

$$r_{us}(1 - t) - dt,$$

154

where r_{us} is the dollar interest rate, then the Belgian firm's expected after-tax dollar cost of borrowing dollars for the year is

$$.08(1 - .42) - .0492 \times .42 = 2.57\%.$$

c. The expected after-tax dollar cost of borrowing LC is

$$r_L \ (1 - d)(1 - t) - d.$$

Substituting in the numbers from the problem yields an after-tax expected dollar cost of borrowing Belgian francs for the year equal to

$$.14(1 - .0492)(1 - .42) - .0492 \times .42 = 5.65\%.$$

This is higher than the 2.57% expected cost of borrowing dollars calculated in 3b. Hence, dollar financing is the less expensive borrowing option on an expected cost basis per annum.

CHAPTER 13

FINANCING FOREIGN TRADE

Summary: The main purpose of this chapter is to describe and analyze the various payment terms possible in international trade along with the necessary documentation associated with each procedure. It also examines the different methods and sources of export financing and credit insurance that are available to the multinational corporation.

I. Payment Terms in International Trade

    A. Every shipment abroad involves a combination of financing by the exporter, the importer, and one or more financial intermediaries.

    B. The five principal means of payment in international trade, ranked in terms of increasing risk to the exporter, are:

        1. Cash in advance.

        2. Letter of credit.

        3. Draft.

        4. Consignment.

        5. Open account.

    C. As a general rule, the greater the protection sought by the exporter, the less convenient the payment terms for the buyer. However, some of the payment procedures provide protection to both parties against commercial and/or political risks.

    D. When choosing among these methods, the exporter must weigh the benefits in risk reduction against the cost of lost sales. Some of the factors that must be included in the exporter's calculation are:

        1. The credit standing of the buyer.

        2. The amount involved.

        3. The competitive situation.

        4. The type of merchandise being shipped.

        5. The trade customs.

6. The cost of lost sales.

7. The financing costs.

8. The current or anticipated exchange controls.

9. The political conditions.

E. Cash in advance offers the exporter the greatest protection because payment is received either before shipment or upon arrival of the goods. Also, it allows the exporter to avoid tying up its own funds.

1. Cash terms are used where:

    a. There is political instability in the importing country (e.g., exchange controls).

    b. The buyer's credit is doubtful.

    c. Goods are made to order.

F. When credit is extended, the letter of credit (L/C), offers the exporter the greatest degree of safety.

1. The letter of credit is a letter addressed to the seller (exporter), written and signed by a bank acting on behalf of the buyer (importer).

2. In the letter of credit, the bank promises that it will honor drafts drawn on itself if the seller (exporter) complies with the L/C's stipulated conditions.

3. The letter of credit represents, therefore, a financial contract between the issuing bank and a designated beneficiary that is separate from the commercial transaction.

4. The advantages to the seller (exporter) include the following:

    a. The L/C eliminates credit risk if the bank issuing it has an excellent credit standing.

    b. The L/C reduces the danger that payment will be delayed or withhold due to exchange controls or other political acts.

    c. The L/C reduces uncertainty.

    d. The L/C guards against pre-shipment risk.

    e. The L/C facilitates financing because it ensures the exporter a ready buyer for its product.

5. The advantages to the buyer (importer) include:

   a. Because payment is only made if the exporter conforms to the specific conditions set forth in the L/C, the importer is able to ascertain that the merchandise is actually shipped, or before, or a certain date by requiring either an on-board bill of lading or an inspection certificate.

   b. Any documents required are carefully inspected.

   c. A L/C is about as good as cash. Thus, the importer can usually demand better credit terms and/or prices.

   d. Some exporters will only sell on a letter of credit. Willingness to provide one expands a firm's sources of supply.

   e. L/C financing may be cheaper, there is no tie up of cash.

   f. If prepayment is required, the importer is in a better position to recover deposits from a bank than from the seller should the seller be unable or unwilling to make a proper shipment.

6. Most L/Cs issued in connection with a commercial transaction are documentary; that is, the seller is required to submit, together with the draft, any necessary invoices or other documents.

7. A non-documentary, or clean, L/C is normally used in other than commercial transactions.

8. A letter of credit can be revocable or irrevocable.

   a. In a revocable L/C payment is arranged, but not guaranteed. It can be revoked without notice, at any time up to the time a draft is presented to the issuing bank.

   b. On the other hand, an irrevocable L/C cannot be revoked without the specific permission of all parties concerned, including the exporter.

   c. Credits between unrelated parties are usually irrevocable; otherwise, the advantage of commitment to pay is lost.

9. A letter of credit can also be confirmed or unconfirmed.

   a. A L/C issued by one bank can be confirmed by another, thus obligating both banks to honor any drafts drawn in compliance.

b. An <u>unconfirmed</u> <u>L/C</u> is the obligation of only the issuing bank.

10. An exporter will prefer the following financing arrangements, ranked in terms of degree of safety for the exporter:

    a. The irrevocable, confirmed L/C.

    b. The irrevocable, unconfirmed L/C.

    c. The revocable L/C.

11. The selection of the type of L/C to use depends on an evaluation of the risks associated with the transaction and the relative costs involved.

12. A <u>transferable</u> <u>L/C</u> is one under which the beneficiary has the right to instruct the paying bank to make the credit available to one or more secondary beneficiaries.

13. An <u>assignment</u>, on the other hand, assigns part or all of the proceeds, except the required documents, to another party.

G. A <u>draft</u> is an unconditional order in writing ordering the importer (buyer) to pay the amount specified on the draft on demand or at a fixed or determinable future date.

1. This instrument, also known as <u>bill</u> <u>of</u> <u>exchange</u>, serves three important functions:

    a. To provide written evidence, in clear and simple terms, of a financial obligation.

    b. To enable both parties to potentially reduce their costs of financing.

    c. To provide a negotiable and unconditional instrument.

2. With a draft, the exporter can employ its bank as a <u>collection</u> <u>agent</u>.

3. The three parties to a draft involve:

    a. The <u>drawer</u> is the party who signs and sends the draft to the second party.

    b. The <u>payer</u> receives the payment.

    c. The <u>drawee</u> is the party to whom the draft is addressed.

4. Drafts may be either sight or time drafts.

    a. <u>Sight</u> <u>drafts</u> must be paid on presentation or else dishonored.

    b. <u>Time</u> <u>drafts</u> are payable at some specified future date. The maturity of a time draft is known as the <u>usance</u> or tenor.

5. A time draft becomes an <u>acceptance</u> after being accepted by the drawee.

    a. If the draft is accepted by a bank, it becomes a <u>banker's acceptance</u>.

    b. If it is drawn on and accepted by a commercial enterprise, it is termed a <u>trade</u> <u>acceptance</u>.

    c. The exporter can either hold the acceptance or sell it at a <u>discount</u> to its bank, to some other bank, or to an acceptance dealer.

6. Drafts can be clean or documentary.

    a. A <u>clean</u> <u>draft</u> is unaccompanied by any papers and normally used only for non-trade remittances.

    b. A <u>documentary</u> <u>draft</u> is accompanied by documents that are to be delivered to the drawee on payment or acceptance of the draft.

H. With a <u>consignment</u>, goods are only shipped, not sold, to the importer (buyer). The exporter (consignor) retains title to the goods until the importer (consignee) has sold them to a third party. This arrangement is normally made only to related companies because of the risks involved.

I. Selling merchandise on <u>open</u> <u>account</u> involves shipping the goods first and billing the importer later.

1. The credit terms are arranged between the buyer and the seller.

2. Because of little evidence of the importer's obligation to pay, this arrangement is made available only to foreign affiliates or customers with a long history of favorable business dealings.

3. The major benefits of open account selling include:

    a. Greater flexibility.

    b. Lower costs because of fewer bank charges.

4. The drawbacks of this arrangement, in turn, are as follows:

    a. High risk.

    b. Increased risk from currency controls.

    c. Low priority in allocating foreign exchange.

J. Exporters can choose between three alternatives to collect overdue accounts.

    1. They can try to collect the account themselves.

    2. They can hire an attorney who is experienced in international law.

    3. They can use the services of a collection agency.

II. Documents in International Trade

A. The most important supporting document required by commercial banks when financing exports is the bill of lading (B/L).

    1. The bill of lading serves three main functions:

        a. It is a contract between the carrier and the shipper (exporter), in which the carrier agrees to carry the merchandise from the port of shipment to the port of destination.

        b. It is the shipper's receipt for the merchandise.

        c. The negotiable B/L, which is the most common document, establishes control over the merchandise.

    2. A bill of lading can be either a straight or an order B/L.

        a. A straight B/L consigns goods to a specific party, usually the importer and is not negotiable nor transferable.

        b. An order B/L consigns goods to the order of a named party, usually the exporter, who retains title until the B/L is endorsed.

    3. The bill of lading can also be classified in several other ways.

        a. An on-board B/L certifies that goods have been placed on board of a vessel.

b. A <u>received-for-shipment</u> <u>B/L</u> acknowledges that goods have been received for shipment.

c. A <u>clean</u> <u>B/L</u> indicates that the goods have been received in good condition.

d. A <u>foul</u> <u>B/L</u> indicates that the goods are damaged or in poor condition.

B. A <u>commercial</u> <u>invoice</u> contains an authoritative description of the merchandise shipped. Also included are the names and addresses of the importer and exporter, the number of packages, the payment terms, the name of the vessel, and others.

C. All shipments going abroad are insured.

1. The insurance contracts used are under an <u>open</u>, or <u>floating</u>, policy in which all shipments made by the exporter is automatically covered.

2. An <u>insurance</u> <u>certificate</u> is made out by the exporter and attached to the forms supplied by the insurance company.

D. A <u>consular</u> <u>invoice</u> is presented to the local consul in exchange for a visa. It does not convey any title to the goods being shipped and is not negotiable.

III. Financing Techniques in International Trade

A. A <u>banker's</u> <u>acceptance</u> is a time draft drawn on a bank. By accepting the draft, the bank makes an unconditional promise to pay the holder of the draft a stated amount on a specified date.

1. An acceptance is created when an importer requests its bank to issue a letter of credit on its behalf, authorizing the foreign exporter to draw a time draft on the bank in payment for the merchandise.

2. Typical maturities on banker's acceptances are 30-, 90-, and 180-days, with the average being 90 days. Maturities can be tailored to cover the entire period needed to ship and dispose of the goods financed.

3. The rates on banker's acceptances are close to those on CDs. In addition, banks charge fees averaging less than 1% per annum.

B. A trade draft can be converted into cash by means of discounting.

   1. The exporter places the draft with a bank or other financial institution and, in turn, receives the face value of the draft less interest and commissions.

   2. The discount rate for trade drafts is often lower than interest rates on overdrafts, bank loans, and other forms of local funding.

   3. Discounting may be done with or without recourse.

      a. With recourse, the bank can collect from the exporter if the importer fails to pay the bill when due.

      b. Without recourse, the bank bears the collection risk if the draft is sold. This is also known as factoring.

C. Forfaiting is the discounting, at a fixed rate without recourse, of medium-term export receivables denominated in fully convertible currencies.

IV. Government Sources of Export Financing and Credit Insurance

   A. Most governments of developed countries provide their domestic exporters with a competitive edge in the form of low-cost export financing and concessionary rates on political and risk insurance.

   B. The Export-Import Bank, or Eximbank, is the only U.S. government agency which finances and facilitates U.S. exports.

      1. The Eximbank is an autonomous agency located within the executive branch of the federal government.

      2. Eximbank loans provide competitive, fixed-rate financing for U.S. export-sales facing foreign competition backed with subsidized official financing.

      3. Eximbank also guarantees the loans made by others. The loan and guarantee programs coverup to 85% of the U.S. export value and have repayment terms of one year or more.

      4. The operations of the EXimbank conform to five basic principles.

         a. Loans are made for the specific purpose of financing the export of goods and services of U.S. origin.

b.   Financing will not be provided unless private capital is unavailable in the amounts required.

c.   Loans must have a reasonable assurance of repayment and must be for projects that have a favorable impact on the country's economic and social well-being.

d.   Fees and premiums charged for guarantees and insurance ar based on the risks covered.

e.   In authorizing loans or other financial assistance, the Eximbank is obliged to take into account any adverse effects on the U.S. economy or balance of payments that might occur.

5.   Interest rates charged on Eximbank loans are based on the rat table of the international arrangement among the 22 members o the Organization for Economic Cooperation and Development (OECD).

6.   Programs provided by the Eximbank include the following:

a.   Direct loans to foreign buyers of U.S. exports.

b.   Intermediary loans to financial institutions which extend loans to foreign buyers. These are structured as "stand by" loan commitments.

c.   Guarantees to provide repayment protection for private sector loans to creditworthy buyers of exported U.S. good and services.

d.   Export-related working capital loans to creditworthy smal and medium-sized businesses.

e.   Preliminary commitments outlining the amount, terms, and conditions, of financing that is extended to importers of U.S. goods and services.

7.   The fees charged by the Eximbank consist of:

a.   A commitment fee to the borrower of $\frac{1}{2}$% p.a. on the unused portion of an Eximbank loan.

b.   A charge to the lender of 1/8% p.a. on the unused portion of a guaranteed loan.

c.   A front-end exposure fee to the exporter which is assessec on each disbursement of a loan by the Eximbank or the guaranteed or intermediary lender.

C. The <u>Private</u> <u>Export</u> <u>Funding</u> <u>Corporation</u> (PEFCO) was formed in 1970 to mobilize private capital for financing the export of big-ticket items by U.S. firms.

   1. PEFCO purchases medium to long-term debt obligations of importers of U.S. products at fixed interest rates.

   2. It finances portfolios of foreign importer loans through the sale of its own securities.

   3. The Eximbank fully guarantees the repayment of all PEFCO foreign obligations.

   4. PEFCO normally extends its credit jointly with one or more commercial banks and the Eximbank.

      a. Maturities vary from 2.5 years to 12 years.

      b. Banks take the short-term maturity and the Eximbank takes the long-term portion of a PEFCO loan.

D. Export financing covered by government <u>credit</u> <u>insurance</u> provides protection against losses from political and or commercial risks.

   1. This insurance serves as collateral for the credit provided and is often indispensable in making the sale.

   2. While having insurance results in lowering the cost of borrowing from private institution, additional security may be required in the form of a guarantee by a foreign local bank or a certificate by the foreign central bank that foreign exchange is available for the repayment of the loan.

   3. The main purpose of the export-credit insurance, though, is to encourage a nation's export sales by protecting domestic exporters against the non-payment by importers.

   4. In the U.S., the export-credit insurance program is administered by the Foreign Credit Insurance Association (FCIA).

      a. The FCIA is a cooperative effort of the Eximbank and a group of 50 of the leading insurance companies.

      b. It offers protection to exporters from political and commercial risks where:

         (1) The private insurers cover the commercial risks.

         (2) The Eximbank covers the political risks.

  c. Any portion of the risks not covered by the FCIA must be self-insured by the exporter.

  d. Under the FCIA base program, lessors of U.S. equipment an services can cover both the stream of lease payments and the fair market value of the products leased abroad.

V. Countertrade

 A. More and more multinational corporations have to resort to countertrade if they want to sell overseas.

  1. Countertrade involves purchasing local products to offset the exports of a firm's own products to this market.

  2. While swapping goods for goods is less efficient, it is often preferable to having no sales in a given market.

 B. Countertrade can take several specific forms:

  1. Barter involves a direct exchange of goods between two parties without the use of money.

  2. Counterpurchase or parallel barter involves the sale and purchase of goods that are unrelated to each others.

  3. Buyback consists of repaying the original purchase price through the sale of a related product.

 C. While countertrading may enable members of cartels, such as OPEC, to undercut an agreed-upon price, it is replete with problems for the firms involved.

  1. The goods that are taken in countertrade are usually undesirable.

  2. The trading details are difficult to work out.

 D. Most countertrade has centered on

  1. the governmental foreign trade organizations (FTOs) of Eastern European countries.

  2. Third World countries.

 E. A major concern of the authorities in countertrading countries is that goods taken in countertrade will cannibalize their existing cash markets.

KEY TERMS

Cash in Advance
Letter of Credit (L/C)
Bill of Lading (B/L)
Inspection Certificate
Documentary L/C
Nondocumentary or Clean L/C
Revocable L/C
Irrevocable L/C
Confirmed L/C
Unconfirmed L/C
Transferable L/C
Assignment
Draft
Drawer
Drawee
Payee
Sight Draft
Time Draft
Usance or Tenor
Acceptance
Banker's Acceptance
Trade Acceptance
Clean Draft
Documentary Draft
Consignment
Open Account
Straight B/L

Order B/L
On-Board B/L
Received-for-Shipment B/L
Clean B/L
Foul B/L
Commercial Invoice
Insurance Certificate
Open, or Floating Insurance
  Policy
Consular Invoice
Discounting
Factoring
Forfaiting
Export-Import Bank (Eximbank)
Private Export Funding
  Corporation (PEFCO)
Export-Credit Insurance
Foreign Credit Insurance
  Association (FCIA)
Countertrade
Barter
Counterpurchase or Parallel
  Barter
Buyback
Foreign Trade Organizations
  (FTOs)

CONCEPTUAL QUESTIONS

QUESTION 1: What are the functions of the various financing arrangements and documents involved in international trade?

ANSWER: The financing techniques used in international trade serve the following four functions: (1) to reduce both buyer and seller risk; (2) to pinpoint who bears those risks that remain; (3) to facilitate the transfer of risk to a third party; and (4) to facilitate financing.

QUESTION 2: Distinguish between the letter of credit, the draft, and the bill of lading.

ANSWER: A letter of credit is a bank guarantee of payment provided that certain stipulated conditions are met. A draft is a written order to pay. And a bill of lading is the document which covers the actual shipment of the merchandise by a common carrier and title.

QUESTION 3:   What is a banker's acceptance?

ANSWER: A banker's acceptance is a time draft drawn on a bank. By
accepting the draft, the bank makes an unconditional promise to pay the
holder of the draft a stated amount on a specified day. Thus, the bank
effectively substitutes its own credit for that of a borrower, and in the
process, it creates a negotiable instrument that may be freely traded.

SELECTED QUESTIONS FROM THE TEXT

QUESTION 3:   One of the purposes of Eximbank is to absorb credit risks on
export sales that the private sector will not accept. Comment on this
purpose.

ANSWER: The private sector is always willing to absorb credit risks, but
not necessarily at a low price. By providing low-cost export credits, the
government causes uneconomical deals to get done. That is, the government
is sending out the wrong signals about the profitability of doing certain
deals. The exporter gets the benefits from any export sales while the
taxpayer gets stuck with the cost of any credit that turns out bad. This
leads to poor foreign credit risks receiving low-cost financing. And
taxpayers are subsidizing these bad risks.

QUESTION 5:   What is countertrade? Why is it termed a sophisticated form
of barter?

ANSWER: Countertrade involves purchasing local products to offset the
exports of their own products to that market. Countertrade is a form of
barter because both involve swapping goods for goods. Countertrade
transactions are often very complex, involving two-way or three-way
transactions, especially where a company is forced to accept unrelated
goods for resale by outsiders. In this way, countertrade is a
sophisticated form of barter; that is, it may involve more than two parties
and a number of transactions.

CURRENT ASSET MANAGEMENT

Summary: This chapter deals with the management of working capital items available to each foreign affiliate. In particular, it discusses the techniques by which the MNC shifts liquid assets among its various affiliates. It also examines the tax and other consequences associated with these maneuvers.

I.   International Cash Management

    A.   The objectives and principles of international cash management are identical to those of domestic cash management.

        1.   International money management is a more complicated task because of a number of external factors which inhibit adjustment and constrain the money manager. These complicating factors include:

            a.   A set of restrictions that impedes the free flow of money in and out of a country.

            b.   Multiple tax jurisdictions.

            c.   Multiple currencies.

            d.   Absence of internationally integrated interchange facilities for moving cash swiftly from one location to another.

        2.   On the other hand, MNCs may have significant opportunities for improving their global cash management.

            a.   Firms can achieve higher returns on short-term investments, otherwise denied to purely domestic firms.

            b.   Tax laws and treaties among countries reduce the tax rate applicable to these returns.

            c.   By managing all corporate funds, overall returns to the firm can be increased while, at the same time, reducing the required level of cash and marketable securities worldwide.

    B.   A fully centralized international cash management system offers a number of advantages.

        1.   The MNC is able to operate with a lower level of cash.

2. The reduction of total assets enhances profitability and reduces financing costs.

3. The headquarters staff, responsible for managing all corporate activities, can identify problems and opportunities that an autonomous unit would not perceive.

4. All decisions can be made on the basis of the overall corporate benefit.

5. The firm may obtain better foreign exchange quotes and better service from its bank by increasing the volume of foreign exchange and other transactions.

6. Greater expertise in cash and portfolio management can be exercised if one group is responsible for these activities.

7. In the event of expropriation or blockage of funds, the firm may lose less because its total assets at risk in a foreign country can be reduced.

C. A key element of international cash management is accelerating the receipt of funds both within a foreign country and across borders. This process is broken down into three steps:

1. Defining and analyzing the different available payment channels.

   a. The full cost of each method must be determine.

   b. The inherent delay in the collection process must be calculated.

2. Selecting the most efficient method.

   a. Cable remittances help companies to minimize delays in receipt of payments and in conversion of payments into cash.

   b. SWIFT is a network of banks throughout the world which allows its member banks to automatically process data by computer.

   c. Cash mobilization centers are centrally located points in regions with large sales volumes. Funds are managed centrally or transmitted to the selling subsidiary.

d. With a <u>lock</u> <u>box</u> <u>system</u>, a local bank or branch of a multinational bank takes and opens the mail that is received one or several times daily. Any deposit a transfer made is immediately reported to the national or regional mobilization office.

e. In <u>direct</u> <u>debiting</u>, or pre-authorized payment, the customer allows its account to be charged periodically by the supplier or the supplier's bank, up to a maximum amount.

f. Rapid transfer of funds can be provided by multinational banks or its correspondent network by arranging <u>same-day</u> <u>value</u> of funds.

3. Giving specific instructions regarding procedures to the firm's customers and banks.

4. Management of disbursements requires a detailed knowledge of individual and country differences as well as the various payment instruments and banking services available worldwide.

D. Whenever foreign affiliates buy from or sell to each other, large amounts of funds flow between these foreign units. A clear incentive for the MNC is to minimize the total volume of intracorporate fund flows, which can be accomplished with <u>payments</u> <u>netting</u>.

1. In netting only the netted amount of any sales and purchases is transferred.

a. <u>Bilateral</u> <u>netting</u> is used when two subsidiaries sell back and forth to each other.

b. Where there is a more complex structure of internal sales, <u>multilateral</u> <u>netting</u> is done.

2. An essential element to payments netting is a centralized control point that can collect and record detailed information on the intracorporate accounts of each participating affiliate at specified time intervals. The control point, or <u>netting</u> <u>center</u>, is a subsidiary company located in a country with minimal exchange controls for trade transactions.

a. The netting center will use an intracorporate payments matrix to determine the net payer or creditor position of each affiliate at the date of clearing.

b. In order to minimize the impact of currency changes on the amounts scheduled for transfer, the exchange rate at which these transactions occur is fixed during the week of netting.

        c.   If a central pool is used for all payments and disbursements, the payers in the system either will remit the local currency equivalent of their net obligations to the pool or remit funds directly to specified recipients.

        d.   The choice of which affiliate(s) each payer pays depends on the relative costs of transferring funds between each pair of affiliates.

        e.   The timing of the transfer of the net payments is very crucial because it can modify the planned cash flows of some affiliates.

   3.   Before a MNC implements a multilateral payments system, it needs to know whether the government has imposed restrictions on netting.

   4.   The feasibility of a netting system can be analyzed by estimating the direct cost savings of the netting system and then comparing it with the costs of implementation and operation.

E.   An important task of international cash management is to determine the levels and currency denominations of the multinational's investment in cash balances and money market instruments.

   1.   Managing a firm's short-term investment portfolio requires:

        a.   A forecast of future cash needs based on the firm's current budget and past experience.

        b.   An estimate of a minimum cash level for the next period.

   2.   Managing these investments successfully largely depends on the selection of appropriate money market instruments. This choice, in turn, will be affected by government regulations, tax laws, and the structure of the market, all of which vary widely.

   3.   A policy of managing liquid assets worldwide must recognize that the value of shifting funds across borders depends on:

        a.   The risk-adjusted yield differential.

        b.   The currency conversion cost.

   4.   Guidelines for globally managing the marketable securities portfolio are stated as follows:

a. Short-term securities in the portfolio should be diversified to maximize the return for a given level of risk.

b. The portfolio must be reviewed daily to determine which securities should be liquidated and what new investments should be made.

c. In revising the portfolio, care should be taken to ensure that the incremental interest earned exceeds the added costs incurred.

d. If a firm needs to be able to quickly convert securities into cash, then marketability should be carefully evaluated.

e. The maturity of the investment should be matched with the projected cash needs of the firm.

f. Opportunities for covered or uncovered interest arbitrage should be carefully considered.

F. Centralized cash management involves the transfer of an affiliate's cash in excess of minimal operating requirements into a central account or cash pool where all corporate funds are managed by corporate staff.

1. With cash pooling, an affiliate is required to hold only the minimum cash balance necessary for transactions purposes.

2. If cash requirements of foreign affiliates are relatively independent of each other, centralized cash management can provide an equivalent degree of protection with a lower level of cash reserves.

3. With pooling, the borrowing needs can be reduced or more excess funds are available for investments where returns will be maximized.

4. If funds are pooled, the exposure arising from holding foreign cash balances can be centrally managed.

5. The larger the pool of funds, the more willing a firm is going to be to invest in cash management expertise.

G. To globally manage a firm's cash and marketable securities, the MNC must devise a good reporting system. This system, in turn, must be able to rely on a cash budgeting system to track and forecast the firm's various cash inflows and cash outflows.

1. The benefit of such a reporting system is the firm's ability effectively manage its affiliates' liquidity and tax position by:

   a. leading and lagging intercompany payments.

   b. Adjusting dividend flows, transfer prices, fees and royalties, and intracorporate loans.

2. A _multinational_ _cash_ _mobilization_ _system_ is designed to optimize the use of funds by tracking current and near-term cash positions. The information gathered can be used to:

   a. Aid a multilateral netting system.

   b. Increase the operational efficiency of a centralized cash pool.

   c. Determine more effective short-term borrowing and investment policies.

H. Good _bank_ _relations_ are important to a company's international ca management effort.

   1. To avoid poor cash management service, many firms conduct ban relations audits.

   2. Some considerations in auditing a company's banks include:

      a. Too many bank relations.

      b. High banking costs.

      c. Inadequate reporting.

      d. Excessive clearing delays.

   3. The company compiles a monthly report that details precisely how much business it is giving to each bank it uses. This information, in turn, can be used to negotiate better terms an better service from its bank.

II. Credit Management

A. Trade credit is made available to customers because the credit granting company expects the investment in accounts receivables t be profitable.

B. In deciding on the appropriate credit policy, the following three major variables need to be considered:

1. <u>Credit</u> <u>terms</u> which need to be closely scrutinized in countries experiencing rapid inflation.

2. <u>Credit</u> <u>standards</u> which vary among countries and quite often are more relaxed than in the home market, especially in countries lacking alternative sources of financing for the small customer.

3. <u>Collection</u> <u>effort</u> is used by firms to isolate and analyze those accounts that are past due.

C. <u>Factoring</u> is used primarily by firms with a substantial export business, and companies too small to afford a foreign credit and collection department.

   1. Factoring involves buying a company's receivable, thereby accelerating their conversion into cash.

      a. Factoring done on a <u>nonrecourse</u> basis means that the factor assumes all the credit and political risks except those which involve disputes between the transacting parties.

      b. In factoring <u>with</u> <u>recourse</u>, all these risks are assumed by the exporter.

   2. By using a factor, the company can ensure that its terms are in accord with local practice and are competitive.

   3. Export factoring fees, which can be quite high, are determined on an individual company basis and are related to:

      a. The annual turnover.

      b. The average invoice size.

      c. The creditability of the claims.

      d. The terms of sale.

   4. Despite these higher costs, the cost of bearing the credit risk associated with a given receivable can be substantially lower to the factor than to the exporter.

D. The credit extension policy of a firm engaged in international business involves the decision as to the amount of credit to extend and the currency in which credit sales are to be billed.

1. If both buyer and seller have access to credit at the same cost and reflect in their decisions anticipated currency changes and inflation, then there should be no difference between receiving additional credit or an equivalent cash discount.

2. There are three situations from which a MNC will benefit if revises its credit terms.

   a. The buyer and seller have different opinions regarding t future course of inflation and currency changes.

   b. The MNC is able to receive credit at a lower risk-adjust cost than does its customer because of market imperfections.

   c. During periods of credit rationing, the affiliate of a M may have access to funds that local competitors do not have, thereby gaining a marketing advantage over its competitors.

3. The following approach can be used by firms to compare the expected costs and benefits associated with extending credit internationally. This approach involves five steps.

   (1) Calculate the current cost of extending credit.

   (2) Calculate the cost of extending credit under the revised credit policy.

   (3) Using the information from steps 1 and 2, calculate the incremental credit costs under the revised credi policy.

   (4) Ignoring credit costs, calculate the incremental profits under the new credit policy.

   (5) If, and only if, the incremental profits are greater than the incremental costs, select the new credit policy, or

   $$\Delta S - \Delta C \geq S \Delta R + \Delta S (R + \Delta R)$$

   where ΔS and ΔC are the incremental sales costs associated with the new credit policy, R is the expected credit cost per unit of sales revenue, and is the incremental change in the expected credit cost.

III. Inventory Management

    A. For a MNC it is much more difficult to control its overseas inventory and realize its inventory turnover objectives because of the following reasons:

        1. Long and variable transit times if ocean transportation is used.

        2. Lengthy customs proceedings and possibilities of dock strikes.

        3. Import controls.

        4. Supply disruption.

        5. Anticipated changes in currency values.

        6. Higher duties.

    B. In addition, inflation, currency changes, and supply disruptions cause greater concern in the multinational firm than its domestic counterpart because financial market constraints and import controls often restrict the multinational in its ability to deal with these problems.

        1. Companies have traditionally responded to such risks with advance purchases of inventory.

        2. However, holding large quantities can be quite expensive.

        3. The inventory manager, in turn, needs to weigh the costs associated with stock-out and future supplies against the probability of disruption.

IV. Appendix 14A: Electronic Means of International Funds Transfers

    A. The Clearing House Interbank Payments System (CHIPS) is a computerized network for transfer of international dollar payments, linking about 140 depository institutions that have offices or affiliates in New York City.

        1. In August 1981, the New York Fed established a settlement account for member banks into which debit settlement payments are sent and from which credit settlement payments are disbursed.

        2. Transfers between member banks are netted out and settled at the close of each business day by sending or receiving FedWire transfers through the settlement account.

a. The FedWire system is operated by the Federal Reserve a is used only for domestic money transfers.

b. FedWire allows almost instant movement of balances as well as the transfer of government securities between institutions having accounts at the Federal Reserve Ban

3. At the closing of the CHIPS network, the CHIPS computer complies a settlement report showing the net debit or credit positions of each participant.

4. These positions are netted out whereby:

a. The settling participant with a debit position transfers its debit amount via FedWire to the CHIPS settlement account.

b. The Clearing House transfers funds via FedWire out of th settlement account to those settling participants with r credit or positions.

KEY TERMS

SWIFT
Cash Mobilization Center
Lock Box System
Direct Debiting
Same-Day Value
Payments Netting
Bilateral Netting
Multilateral Netting

Netting Center
Cash Pooling
Multinational Cash Mobilizatio
Credit Management
Factoring
Credit Extension Policy
Inventory Management
CHIPS

CONCEPTUAL QUESTIONS

QUESTION 1: How do MNCs handle their inventories and accounts receivable

ANSWER: Inventory and accounts receivable management in the MNC involves cost-minimizing strategy of investing in these assets up to the point at which the marginal cost of extending another dollar of credit or purchasi one more unit of inventory is just equal to the additional expected benefits to be derived. These benefits accrue in the form of maintaining or increasing the value of other current assets, such as cash and marketable securities, increasing sales revenue, or reducing inventory stock-out costs.

SELECTED QUESTIONS FROM THE TEXT

QUESTION 1b: What are the advantages and disadvantages of centralizing the cash management function?

ANSWER: The advantages of centralizing the cash management function include:

1. The corporation can operate with a smaller amount of cash; pools of excess liquidity are absorbed and eliminated. Each operation will maintain transactions balances only and not hold speculative or precautionary ones.
2. By reducing total assets, financing costs are reduced and profitability is enhanced.
3. The headquarters staff, with its purview of all corporate activity, can recognize problems and opportunities that an individual unit might not perceive.
4. All decisions can be made using the overall corporate benefit as the criterion.
5. By increasing the volume of foreign exchange and other transactions done through headquarters, banks provide better foreign exchange quotes and better service.
6. Greater expertise in cash and portfolio management exists if one group is responsible for these activities.
7. The corporation's total assets at risk in a foreign country can be reduced. Less will be lost in the event of an expropriation or the promulgation of regulations restricting the transfer of funds.

The principal disadvantage of centralization is that it entails costs, which are both explicit and implicit. The explicit continuing costs are those related to the additional management time and expanded communications necessitated by the centralized management. There are also costs of a more implicit nature, those related to the behavioral problems resulting from more centralized control. Affiliates might resent the tighter control necessary. In addition, rigid centralization provides no incentive for local managers to take advantage of specific opportunities that only they may be aware of.

QUESTION 3: Suppose a subsidiary is all equity financed and hence has no interest expenses. Does it still make sense to charge the local managers for the working capital tied up in their operations? Explain.

ANSWER: Yes. Otherwise, the subsidiary's management is not motivated to carefully scrutinize the level of working capital to trade off its costs and benefits. The point is that working capital has an opportunity cost regardless of how it is financed and managers should be charged for the cost of capital tied up in all the assets they use. In this way, subsidiary managers will be more likely to weigh the costs of adding to working capital against its benefits.

PROBLEM 1: A $1.5 billion Italian multinational manufacturing company h
a total of $600 million in intercompany trade flows and settles accounts
13 currencies. It also has about $400 million in third-party trade flow
Intercompany settlements are all made manually, there are no predefined
remittance channels for either intercompany or third-party accounts are
identical. What techniques might help this company better manage its
affairs?

SOLUTION: Several techniques that might help this company better manage
its affairs are as follows:

1. Define and analyze the different available payment channels.
2. Select the most efficient method (which can vary by country and
   customer).
3. Give specific instructions regarding payment procedures to the
   firm's customers and banks.
4. Use multilateral netting.
5. Determine the currency of invoice and payment by reference to wl
   is available and what is needed for the system as a whole.
6. Use treasury work stations to keep track of liquidity world wide

PROBLEM 8: Twenty different divisions of Union Carbide sell to thousands
of customers in more than 50 countries throughout the world. The procee
are received in the form of drafts, checks, and letters of credit.
Controlling the flow of funds from each transaction is an extremely compl
task. Union Carbide wants to reduce the collection float to improve its
cash flows. What are some techniques that might help to achieve this
objective?

SOLUTION: To reduce days sales outstanding (DSO) so as to reduce
collection float, Union Carbide must identify where the delays are. Are
the delays caused by customers, foreign banks, or the exporter itself?
What are the relative magnitudes of each type of delay and can simple
changes eliminate significant portions of float?
    As most companies have found, Union Carbide will probably be able to
reduce its collection float by modifying the way it prepares and mails ou
documents, changing customer payment methods, and concentrating its
collection activity in far fewer banks.
    Here are some techniques that can help to reduce float:

1. Date drafts when goods are shipped, not several days later.
2. Have customers remit funds by wire transfer instead of by check.
3. Have foreign banks remit funds by SWIFT or cable transfer rather
   than by check.
4. Cut the banking chain to a minimum so that an international mone
   transfer passes through as few banks as possible between the tin
   it is initiated by the customer and the time the payment
   instruction arrives at the U.S. collecting bank.

5. Have U.S. collecting banks speed up the process of crediting Union Carbide with goods funds after receiving payment instructions or receiving check deposits.
6. Pay close attention to high value transfers and make special arrangements where necessary to expedite these transfers.
7. Convert the customer's payment into dollars in the importer's country if it is cheaper and/or quicker to do so there.
8. Maintain accounts in the currencies of customers where doing so will expedite clearing of payments.

PROBLEM 10: Cypress Semiconductor, a California firm, is trying to decide whether to shift production overseas of its relatively expensive integrated circuits (they average around $8 each). Offshore assembly would save about 8.2¢ per chip in labor costs. Buy by producing offshore, it would take about five weeks to get the parts to customers, in contrast to one week with domestic manufacturing. Thus, offshore production would force Cypress to carry another four weeks of inventory. In addition, offshore production would entail combined shipping and customs duty costs of 2.5¢. Suppose Cypress's cost of funds is 15%. Will it save money by shifting production offshore?

SOLUTION: Ignoring any problems associated with distance, the net benefit to Cypress of shifting production abroad will equal

Labor cost savings - (shipping + customs duty + cost of money tied up in inventory)

The key here is to estimate the final term. By producing abroad, Cypress will be forced to carry another four weeks of inventory. At an annual cost of funds equal to 15% and an average cost per chip of $8, the added inventory-related interest expense associated with overseas production is found as follows:

$$\text{Added interest expense} = \begin{array}{c}\text{opportunity cost}\\\text{of funds}\end{array} \times \begin{array}{c}\text{added time}\\\text{in transit}\end{array} \times \begin{array}{c}\text{cost per}\\\text{part}\end{array}$$

$$= .15 \times (4/52) \times \$8$$

$$= \$.092.$$

Returning to the equation above, the net benefit to Cypress of offshore production equals

$$8.2¢ - (2.5¢ + 9.2¢) = -3.5¢.$$

Hence, it is not worthwhile to shift production abroad. The high inventory cost alone will more than offset the labor cost savings.

CHAPTER 15

MANAGING THE MULTINATIONAL FINANCIAL SYSTEM

Summary: This chapter analyzes the benefits, costs, and constraints associated with the multinational financial system. It involves (1) identifying the conditions which will lead to increasing the value of the firm if this system is used, (2) describing and evaluating the various channels for moving money and profits internationally, and (3) specifying the design principles for a global approach to managing international fund transfers.

I. The Value of the Multinational Financial System

    A. Multinational corporations possess a unique characteristic: the ability to shift funds and profits among its various units through internal financial transfer mechanisms.

    B. While there is no such counterpart to a purely domestic firm, international fund transfers confer advantages to the MNC for two main reasons:

        1. The wide variation in national tax systems.

        2. The significant costs and barriers associated with international financial transfers.

    C. Thus, multinational corporations are presented with three different types of arbitrage opportunities.

        1. _Tax arbitrage_. The tax burden of a MNC can be reduced by shifting profits:

            a. From units located in high-tax nations to units in lower-tax nations.

            b. From units in a taxpaying position to units with losses.

        2. _Financial market arbitrage_. The ability to transfer funds among units may enable MNCs to:

            a. Circumvent exchange controls.

            b. Earn higher risk-adjusted returns on excess funds.

            c. Reduce their risk-adjusted borrowed funds.

            d. Tap previously unavailable capital sources.

3. <u>Regulatory system arbitrage</u>. Where subsidiary profits are a function of government regulations or union pressure, the MNC may be able to disguise true profitability by reallocating profits among units.

D. A fourth arbitrage opportunity is presented when a subsidiary may be permitted to negate the effect of credit restraint or controls in its country of operation.

II. Intracorporate Fund-Flow Mechanism: Costs and Benefits

A. A MNC can be viewed as <u>unbundling</u> the total intracorporate transfer of funds between each pair of affiliates into separate flows corresponding to the nature of payment.

B. The total tax liability on fund transfers is dependent on the tax regulations of both the host and home countries.

1. The host country ordinarily has two types of taxes that directly affect tax costs:

a. Corporate income taxes.

b. Withholding taxes on dividend, interest, and fee remittances.

2. In addition, some countries (West Germany and Japan) tax retained earnings at a different (usually higher) rate than earnings paid out in the form of dividends.

3. Many home countries, including the U.S., tax income remitted from abroad at the regular corporate income tax rate. If this rate is higher than the foreign tax rate, dividends and other payments will entail an incremental tax cost.

4. However, a number of countries, such as Canada, the Netherlands, and France, do not impose any additional taxes on foreign-source income.

5. To offset the additional taxes, most countries, including the U.S., provide <u>tax credits</u> for affiliate taxes already paid on the same income.

6. <u>Tax treaties</u> between countries have been established to avoid double taxation of the same income.

7. In the U.S., MNCs are also required to pay taxes on certain types of unremitted foreign profits, as set forth in the U.S. Revenue Act of 1962.

C. The pricing of intracorporate exchange of goods and services is
    one of the most sensitive and probably most misunderstood area i
    multinational financial management.

    1. Transfer pricing is used by MNCs to influence the amount an
        direction of intracorporate transfers.

    2. Effective utilization of this tool, however, is increasingly
        subjected to legal and administrative constraints imposed by
        home and host governments.

D. Transfer pricing can be, and has been, used by MNCs to accomplis
    one or more of the following objectives.

    1. Reducing taxes and tariffs.

        a. A MNC may be able to shift profits from a higher to a
            lower tax jurisdiction or shift tax-paying profits of on
            unit to one with losses.

        b. If the objective is to minimize corporate taxes, a basic
            rule of thumb can be followed:

            (1) If $t_A > t_B$, set the transfer price as low as
                possible.

            (2) If $t_A < t_B$, set the transfer price as high as
                possible.

            where: t_A = marginal tax rate of Affiliate A
                    t_B = marginal tax rate of Affiliate B

        c. The higher a tariff relative to the income tax
            differential, the more desirable it is to set a low
            transfer price.

        d. Costs associated with using transfer pricing for tax
            reduction take the form of legal fees, executive time, a
            penalties.

        e. Most countries have specific regulations governing
            transfer prices. The U.S. government is calling for arm
            length prices, which are determined by a willing buyer a
            a willing unrelated seller. There are four alternative
            transfer pricing methods ranked by their apparent
            acceptability to the Department of the Treasury:

            (1) Comparable uncontrolled price method. Under this
                method, the transfer price is set by direct referenc
                to prices used in similar transactions between two
                unrelated firms.

(2) Resale price method. Under this method, the transfer price is set by reducing the price charged to an independent purchaser by an appropriate markup.

(3) Cost-plus method. This method adds an appropriate profit markup to the seller's cost.

(4) Another appropriate method. In some cases, it may be appropriate to use a combination of the above methods or use still other methods, such as the comparable profits and net yield methods.

2. Transfer pricing is used even more to by pass exchange restrictions, as shown by a study by Robbins and Stobaugh.

3. At times, transfer prices are used to channel profits to an affiliate with the purpose of bolstering its credit rating.

4. Funds in weak-currency nations are sometimes syphoned off through transfer price adjustments to reduce exchange risk exposure. However, transfer pricing is only useful if:

a. The currency is blocked.

b. Tax advantages are independent of the exchange risk benefits.

5. Conflicts over transfer pricing often arise when one of the affiliates involved is a joint venture. The outside partner is often suspicious that transfer pricing is used to shift profits from the joint venture to a wholly-owned subsidiary where, in fact, they should be shared.

6. Where profits are a function of government regulations, the MNC can use transfer pricing to disguise the true profitability of its affiliate, enabling it to justify higher prices and exploit its monopolistic position more fully.

E. A multinational corporation may use a reinvoicing center to disguise profitability, avoid the scrutiny of governments, and coordinate transfer pricing policy.

1. The reinvoicing center takes title to all goods sold by one corporate unit to another affiliate or to a third-party customer, although the goods move directly from the factory or warehouse location to the purchaser. The center pays the seller and, in turn, is paid by the purchasing unit.

2. A reinvoicing center can be advantageous for the following reasons.

    a. With price quotations coming from only one location, it easier and quicker to implement decisions to have prices reflect changes in currency values.

    b. It provides greater flexibility when choosing an invoic currency.

    c. By requesting an affiliate to pay in other than its loca currency, the MNC can avoid the costs of converting from one currency to another and then back again.

3. Some disadvantages associated with a reinvoicing center include

    a. Increased communications costs due to the geographical separation of marketing and sales from the production centers.

    b. Increased suspicion by tax authorities of transactions with an affiliated trading company located in a tax have

F. Management services, such as professional advice, allocated overhead, patents, and trademarks, are often unique and, therefore, are without a reference market price. Because of thi pricing difficulty, these corporate resource can be used as additional routes for international fund flows by varying the fe and royalties charged for the use of these intangible factors of production.

1. Transfer prices for services have the same tax and exchange control effects as those for transfer prices on goods, but they are often subject to even greater scrutiny.

    a. The host country is less likely to object to transfers i fees and royalties have been specified in a written agreement (e.g., payments for industrial know-how).

    b. Should restrictions exist in a host country, they are mo likely to be modified to permit a fee for technological knowledge than to allow for dividends.

2. According to a survey by Shapiro (1977), the three most commonly practiced methods of moving funds from countries wi exchange controls are royalties, licensing payments, and management fees. These techniques are most commonly employe in Latin America.

3. The most common approach used by MNCs to setting fee and royalty charges is for the parent to decide on a desired amount of total fee remittances from the overseas operations and then to assign these charges on the basis of subsidiary sales or assets.

   a. Sometimes this method involves establishing identical licensing agreements with all foreign units.

   b. This method gives these charges the appearance of a legitimate and necessary business expense, thereby aiding in overcoming currency controls.

   c. Governments prefer prior agreements and predictable payment flows; a sudden change in licensing and service charges is likely to be looked at with suspicion.

G. A highly favored method of transferring funds among affiliates is an acceleration (leading) or delay (lagging) in the payment of inter-affiliate accounts, by modifying the credit terms extended by one unit to another.

   1. The value of leading and lagging depends on the opportunity cost of funds to both the paying unit and the recipient.

   2. The advantages of leading and lagging over direct intra-corporate loans include the following:

      a. No formal note of indebtedness is needed, and the amount of credit can be adjusted up or down by making the necessary adjustments in the credit terms. Governments do not always allow such freedom on loans.

      b. Governments are less likely to interfere with payments on intra-corporate accounts than on direct loans.

      c. While intra-corporate accounts are interest free up to six months (Section 482), interest must be charged on all intra-corporate loans.

   3. Government controls on intracorporate credit terms are often tight and subject to abrupt changes.

   4. Leading and lagging is simple in concept but difficult in practice. Operating a comprehensive, multilateral leading and lagging system on a continuing basis requires one or more sophisticated individuals as well as timely information.

      a. Changes in credit terms will require the MNC to adjust its netting schedule as well as its estimates of cash balances held by the affected affiliates.

b. Problems can also arise from the various distortions th[...] these adjustments can cause to affiliate profits and investment bases.

H. A principal method of financing foreign operations and moving funds internationally is to engage in intracorporate lending activities. Intra-corporate loans are more valuable to the fir[...] than arm's length transactions only if at least one of the following market distortions exist: Credit rationing, currency controls, differential tax rates among countries.

1. Direct loans are straight extensions of credit from the par[...] to an affiliate or from one affiliate to another.

2. Back-to-back loans, also called fronting loans or link financing, are employed to finance affiliates located in notions with high interest rates or restricted capital markets.

   a. In a typical arrangement, the parent company deposits funds with a bank in country A that, in turn, lends the money to a subsidiary in country B.

   b. Thus, a back-to-back loan is an intra-corporate loan channeled through a bank.

   c. Because the parent's deposit collateralizes the loans, is viewed by the bank as riskfree.

   d. The bank acts as an intermediary or a front; compensati[...] is provided by the margin between the borrowing rate an[...] the lending rate.

   e. The advantages of a back-to-back loan over a direct intracorporate loan are as follows:

      (1) Because of different withholding tax rates to inter[...] paid to a foreign parent and interest paid to a financial institution, a cost saving in the form of lower taxes may be available with a back-to-back lo[...]

      (2) Back-to-back financing provides better protection t[...] does an intracorporate loan against expropriation t[...] does an intracorporate loan against expropriation and/or exchange controls.

   f. The costs of a back-to-back loan are evaluated in terms all interest, tax, and currency effects that accrue to both the borrowing and lending units, which then are converted to the home currency.

g. Variations on the back-to-back loan include

   (1) The parent depositing dollars while the bank lends out local currency.

   (2) A foreign affiliate placing the deposit in any of several currencies with the bank loan denominated in the same or a different currency.

h. Users of the back-to-back loan include:

   (1) U.S. companies that have accumulated sizable amounts of money in "captive" insurance firms.

   (2) Holding companies in low-tax countries.

i. Back-to-back arrangements can be used to:

   (1) Recycle accumulate funds indirectly.

   (2) Access blocked currency funds, without physically transferring them.

3. A technique related to the back-to-back loan is the <u>trust escrow agreement</u>.

   a. Under this arrangement, a parent opens a trust account with an international bank. These funds are then deposited in the bank's name with a foreign bank which, in turn, loans the funds to the parent's local affiliate.

   b. This techniques offers the following advantages:

      (1) It facilitates the repayment of the loan.

      (2) It allows greater flexibility in setting interest rates.

      (3) The local subsidiary benefits by appearing to borrow at arm's length from a local bank.

      (4) The foreign government receives a temporary inflow of foreign exchange.

4. A <u>parallel loan</u> is a method of effectively repatriating blocked funds, circumventing exchange control restrictions, avoiding a premium exchange rate for investments abroad, financing foreign affiliates without incurring additional exchange risk, or obtaining foreign currency financing at attractive rates.

a. Under this arrangement, the parent company, A, will exten a loan in its home country and its home currency to a subsidiary of B, whose foreign parent company, in turn, will lend the local currency equivalent in its country to the subsidiary of A.

b. Draw downs, repayments of principal, and payments of interest are made simultaneously.

c. The differential between the interest rates on the two loans is determined by the cost of money in each country and anticipated changes in currency values.

d. The parties to a parallel loan must agree on:

    (1) The spread between the home and foreign currency interest rates.

    (2) Maturity.

    (3) The principal amount.

    (4) A topping-up clause dealing with currency fluctuations.

    (5) Repayment of principal.

I. With the granting of intracorporate loans, the MNC can use the compensating balances to effect partial fund transfers.

1. When a U.S. bank extends funds to a firm, it charges interest on the full amount of the loan and also requires that a specified amount of compensating balances be kept on deposit in the bank.

2. A foreign bank generally lends on an overdraft basis with the firm paying full interest only on that portion drawn down, plus a commitment fee on the unused portion of the loan.

3. U.S. dollar accounts held in the bank's branches for transaction purposes by the parent company's affiliates aroun the world can be used toward satisfying the compensating balance requirement. A costless shift of funds can then be attained by changing the composition of these accounts.

J. _Dividends_ are the most important means of transferring funds from foreign affiliates to the parent company.

1. The studies by Robbins and Stobaugh and Zenoff (1968) reveale the importance of a parent company's dividend payout ratio.

a. Some firm's require the same payout ratio as the parent's rate for each of their subsidiaries.

b. Others set a target payout ratio as a percentage of overall foreign-source earnings, without attempting to receive the same percentage from each subsidiary.

c. The reason for focusing on the parent's payout ratio is that the subsidiaries should contribute their share of the dividend paid to the shareholders.

d. Whenever a parent establishes a uniform payout ratio for each unit, rather than an overall target, it is effectively trying to persuade foreign governments, particularly those of LDCs, that these payments are necessary rather than arbitrary.

2. When a MNC decides on the dividend payment by its subsidiaries, the following factors are taken into consideration.

a. Financial statement effects. Because the foreign earnings of unconsolidated affiliates were recognized on the parent company's income statement only when they were repatriated as dividends, fees, royalties, or some other form of profit remittance, many of these firms adjusted their subsidiaries' dividend payments in order to achieve their targeted earnings growth. However, most MNCs have stopped making these adjustments because they now consolidate their foreign units, thereby recognizing income overseas as soon as it is earned.

b. Tax effects. A major consideration behind the dividend decision is the effective tax rate on payments from different affiliates. By varying payout ratios among the foreign subsidiaries, the MNC can reduce its total tax burden.

c. Financing requirements. Dividend payments also lead to liquidity shifts. The value of moving these funds is dependent on the differences in opportunity costs of money among the various units of the MNC.

d. Exchange risk. Companies which anticipate a devaluation seem to be willing to accelerate their dividend payments. Other firms hedge their declared dividends through a forward sale that is timed to coincide with the payment of the dividend.

e. Exchange <u>controls</u>. A number of firms attempt to reduce the danger of currency controls by maintaining a record consistent dividends. Some companies even set a unifor dividend payout ratio throughout the corporate system t set a global pattern.

f. <u>Joint venture</u>. The presence of local partners may constrain a MNC in its ability to adjust its dividend policy according to global factors.

K. While corporate funds overseas, whether <u>debt</u> or <u>equity</u>, require the same rate of return as the firm's cost of capital, the appropriate ratio of parent company loans to parent equity can an important factor in determining the firm's ability to withdr funds from abroad and of the cost of doing so.

1. Multinational corporations generally prefer loans to equity for several reasons.

a. Parent company loans to foreign subsidiaries are often regarded by the host nation and local creditors as equivalent to equity investments.

b. It is much easier for the firm to repatriate funds in th form of interest and principal than as dividends or reductions in equity because the latter flow of funds ar more closely controlled by the host governments.

c. Using intracorporate loans over equity investments provides the possibility of reducing taxes.

2. However, firms do not have complete freedom in choosing thei appropriate debt-to-equity ratios abroad for the following reasons.

a. Choosing a debt-to-equity ratio is frequently open for negotiation with the host governments.

b. Dividends are often restricted to a fixed percentage of the firm's equity base.

c. Some host governments might restrict a subsidiary's loca borrowing to a certain percentage of the parents equity.

d. Local banks may also set limits on an affiliate's debt-t equity ratio.

e. In addition, loan repayments may be treated as constructive dividends by the IRS and taxed accordingly the subsidiary is felt to be too thinly capitalized.

3. Firms usually use guidelines, such as 50% of total assets or fixed assets, in determining the amount of equity to provide their subsidiaries.

L. Firms often have the option of selecting the currencies in which to invoice interaffiliate transactions. The choice of the invoicing currency will have an impact on the following two variables.

1. Tax effects. The particular currency or currencies in which intracorporate transactions are invoiced can affect the after-tax profits if currency fluctuations are anticipated.

2. Exchange controls. The choice of the invoicing currency can also enable a MNC to remove some blocked funds from a country that has currency controls.

III. Designing a Global Remittance Policy

A. It is the task of the international financial executive to coordinate the use of the various financial linkages so as to maximize the value of the firms as a whole. This task involves the following four interrelated decisions:

1. How much money (if any) to remit.

2. When to do so.

3. Where to transmit those funds.

4. Which transfer method(s) to use.

B. To take advantage of its internal financial system, the MNC must conduct a systematic and comprehensive analysis of the available remittance options and their associated costs and benefits.

C. A number of factors which strongly affect a firm's ability to benefit from its internal financial transfer system include:

1. The number of financial links.

2. The volume of interaffiliate transactions.

3. The foreign affiliate ownership pattern.

4. The degree of product and service standardization.

5. Government regulations.

D. To take full advantage of its global financial system, the MNC needs detailed information on the following factors:

1. Affiliate financing requirements.

2. Sources and costs of external credit.

3. Local investment yields.

4. Expected currency changes.

5. Available financial channels.

6. Volume of interaffiliate transactions.

7. Relevant tax factors.

8. Government restrictions and regulations on fund flows.

E. Although the goal of a global financial system is to increase after-tax global profits, the actual result may be to destroy incentive systems based on profit centers and cause confusion a computational chaos. Subsidiaries may not cooperate when asked to undertake actions that will benefit the corporation as a whole but will adversely affect their own performance valuation

IV. Appendix 15A: Managing Blocked Currency Funds

A. A host government with balance-of-payments difficulties is likel; to impose currency controls that block the transfer of funds to nonresidents.

B. The management of blocked funds can be considered a three-stage process.

1. Pre-investment planning which includes analyzing the effects of currency controls on investment returns and structuring the operation so as to maximize future remittance flexibility.

2. Developing a coordinated approach to repatriating blocked funds from an ongoing operation. Firms can transfer funds being generated:

a. Directly as cash.

b. Indirectly through special financial arrangements.

c. In the form of goods and services purchased locally for use elsewhere.

3. <u>Maintaining</u> <u>the</u> <u>value</u> <u>of</u> <u>those</u> <u>funds</u> that, despite all efforts, cannot be repatriated. The company then has the choice of placing the funds in:

   a. Long-term, il-liquid investments, such as new plant and equipment.

   b. Fairly liquid, short-term assets, such as local-currency-denominated securities.

KEY TERMS

Tax Arbitrage	Fees
Financial Market Arbitrage	Royalties
Regulatory System Arbitrage	Leading and Lagging
Unbundling	Intracorporate Loans
Tax Credits	Direct Loans
Tax Treaties	Back-to-Back Loans
U.S. Revenue Act of 1962	Fronting Loans
Transfer Pricing	Link Financing
Arm's Length Price	Trust Escrow Agreement
Comparable Uncontrolled Price Method	Parallel Loans
Resale Price Method	Dividends
Cost-Plus Method	Blocked Currency Funds
Reinvoicing Center	

CONCEPTUAL QUESTIONS

QUESTION 1: What are some of the objectives of using internal financial transfer mechanisms?

ANSWER: Corporate objectives associated with fund-shifting techniques include financing foreign operations, reducing interest costs, reducing tax costs, removing blocked funds, and reducing exchange risk.

SELECTED QUESTIONS FROM THE TEXT

QUESTION 1: An increase in the payment of dividends from a foreign affiliate: (a) can lead to a decrease in total U.S. taxes, (b) will invariably lead to an increase in U.S. taxes.

ANSWER: If the dividends are being paid by an affiliate whose income tax rate exceeds 34%, the parent will receive a foreign tax credit that can be used to offset U.S. tax owed on other foreign source income. If these credits are actually used, payment of the dividend will lead to reduction in U.S. taxes owed.

QUESTION 2: Where does the value of an MNC's multinational financial system reside?

ANSWER: The multinational financial system gives the MNC the ability to engage in tax arbitrage, financial market arbitrage, and regulatory syste arbitrage.

QUESTION 4: Leading and lagging is primarily of value because of: (a) t regulations, (b) foreign exchange risk, (c) expropriation risk, (d) exchange and capital controls, (e) all of the above factors.

ANSWER: Leading and lagging has minimal impact on taxes and is of little value in currency risk management since companies can hedge their exchang risk in other ways. Expropriation risk can be managed, if need be, by shifting assets out of the country. The major value of leading and laggi is to enable firms to elude exchange and capital controls.

QUESTION 5: What are the principal advantages of investing in foreign affiliates in the form of debt instead of equity?

ANSWER: By investing in the form of debt rather than equity, companies m be able to reduce their taxes (because principal repayments are treated a a return of capital and are not taxed) and to avoid currency controls (because governments are more reluctant to block loan repayments, even to parent, than dividend payments).

SELECTED PROBLEMS FROM THE TEXT

PROBLEM 5: Suppose that, in the section on dividends, International Products has $500,000 in excess foreign tax credits available. How will this affect its dividend remittance decision?

SOLUTION: Even if International Products has $500,000 in excess foreign tax credits available, the company should still pay dividends out of its West German affiliate. Since the French tax rate exceeds 46%, IP does not pay U.S. tax on dividends from France. Hence, paying dividends out of France does not save any U.S. taxes. If the dividend is paid by the Irish affiliate, there is a savings of $460,000. This brings worldwide taxes down to $2,020,000. But this still exceeds worldwide taxes of $1,910,000 if the dividend is paid by the West German affiliate.

PROBLEM 8: Suppose GM France sells goods worth $2 million monthly to GM Denmark on 60-day credit terms. A switch in credit terms to 90 days will involve a one-time shift of how much money between the two affiliates?

SOLUTION: Under the old 60-day terms, GM France is carrying two month's worth of sales as receivables or $4 million. By switching credit terms to 90 days, GM France will now carry receivables equal to three month's worth of sales or $6 million. The net result is a transfer of $2 million from G France to GM Denmark.

PROBLEM 9:   Suppose a firm earns $1 million before tax in Spain.   It pays
Spanish tax of $0.52 million and remits the remaining $0.48 million as a
dividend to its U.S. parent.   Under current U.S. tax law, how much U.S. tax
will the parent owe on this dividend?

SOLUTION: Under current U.S. tax law, the firm's U.S. tax owed on the
dividend payment is calculated as follows:

Dividend	$480,000	
Spanish tax paid		520,000
		————
Included in U.S. taxable income		
$1,000,000 U.S. tax @ 34%		340,000
Less U.S. indirect tax credit		520,000
		————
Net U.S. tax owed		(180,000)

As a result of paying Spanish tax at a rate that exceeds the U.S. tax rate
of 34%, the company receives a foreign tax credit for $180,000 that can be
used to offset U.S. taxes owed on other foreign source income.

PROBLEM 10:   Suppose Affiliate A sells 10,000 chips monthly to Affiliate B
at a unit price of $15.   Affiliate A's tax rate is 45%, and Affiliate B's
tax rate is 55%.   In addition, Affiliate B must pay an ad valorem tariff of
12% on its imports.   If the transfer price on chips can be set anywhere
between $11 and $18, how much can the total monthly cash flow of A and B be
increased by switching to the optimal transfer price?

SOLUTION: For each $1 increase in income shifted from B to A, A's taxes
rise by $.45.   At the same time, B must pay an extra $.12 in tariffs.   The
before-tax increase of $1.12 in B's cost gives it a tax writeoff worth

$$\$1.12 \times .55 = \$.616.$$

By shifting $1 in income from B to A, the effect is to lower B's tax
payments by $.616 and raise its tariffs by $.12, a net decrease in tax plus
tariff payments of $.496.   The net effect of switching $1 in income from B
to A is to lower tax plus tariff payments to the world by

$$\$.496 - .45 = \$.046.$$

Thus, the transfer price should be set as high as possible in order to
shift as much income to A from B as possible.   The new transfer price
should, therefore, be set at $18, a $3 increase over the old transfer
price. The resulting increase in monthly cash flow is

$$\$.046 \times 3 \times 10,000 = \$1,380.$$

CHAPTER 16

CORPORATE STRATEGY AND FOREIGN INVESTMENT ANALYSIS

Summary: This chapter examines the foreign direct investment decision and identifies those market imperfections that lead firms to become multinational. Only if these imperfections are well understood can a firm determine which foreign investments are likely to have positive net present values. In addition, this chapter analyzes corporate strategies for international expansion and foreign investment analysis.

I. Theory of the Multinational Corporation

    A. An explanation for the existence of multinational corporations can be found in the theory of industrial organization, which focuses o imperfect product and/or factor markets.

        1. This theory points to certain general circumstances under which each form of entry is the preferred alternative for exploiting foreign markets.

        2. According to this theory, MNCs have <u>intangible capital</u> in the form of trademarks, patents, general marketing skills, and other organizational skills.

            a. If this intangible capital takes the form of products without adaptation, then <u>exporting</u> may be the preferred alternative to entering a foreign market.

            b. If the intangible capital takes the form of specific product or process technologies, then foreign direct investment will take the form of <u>licensing</u>.

            c. Often the intangible capital takes the form of organizational skills, in which case the MNC would attempt to capitalize on this form of market imperfection by establishing <u>foreign affiliates</u>.

        3. Foreign direct investment, or <u>internalization</u>, is economically feasible only if the firm possesses a valuable asset and is better off directly controlling the use of the asset than selling or licensing it.

        4. To survive as MNCs, firms must create and preserve effective barriers to direct competition in product and factor markets worldwide.

B. An alternative explanation for firms expanding abroad can be found in the existence of financial market imperfections.

    1. International diversification is an even more important financial motif for foreign direct investment.

        a. Being able to operate in a number of countries whose economic cycles are not perfectly correlated, should reduce the variability of MNC earnings.

        b. Most of the economic and political risks specific to MNCs are unsystematic in nature and can be eliminated through diversification.

    2. Corporate international diversification will be advantageous to shareholders only if there are barriers to direct international portfolio diversification by individual investors, such as:

        a. Legal, informational, and economic impediments that serve to segment capital markets.

        b. Lack of liquidity.

        c. Currency controls.

        d. Specific tax regulations.

        e. Relatively less-developed capital markets abroad.

        f. Exchange risk.

        g. Lack of readily accessible and comparable information on potential foreign security acquisitions.

    3. There are several ways in which U.S. investors can diversify into foreign securities.

        a. A small number of foreign firms have their stocks listed on the NYSE or the ASE.

        b. Investors can also buy foreign stocks in their home markets.

        c. Investors can buy foreign equities traded in the U.S. in the form of

            (1) American Depository Receipts (ADRs) which one certificates issued by a U.S. bank as a convenience to investors in lieu of the underlying shares it holds in custody.

(2) <u>American</u> <u>shares</u> which are securities certificates issued in the U.S. by a transfer agent on behalf of t foreign issuer.

II. The Strategy of Multinational Enterprise

A. Some firms create barriers to entry by continually introducing n products and differentiating existing ones, both at home and abroad. The behavior of these firms can be explained by the <u>product</u> <u>life</u> <u>cycle</u> <u>theory</u> of international trade.

1. Production often occurs in the country for whose market the innovation was designed, regardless of cost, due to price insensitive demand and the need to react quickly to changing market conditions.

a. Early in the product's life cycle, export orders are received from countries with similar demand structures a income levels.

b. As the product matures and potential competitors enter t market both at home and abroad, the market leaders begin to produce in their foreign markets.

c. With product standardization comes price competition; co reduction becomes a dominant strategic concern. Production is shifted to low-cost, primarily developing countries for export back to the home country and other foreign countries.

2. The decision to invest abroad should not only depend on the desire to protect and prolong an innovational lead but also the relative labor and transportation costs, economies of scale, currency changes, legal factors, and tax factors.

B. Mature multinationals maintain their international viability by creating the same entry barriers internationally as those that allowed them to remain domestic oligopolists.

1. Strategies designed to differentiate products, reduce costs, and keep out actual and potential competitors include:

a. Taking advantage of massive advertising and highly developed marketing skills.

b. Exploiting economies of scale in production and transportation.

      c.   Taking advantage of economies in scope in production, advertising, and distribution.

      d.   Taking advantage of the learning curve.

  2. Strategies designed to reduce instability and foster cooperation in the industry include:

      a.   Follow-the-leader behavior in entering new countries or new product lines.

      b.   Joint ventures among members of the oligopoly.

      c.   Pricing convention.

      d.   Cross-investment.

C. Multinationals that have eroded the competitive advantage in their product lines or markets can choose to follow these strategies.

  1. Entering new markets where imperfections still exist. For example, less-developed countries which are more concerned with promoting import-substituting industries than with economic efficiency may provide market-oriented firms to exploit new marketing opportunities. Other solutions include product differentiation or cartelization of the industry.

  2. Seeking out lower cost production sites.

  3. Dropping old products and turning corporate skills to new products.

D. While many firms are capable of becoming and remaining multinationals, often that decision is not a matter of choice but one of survival.

  1. If <u>cost</u> is a key consideration then firms may follow a strategy to develop a global scanning capability to seek out lower-cost production sites or production technologies worldwide.

  2. To take advantage of <u>economies</u> <u>of</u> <u>scale</u>, firms are required to compete effectively in the global marketplace.

  3. Some firms enter foreign markets for the purpose of <u>gaining information</u> <u>and</u> <u>experience</u> that can be used successfully elsewhere.

  4. Supplier of goods and services to multinational corporations will often <u>follow</u> <u>their</u> <u>customers</u> abroad to better serve and guarantee them a continuing flow of products.

E. Several corporate policies with the purpose of reducing or avoiding risk may be encountered by multinationals at any stage of their development.

1. In a world characterized by possible strikes and political risks, firms tend to follow a policy of <u>multiple</u> <u>sourcing</u>. A number of benefits to the firm include:

   a. The potential leverage that can be exerted against unions and governments by threatening to shift production elsewhere.

   b. The additional safety achieved by having several plants capable of supplying the same product.

   c. The option of switching production from one location to another to take advantage of transient unit-cost differences arising from real exchange rate changes or new labor contracts.

2. An alternative to multiple production facilities is to locate one or more large export-oriented plants in <u>stable</u> <u>environments</u>, even though expected costs may not be minimized.

3. A number of companies locate facilities in countries only to maintain good relations with the host country.

4. For a number of firms, particularly those headquartered in Europe, the desire for foreign direct investment in the U.S. is based on two additional motivating forces.

   a. One is the fear of Soviet expansionism and the resulting loss of all European investments.

   b. The other is the attractiveness of operating in the U.S. with its free-market orientation and political stability.

III. Designing a Global Expansion Strategy

A. For many firms, international operations have become an important source of profits, and as these companies become more aggressive, it will become apparent that their domestic survival is increasingly dependent on their success overseas.

B. The design of a global corporate strategy involves three interrelated aspects.

1. A company must define a set of corporate <u>objectives</u> so that managers have a clear understanding about:

a. How these objectives fit together.

b. What tradeoffs should be considered among the various conflicting objectives.

c. What is expected of the managers themselves.

2. Next, management must devise policies that are congruent with the established objectives. The emphasis must be on systematically pursuing policies and investments consistent with worldwide survival and growth. This approach involves five interrelated elements.

a. It requires an awareness of those investments that are likely to provide the highest return in terms of profitability.

b. A global approach to investment planning, in turn, necessitates a systematic evaluation of individual entry strategies in foreign markets, a comparison of the alternatives, and the selection of the optimal mode of entry.

c. A key element is the continual audit of the effectiveness of current entry modes.

d. A systematic investment analysis requires the use of appropriate evaluation criteria.

e. In the final step, the firm must estimate the longevity of its particular form of competitive advantage.

3. In order to carry out the agreed-upon policies, the firm must have the corporate resources.

C. A key element behind any global strategy is management's commitment to becoming or remaining a multinational corporation, which involves:

1. Developing reasonable international business objectives and policies.

2. Communicating and selling them to the rest of the organization by adjusting the evaluation and control system.

3. Devising an intelligence system that will scan the world and understand it, along with the people who are experienced in international business and who know how to use the information generated by the system.

IV. Appendix 16A: Corporate Strategy and Joint Ventures

   A. International joint ventures have become an attractive
       alternative to building production facilities overseas. The
       great benefits of entering into a joint venture include the
       following.

       1. Access to markets otherwise not penetrable to foreign firms.

       2. Low manufacturing costs.

       3. Improved access to technology.

       4. Economies of scale in production and production development.

   B. Despite the potential benefits of joint ventures, some MNCs
       follow strategies that mitigate against such partnerships. These
       strategies are:

       1. Use of marketing techniques to differentiate products.

       2. Production rationalization to reduce manufacturing costs.

       3. Control of raw materials.

       4. New product development.

   C. The decision to enter into a joint venture must be systematically
       analyzed in terms of the likelihood of the joint venture's
       success.

       1. Firms that are forced into joint ventures can be successful in
           markets separated by trade barriers from other markets.

       2. An alternative to foreign direct investment is to sell
           managerial expertise in the form of a management contract.
           While this unbundling of services reduces the political and
           economic risks, firms believe they can take better advantage
           of market imperfections and earn higher returns through direct
           investment.

KEY TERMS

Internalization   Product Life Cycle Theory
Product and Factor Market Imperfections   Economies of Scale
Financial Market Imperfections   Knowledge Seekers
American Depository Receipts (ADRs)   Follow the Customer
American Shares   Multiple Sourcing

QUESTION 1: If survival is a motive, what are the key consideration of firms becoming and remaining multinational?

ANSWER: The following key considerations consist of

1. Cost. Firms may follow a strategy to develop a global scanning capability to seek out lower-cost production sites or production technologies worldwide.
2. Economies of scale. To compete effectively in the global marketplace, firm are required to take advantage of economies of scale in production, marketing, finance, organization, and management.
3. Knowledge seekers. Some firms enter foreign markets for the purpose of gaining information and experience that can be used successfully elsewhere.
4. Follow-the-customer. Supplier of goods and services to multinational corporations will often follow their customers abroad to better serve and guarantee them a continuing flow of products.

QUESTION 2: Explain the product life cycle theory of international trade.

ANSWER: The product life cycle theory can be used to explain why some firms create barriers to entry by continually introducing new products and differentiating existing ones, both at home and abroad. Production often occurs in the country for whose market the innovation was designed, regardless of cost, due to price insensitive demand and the need to react quickly to changing market conditions.

1. Early in the product's life cycle, export orders are received from countries with similar demand structures and income levels.
2. As the product matures and potential competitors enter the market both at home and abroad, the market leaders begin to produce in their foreign markets.
3. With product standardization comes price competition; cost reduction becomes a dominant strategic concern. Production is shifted to low-cost, primarily developing countries for export back to the home country and other foreign countries.

SELECTED QUESTIONS FROM THE TEXT

QUESTION 7: What factors help determine whether a firm will export its output, license foreign companies to manufacture its products, or set up its own production or service facilities abroad? Identify the competitive advantages that lead companies to prefer one mode of international expansion over another.

ANSWER: Here are some factors involved in deciding how to enter a market

1. **Production economies of scale.** If these are important, then exporting might be the appropriate answer.
2. **Trade barriers.** Companies that might otherwise be inclined to export to a market may be forced by regulations to produce abroad, either in a wholly-owned operation, a joint venture, or through a licensing arrangement with a local manufacturer.
3. **Transportation costs.** These have the same effect as trade barriers. The more expensive it is to ship to a market, the more likely it is that local production will take place.
4. **Size of the foreign market.** The larger the local market, the more likely local production is to take place, particularly if there are significant production economies of scale. Conversely, with smaller markets, exporting is more likely to take place.
5. **Production costs.** The real exchange rate, wage rates, and other cost factors will also play a part in determining whether exporting or local production takes place.
6. **Intangible capital.** If the MNC's intangible capital is embodied in the form of products, then exporting will generally be preferred. If this intangible capital takes the form of specific product or process technologies that can be written down and transmitted objectively, then foreign expansion will usually take the licensing route. But if this intangible capital takes the form of organizational skills that are inseparable from the firm itself, then the firm is likely to expand overseas via direct investment.
7. **Necessity of a foreign market presence.** By investing in fixed assets abroad, companies can demonstrate to local customers their commitment to the market. This can enhance sales prospects.

QUESTION 9: What are the important advantages of going multinational? Consider the nature of global competition.

ANSWER: Some important advantages of going multinational are:

1. Taking fuller advantage of economies of scale in production and research and development.
2. Taking fuller advantage of economies of scope in marketing and R&D.
3. Taking advantage of lower cost sources of production.
4. Posing a credible retaliatory threat against foreign competitors
5. Gaining information and experience that is expected to prove useful elsewhere.
6. Keeping domestic customers who become multinational by following them abroad and guaranteeing them a continuing product flow.
7. Diversifying revenues and costs so as to reduce operating risk.

QUESTION 12: Given the added political and economic risks that appear to exist overseas, are multinational firms more or less risky than purely domestic firms in the same industry? Consider whether a firm that decides not to operate abroad is insulated from the effects of economic events that occur outside the home country.

ANSWER: Individual foreign projects may face more political and economic risks than comparable domestic projects. Yet, multinationals are likely to be less risky than purely domestic firms. The reason is that much of the risk faced overseas is diversifiable risk. Moreover, by operating and producing overseas, the multinational firm has diversified its cost and revenue structure relative to what it would be if it were a purely domestic firm producing and selling in the home market. It is important to note that domestic firms are not insulated from economic changes abroad. For example, domestic firms face exchange risk since their competitive position depends on the cost structure of their foreign competitors as well as their domestic competitors. Similarly, changes in the price of oil and other materials abroad immediately lead to changes in domestic prices.

SELECTED PROBLEMS FROM THE TEXT

PROBLEM 3: Airbus Industrie, the European consortium of aircraft manufacturers, buy jet engines from U.S. companies. According to a recent story in The Wall Street Journal, "as a result of the weaker dollar, the cost of a major component (jet engines) is declining for Boeing's biggest competitor." The implication is that the lower price of engines for Airbus gives it a competitive advantage over Boeing. Assess the validity of this statement. Will Airbus now be more competitive relative to Boeing?

SOLUTION: This statement is misleading because engine prices are being measured in dollar terms for Boeing and European currency terms for Airbus. Since the cost of engines, when measured in the same currency, is the same for both Boeing and Airbus currency changes have no effect here. But other costs measured in the same currency will now be lower for Boeing than for Airbus. Therefore, a falling dollar will place Airbus at a competitive disadvantage relative to Boeing.

PROBLEM 4: Nordson Co. of Amherst, Ohio, a maker of painting and glue equipment, exports nearly half its output. Customers value its reliability as a supplier. Because of an especially sharp run-up in the value of the dollar against the French franc, Nordson is reconsidering its decision to continue supplying the French market. What factors are relevant in reaching a decision?

SOLUTION: The problem tells us that customers value Nordson's reliability as a supplier. If Nordson cuts and runs in France, other customers will take it as a signal as to how it is likely to respond elsewhere when the going gets tough. This will hurt Nordson's sales to customers in other countries.

Nordson must also consider the chance that at some point in the futu
the dollar will decline, making it more profitable to service the French
market. But if it exits the market now, reentry at a later date will be
especially difficult. In addition to dealing with customer ill will,
Nordson will have to rebuild its distribution and service network. Thus,
exiting the market today will destroy a valuable option to sell in the
French market when the dollar turns down.

PROBLEM 5: Tandem Computer, a U.S. maker of fault-tolerant computers, is
thinking of shifting virtually all the labor-intensive portion of its
production to Mexico. What risks is Tandem likely to face if it goes ahe
with this move?

SOLUTION: If Tandem Computer shifts virtually all the labor-intensive
portion of its production to Mexico it will face several risks.

1. **Quality control.** Customers are buying its machines because they
    can't tolerate downtime. Tandem faces the risk that it will be
    unable to ensure the same quality workmanship in Mexico as in th
    United States.
2. **On time delivery.** When a customer needs a machine, the customer
    needs it quickly. If there are border problems with customs or
    delays on Mexican highways or railroads, Tandem may be unable to
    deliver machines on time to customers. This makes it a less
    reliable supplier, which could hurt its sales.
3. **Production disruptions.** The Mexican government may at a later
    date restrict Tandems's ability to import necessary machinery or
    parts, thereby forcing it to use Mexican products. This would
    disrupt production and possibly lower quality standards as well.
    Labor strikes or lost or damaged shipments of materials would
    also disrupt production.
4. **Exchange risk.** If the Mexican government insists on controlling
    the exchange rate, and not allowing the peso to devalue in line
    with high Mexican inflation, the dollar costs of production in
    Mexico will rise.
5. **Political risk.** The Mexican government may tamper with tax rates
    sourcing of materials, shipments, customs duties, and the like.
    Similarly, the U.S. government may impose higher duties on
    labor-intensive imports from Mexico at the instigation of
    American labor unions seeking to stifle low-wage competition from
    Mexicans.

CAPITAL BUDGETING FOR THE MULTINATIONAL CORPORATION

Summary: Capital budgeting for the multinational corporation is complicated by a variety of problems that are rarely, if ever, encountered by domestic firms. This chapter examines a number of such problems, including differences between parent and project cash flows, foreign tax regulations, expropriation, blocked funds, exchange rate changes and inflation, project-specific financing, and differences between the basic business risk of foreign and domestic projects. The major principle behind the methods to cope with these complications is to maximize the use of available information while reducing arbitrary cash flow and cost of capital adjustments.

I. Basics of Capital Budgeting

    A. Given a set of investment opportunities compiled by the firm, it must select that investment which maximizes the company's value to the shareholders.

    B. This evaluation and selection process requires a set of rules and criteria that enables managers to determine whether to accept or reject a given investment opportunity.

    C. It is generally agreed that the net present value (NPV) is the most appropriate evaluation technique since its application is consistent with the goal of maximizing shareholder wealth.

        1. The net present value is defined as the present value of future cash flows (x_t), discounted at an appropriate discount rate (k) minus the initial investment (I_0).

           a. If projects are independent, then all these projects with a positive NPV will be accepted while those with a negative NPV will be rejected.

           b. If two projects are mutually exclusive, then the project with the highest NPV, given that it is positive, will be accepted.

        2. Mathematically, the NPV is shown as

$$NPV = -I_0 + \sum_{t=1}^{n} \frac{x_t}{(1 + k)^t} .$$

3. The NPV rule has a number of desirable properties.

   a. The NPV criterion evaluates investments in the same way as investors do. Thus, it is consistent with the goal of shareholder wealth maximization.

   b. The NPV method focuses on cash rather than accounting profits.

   c. It emphasizes the opportunity cost of the money invested.

   d. It recognizes that cash inflows should be greater than cash outflows plus the interest that could have been earned by investing the money elsewhere.

   e. The NPV technique obeys the value additivity principle, which states that the NPV of a set of independent projects is just the sum of the NPVs of the individual projects. Thus, each project can be valuated on its own.

D. The most important and also the most difficult part of the investment analysis is to estimate the cash flows associated with the project; that is, the cost of funding the project, the cash inflows generated during the life of the project, and the terminal cash flows of the project.

   1. An important principle underlying the cash flow estimation is that cash flows should be measured on an incremental basis. In other words, only the additional dollar invested today is what really matters.

   2. The distinction between total and incremental cash flows is crucial, because incremental cash flows can differ from total cash flows for a variety of reasons:

      a. Cannibalization is a phenomenon in which a new product or production facility takes away sales from existing product or production. The estimated profits on the new investment must, therefore, be reduced by the amount of the lost sales.

      b. Sales creation occurs when an investment created, or was expected to create, additional sales of existing products. In computing the project's cash flows, any additional sales and associated incremental cash flows should be attributed to the project.

      c. The project costs must include the true economic or opportunity cost of any resource required for the project, regardless of whether the firm already owns the resource or has to acquire it.

d. Any sunk costs or past expenditures on a project should not influence the decision whether to continue or terminate the project.

e. Transfer prices at which goods and services are traded internally can significantly distort the profitability of a proposed investment. Where possible, prices used to evaluate project inputs or outputs should be market prices. If no market exists for the product, the firm must evaluate the project based on the cost savings or additional profits to the firm.

f. A project should be charged only for the additional expenditures, which appear in the form of fees and royalties, attributable to the project.

3. In general, incremental cash flows associated with a project can be found only by subtracting worldwide corporate cash flows with the investment from corporate cash flows without the investment.

E. The discount rate in the NPV formula is the firm's weighted average cost of capital where the weights are based on the proportion of the firm's capital structure accounted for by each source of capital.

1. This discount rate is appropriate only if the financial characteristics and the business risk are similar for all investments undertaken by the firm.

2. Projects with different risks, however, are likely to possess differing debt capacities with each project, therefore requiring a separate financial structure.

3. The cost of borrowing may also differ because of project-specific loans at concessionary rates or higher-cost foreign funds due to home country exchange controls.

4. The weighted average cost of capital can be modified to reflect deviations from the firm's typical investment.

5. For some companies, there is no norm. Project risk and financial structure vary by country, raw material, production stage, and position in the life cycle of the project.

F. An alternative approach is to discount future cash flows at a rate that reflects only the business risks of the project and abstracts from the financing effects. This rate is the all-equity rate which would apply to projects financed by equity.

1. The all-equity rate, k^*, can be used by viewing the value of project as being equal to the sum of:

   a. The present value of the project's cash flows after taxes but before financing costs, discounted at k^*;

   b. The present value of tax savings on debt financing (T_t);

   c. The present value of any savings or penalties on the interest costs associated with project-specific financing (S_t).

2. Using this approach, the NPV is:

$$APV = -I_0 + \sum_{t=1}^{n} \frac{X_t}{(1 + k^*)^t} + \sum_{t=1}^{n} \frac{T_t}{(1 + i_d)^t} + \sum_{t=1}^{n} \frac{S_t}{(1 + i_d)^t}$$

where i_d is the before-tax cost of dollar debt.

3. The last two terms in the equation are discounted at i_d to reflect the relatively certain value of the cash flows due to tax shields and interest savings (penalties).

4. The all-equity cost of capital equals the required rate of return on a specific project.

II. Issues in Foreign Investment Analysis

A. In most situations a substantial difference exists between project and parent cash flows due to such factors as tax regulations and exchange controls. Given this appreciable difference on what basis should a project be evaluated?

   1. Cash flows to the parent can take the form of:

      a. Project expenses (management fees and royalties).

      b. Additional sales created by the project.

      c. Transfer price adjustments shifting profits to other subsidiaries.

   2. Cash flows of a project will consist of only those project cash flows accruing locally. These cash flows, in turn, are evaluated without considering its consequences on the economic situation of the rest of the corporation.

B. The _relevant_ cash flows to use in project evaluation will consist
    of onlof the back value of expropriated asse, repatriated not of
    any transfer costs because only accessible funds to the parent can
    be used to pay dividends and principal and interest payments as
    well as for reinvestment.

C. A three-stage financial analysis of foreign investments is
    suggested.

    1. Stage I: Project cash flows are computed and analyzed from
        the viewpoint of the subsidiary or affiliate as if it were a
        separate entity.

    2. Stage II: The project is evaluated on the basis of specific
        forecasts of cash flows concerning the magnitude, timing, and
        form of transfers to the parent. It also necessitates
        information about taxes and other expenses which will be
        incurred in the transfer process.

    3. Stage III: The analysis from the viewpoint of the parent
        company is widened to include indirect benefits and costs that
        are attributable to the foreign project (e.g., increases or
        decreases in export sales by other affiliates).

D. Project cash flows should be estimated on an incremental basis
    which entails adjusting cash flows for:

    1. The effects of transfer pricing and fees and royalties, and

    2. The global costs and benefits that are not reflected in the
        project's financial statements.

E. Project cash flows should be estimated on an after-tax basis,
    which involves determining when and what taxes must be paid on
    foreign-source income.

    1. Actual taxes paid are a function of:

        a. The time and remittance.

        b. The form of remittance.

        c. The foreign income tax rate.

        d. The existence of withholding taxes.

        e. The treaties between home and host countries.

        f. The existence and usability of foreign tax credits.

2. A simple approach in calculating the tax liabilities of the foreign investment assumes that:

    a. The maximum amount of funds available for remittance each year is actually remitted.

    b. The tax rate applied to these cash flows is the higher of the home or host country rate.

F. The foreign investment decision is impacted by various political and economic risks, which must be incorporated in the capital budgeting analysis either by adjusting the discount rate or payback period or by adjusting the cash flows in each year.

    1. Multinational corporations have traditionally translated the additional risks of overseas investments by adjusting the hurdle rate upward or adjusting the payback period downward for riskier projects.

        a. Both approaches are attractive because it is:

            (1) Simple--there is no need for elaborate or time-consuming cash flow forecasting based on various assumptions.

            (2) Rigorous--those marginal projects are rejected which would result in substantial losses.

        b. However, neither of the approaches lends itself to a careful evaluation of the actual impact of a particular risk on investment returns.

            (1) Both methods ignore the magnitude and timing of risks and their implications for the projected cash flows.

            (2) The risk premium is arbitrarily chosen.

            (3) The meaning of the net present value is distorted by penalizing future cash flows relatively more heavily than current ones.

    2. Instead, adjusting cash flows makes it possible to fully incorporate all available information about the impact of a specific risk on the future returns from a project.

        a. Uncertainty absorption is a cash flow adjustment technique by which each year's cash flows are reduced by an amount equivalent to a risk or an insurance premium, whether or not such protection is purchased.

(1) Political risks, such as expropriation or currency inconvertibility, can be insured through the Overseas Private Investment Corporation.

(2) Economic risks, such as currency fluctuations, can be hedged in the forward market.

(3) The major difficulties of this approach are that:

- Political risk insurance covers only a fixed portion of the back value of expropriated assets.

- For some political risks, insurance is not available (e.g., restrictions imposed on imports of raw material).

- Forward covers are typically available only for the first two years of the life of a project and only for a limited amount of currencies.

- It works well if local currency cash flows are fixed.

b. An alternative approach is to adjust only the <u>expected values</u> of future cash flows to reflect the specific impact of a given risk.

(1) This procedure assumes that risks are unsystematic.

(2) As long as the systematic risk of a proposed investment remains unchanged, adjusting cash flows rather than the discount rate is a superior procedure.

c. Under the <u>certainty equivalent</u> method risk-adjusted cash flows are discounted at the riskfree rate.

(1) This approach requires generating certainty equivalent cash flows for which no satisfactory procedure has yet been developed.

(2) It also involves losing some information on the valuation of future cash flows that is provided by shareholders in the form of their required rates of return on a typical firm investment.

G. In order to evaluate foreign cash flows, it is necessary to abstract from offsetting inflation and exchange rate changes. Two methods, which yield the same result, can be used.

1. All foreign currency cash flows in nominal terms are converted into nominal home currency terms and then discounted at the nominal domestic required rate of return.

2. Alternatively, nominal foreign currency cash flows can be converted into real home currency terms and then discounted at the real domestic required rate of return.

III. Political Risk Analysis

A. The general approach to incorporating political risk in the capital budgeting analysis involves adjusting the cash flows of the project to reflect the impact of a particular political event on the present value of the project to the parent.

B. Cash flow adjustments can also be made for the cases of expropriation and exchange controls.

1. If the probability of expropriation is P_h in year h and zero in all other years, and if G_h is the expected value of the net compensation provided, then the expected net present value of a project is equal to

$$- I_0 + \sum_{i=1}^{h-1} \frac{x_i}{(1 + k^*)^i} + (1 - P_h) \sum_{i=h}^{n} \frac{x_i}{(1 + k^*)^i} + P_h \frac{G_h}{(1 + k^*)^h}$$

where k^* is the all-equity rate.

2. The same approach can be used to incorporate the likelihood of the imposition of exchange controls in any future period, i, with probability b_i, along with a probability distribution describing the lifting of these controls. If blocked funds cannot be repatriated, then a compensation value would have to be determined and included in the analysis.

IV. Growth Options and Project Evaluation

A. Any investment that requires an additional infusion of funds for its completion and often an uncertain payoff can be viewed as a call option.

1. Any opportunities a firm may have to invest capital so that it can increase the profitability of its existing product lines and benefit from expanding into new products and markets may be thought of as growth options.

2. A firm's ability to capitalize on its managerial talent, experience in a particular product line, its brand name, technology, or other resources may provide valuable but uncertain future opportunities.

B. Investments that embody discretionary follow-up projects must be valued with an expanded net present value rule that takes into account the accompanying options.

   1. The value of an option to undertake a follow-up project is equal to the expected project NPV, using the conventional discounted cash flow analysis, plus the value of the discretion associated with undertaking the project.

   2. The value of discretion to invest or not to invest in a project depends on the following variables.

      a. The length of time a project can be defined.

      b. The risk of the project.

      c. The level of interest rates.

      d. The proprietary nature of the option.

KEY TERMS

Net Present Value (NPV)
Value Additivity Principle
Incremental Cash Flows
Cannibalization
Sales Creation
Opportunity Cost
Sunk Cost
Transfer Pricing
Fees and Royalties
Weighted Average Cost of Capital

All-Equity Rate (k*)
Adjusted Present Value (APV)
Risk-Adjusted Discount Rate
Uncertainty Absorption
Adjusted Expected Value
Certainty Equivalents
Expropriation
Blocked Funds
Growth Options

CONCEPTUAL QUESTIONS

QUESTION 1: Explain the value additivity principle.

ANSWER: The value additivity principle states that the NPV of a set of independent projects is just the sum of the NPVs of the individual projects. Thus, each project can be evaluated on its own. This can also be shown as follows:

$$NPV\ (AB) = NPV\ (A) + NPV\ (B).$$

QUESTION 2:   How can incremental cash flows differ from total cash flows?

ANSWER: Incremental cash flows differ from total cash flows for the following reasons:

1. **Cannibalization** occurs when a new product or production facility takes away sales from existing products or production.
2. **Sales creation** occurs when an investment created, or was expected to create, additional sales of existing product.
3. **Opportunity cost** which is the true economic cost of any resource required for the project, regardless of whether the firm already owns the resource or has to acquire it.
4. **Sunk cost** or past expenditures on a project should not influence the decision whether to continue or terminate the project under consideration.
5. **Transfer prices** are those prices at which goods and services are traded internally.
6. **Fees and royalties** which are expenditures attributable to the project.

QUESTION 3:   What approaches are used by MNCs to incorporate the addition economic and political risks in the capital budgeting analysis?

ANSWER: Traditionally, MNCs have translated the additional risks of overseas investments by adjusting the hurdle rate upward or downward or adjusting the payback period downward for riskier projects. While these approaches are fairly simple and rigorous, they do not evaluate the actua impact of a particular risk on investment returns.

On the other hand, adjusting cash flows makes it possible to fully incorporate all available information about the impact of a specific risk on the future returns from a project. The three cash flow adjustment techniques are the uncertainty absorptions, expected values, and uncertainty equivalents.

SELECTED QUESTIONS FROM THE TEXT

QUESTION 1:   Relevant cash flows from the parent's standpoint when valuing a foreign project equal: (a) project cash flows received by the subsidiary, (b) project cash flows received by the parent, (c) project cas flows that can be repatriated to the parent, (d) all of the above, (e) nor of the above.

ANSWER: The correct answer is incremental cash flows accruing to the parent company. These incremental cash flows are not necessarily project cash flows because of cannibalization, sales creation, and other factors. Hence, the answer to this question is e), none of the above.

QUESTION 4:   If PPP and the international Fisher effect hold, then a
capital budgeting analysis can be conducted by: (a) discounting real
foreign currency cash flows at the real domestic rate, (b) discounting
nominal dollar cash flows at the real domestic rate, (c) discounting
nominal foreign cash flows at the real foreign rate, (d) discounting real
dollar cash flows at the nominal dollar rate, (e) none of the above.

ANSWER: The correct answer is a).   The other answers involve mixing and
matching real and nominal magnitudes, which leads to incorrect valuations.

SELECTED PROBLEMS FROM THE TEXT

PROBLEM 1:   Suppose a firm projects a $5 million perpetuity from an
investment of $20 million in Spain.   If the required return on this
investment is 20%, how large does the probability of expropriation in year
4 have to be before the investment has a negative NPV?   Assume that all
cash inflows occur at the end of each year and that the expropriation, if
it occurs, will occur prior to the year-4 cash inflow or not at all.
There is no compensation in the event of expropriation.

SOLUTION: This problem can be solved by breaking the cash flow stream into
two components--one component if expropriation takes place and the other if
no expropriation takes.   The expected value of these streams is found by
multiplying the first component by the probability that expropriation will
take place and the other component by the probability that expropriation
will not take place.   Note that the cash flow streams are identical prior
to year 4.   All numbers are in millions of dollars.

Year	0	1	2	3	4	5+
Cash flow with expropriation	$20	$5	$5	$5	0	0
Cash flow if no expropriation	20	5	5	5	5	5

If the probability of expropriation in year 4 is p, then the expected cash
flows associated with this investment are:

Year 0	1	2	3	4	5+
- $20	$5	$5	$5	$5(1 - p)	$5(1 -p)

The net present value of these cash flows, discounted at a 20% required
return, is

$$NPV = -20 + 5/1.2 + 5/(1.2)^2 + 5/(1.2)^3 + 5(1 - p)/(1.2)^4$$
$$+ \ldots + 5(1 - p)/(1.2)^t + \ldots$$
$$= -20 + 5/.2 - (5p/.2)/(1.2)^3$$
$$= -20 + 25 - 14.68p$$

Setting this quantity equal to 0 yields a solution of p = 34.1%. This means that the probability of expropriation has to be 34.1% before the investment no longer has a positive NPV.

PROBLEM 2: Suppose a firm has just made an investment in France that wi generate $2 million annually in depreciation, converted at today's spot rate. Projected annual rates of inflation in France and in the United States are 7% and 4%, respectively. If the real exchange rate is expect to remain constant and the French tax rate is 50%, what is the expected real value (in terms of today's dollars) of the depreciation charge in y 5, assuming that the tax write-off is taken at the end of the year?

SOLUTION: If the real exchange rate is expected to remain constant, the the real dollar value of the French franc is expected to decline at the same rate as the real franc value, namely the 7% French inflation rate. Hence, the real dollar value of the depreciation tax writeoff will decli at the rate of 7% per annum. If the French tax rate is 50%, then a depreciation charge of $2 million is worth $1 million in today's dollars If the real dollar value of this writeoff is declining at the rate of 7% annually, then its real value in year 5, given that the writeoff is take at the end of the year, is

$$\$1,000,000/(1.07)^5 = \$712,986.$$

CHAPTER 18

THE COST OF CAPITAL FOR FOREIGN INVESTMENTS

Summary: In evaluating the profitability of foreign projects, the multinational corporation must decide on the appropriate cost of capital. To the extent that the multinational firm has access to a wide variety of financial capital markets, the required rate of return on foreign projects may be higher, lower or the same as that for domestic projects. The purpose of this chapter, therefore, is to examine the process for determining the cost of capital for a specific foreign project rather than for the firm as a whole.

I.   The Cost of Equity Capital

   A.   The cost of equity capital for a firm is defined as the minimum rate of return that investors expect to receive from holding the firm's stock.

   B.   The cost of equity capital is also the rate used to capitalize total corporate cash flows. As such, it is a weighted average of the required rates of return on the firm's individual activities.

   C.   To use the cost of equity capital as a measure of the required return on equity investments in future projects, these projects must be of similar risk to the average of those being already undertaken by the firm.

   D.   The project-specific required return on equity can be determined in two ways.

      1.   The capital asset pricing model (CAPM)

         a.   According to this model, an equilibrium relationship exists between the asset's required return and its associated risk.

$$E(R_i) \ = \ R_f \ + \ \beta_i \ [E(R_m) - R_f]$$

         where: $E(R_i)$ =   equilibrium expected return for asset i.
                    β_i =   cov $(R_i, R_m)/\sigma^2(R_m)$, where cov (R_i, R_m) refers to the covariance between returns on security i and the market portfolio and $\sigma^2(R_m)$ is the variance of returns on the market portfolio.

$$E(R_m) = \text{expected return on the market portfolio}$$

$E(R_m)$ = expected return on the market portfolio consisting of all risky assets.

R_f = rate of return on a riskfree asset, usually measured as the yield on a 30-da U.S. government Treasury bill.

b. The relevance of CAPM is based on the notion that intelligent risk-averse investors will seek to diversify their risks, and as a consequence, the only risk that will be rewarded with a risk premium is systematic risk, as measured by beta.

c. There are three principal problems with using the CAPM.

(1) The major empirical problem lies in identifying the relevant market portfolio.

(2) Another potential empirical difficulty lies in estimating project betas because of the frequent lack of historical returns on comparable projects.

(3) And a major theoretical problem is related to whether the investors do differentiate between systematic and unsystematic risk.

2. Dividend valuation model

a. According to this model,

$$k_e = \frac{D_1}{P_0} + g$$

where: k_e = cost of equity capital.
D_1 = expected dividend in year 1.
P_0 = current stock price.
g = average expected annual dividend growth rate.

b. The dividend growth rate, g, can be estimated using either historical data or, if the past is not considered to be a reliable indicator of future performance, expectations of future earnings and resulting dividends.

E. The resulting estimates of the required return on equity capital, using either of these methods, apply only at the corporate level o to investments with returns and financial characteristics that are expected to be similar to those of the firm's typical investment.

F. If the characteristics of a project diverge from the corporate norm, then the estimates of the cost of equity for the firm as a whole are useless in calculating project-specific required returns on equity.

II. The Weighted Cost of Capital for Foreign Projects

A. The required rate of return on equity for a particular investment assumes that the financial structure and business risk of a project are similar to that for the firm as a whole.

B. This cost of equity capital, k_e, is then combined with the effective cost of debt, i_d ($- t$), to yield a weighted average cost of capital for the parent and the project, k_o, calculated as

$$k_o = (1 - L) k_e + L i_d (1 - t)$$

where L is the parent's target debt ratio.

C. This cost of capital is then used as the discount rate in evaluating the profitability of foreign investments.

D. For many investments, however, project risk and project financial structure can vary from the parent norm. In these situations, it is necessary to adjust the various costs and weights of the different cost components to reflect the actual values.

   1. The calculation of a project's weighted average cost of capital requires first to compute the individual cost of each component.

      a. The required rate of return on parent company funds is the firm's marginal cost of capital, k_o. Thus, parent funds invested overseas should earn the parent's marginal cost of capital provided that the foreign investments undertaken do not change the overall riskiness of the MNC's operations.

      b. The cost of retained earnings overseas, k_s, is a function of dividend withholding taxes, tax deferral, and transfer cost. If T is equal to the incremental taxes owed on earnings repatriated by the parent, then

      $$k_s = k_e (1 - T) .$$

      c. The after-tax dollar cost of borrowing locally, r_f, is equal to the sum of the after-tax interest expenses plus the exchange gain or loss.

223

2. With no change in risk characteristics, a project's weighted cost of capital equals:

$$k_e = k_0 - a(k_e - k_s) - b[i_d(1 - t) - r_f]$$

where:
$$k_0 = \text{parent's marginal cost of capital}$$
$$i_d(1 - t) = \text{parent's after-tax cost of debt}$$
$$k_e = \text{parent's cost of equity capital}$$
$$k_s = \text{subsidiary's cost of retained earnings}$$
$$r_f = \text{expected after-tax dollar cost of foreign debt}$$
$$E_f = \text{amount of subsidiary's retained earnings}$$
$$D_f = \text{amount of foreign debt}$$
$$I = \text{total funds needed to finance a new investment for the subsidiary}$$
$$a = E_f / I$$
$$b = D_f / I$$

3. If an investment changes the parent's risk characteristics in such a way that its cost of equity capital is k_e' rather than k_e, the project's weighted cost of capital equals

$$k_e = k_0 + (1-L)(k_e' - k_e) - a(k_e' - k_s) - b[i_d(1 - t) - r_f] \; .$$

III. The All-Equity Cost of Capital for Foreign Projects.

A. Instead of adjusting the parent's weighted average cost of capital for a foreign investment, as alternative is to use the all-equity cost of capital, k_*, which abstracts from the project's financial structure and is based solely on the riskiness of the project's cash flows.

B. The all-equity cost of capital can be calculated using CAPM.

$$k^* = R_f + \beta^*[E(R_m) - R_f]$$

where β^* is the beta associated with the unleveraged cash flows.

C. The estimation of β^* is often very difficult, requiring the firm to use guess-work based on theory. However, if the project is of similar risk to the average project undertaken by the firm, it is possible to estimate β^* by reference to the firm's stock price beta, β_e.

1. β_e is that beta which appears in the estimate of the firm's cost of equity capital, k_e, using CAPM:

$$k_e = R_f + \beta_e[E(R_m) - R_f] \; .$$

2. β_e can be transformed into β^* by separating out the effects of debt financing or unlevering beta, which can be accomplished by using the following approximation:

$$\beta^* = \frac{\beta_e}{[1 + (1 - t)(D / E)]} \, .$$

IV. Discount Rates for Foreign Projects

A. To the extent that MNCs are uniquely able to supply low-cost international diversification, investors may be willing to pay a premium price for their shares.

   1. This possibility would translate into investor willingness to accept a lower rate of return on shares of a MNC than on shares of a single-country firm.

   2. Consequently, the risk premium applied to foreign projects may be lower than the risk premium for domestic ones.

   3. The net effect may be to enable a MNC to accept overseas projects that would otherwise be unattractive.

B. It is surprising to find that the less-developed countries, where political risks are greatest, provide maximum diversification benefits. The reason is that the economies of LDC are less likely to be closely linked to the U.S. economy or other home-country economy. On the other hand, the economic cycles of the developed countries are more closely correlated with each other.

C. An important issue related to the selection of a discount rate for foreign investments is choosing the relevant market portfolio for evaluating a project's beta coefficient.

   1. Selecting the appropriate market portfolio is important because a risk that is systematic in the context of the home-country market portfolio may well be diversifiable in the context of the world portfolio.

      a. If the domestic market portfolio is used to estimate beta, the required rate of return will be higher than if beta were estimated using the world market portfolio.

      b. The choice of a base portfolio can, therefore, affect the present value of a project and hence its acceptability.

   2. The appropriate market portfolio to use in estimating beta depends on whether capital markets are globally integrated or not.

a. If capital markets are fully integrated, then the correct choice is the world portfolio.

b. If capital markets are segmented, then the correct choice is the domestic portfolio.

3. World capital markets are said to be fully integrated as long as security prices offer all investors worldwide the same trade-off between systematic risk and real expected return.

4. A U.S. manager should estimate the betas of international projects against the U.S. market portfolio for two reasons:

a. It ensures comparability of foreign projects with domestic projects that are evaluated using betas calculated relative to a U.S. market index.

b. The relatively minor amount of international diversification attempted by U.S. investors suggest that the relevant portfolio is the U.S. market portfolio.

5. This reasoning implies that the required rate of return on a foreign project may well be lower, and is likely to be higher than the required rate of return on a domestic project. Thus applying the same discount rate to a project overseas as would be applied against a similar domestic project will probably yield a conservative estimate of the relative systematic riskiness of the project.

D. Ali Fatemi (1984) studied the effects of foreign operations on the cost of equity capital. He compared the performance of two stock portfolios: (1) a portfolio of MNCs, and (2) a portfolio of purely domestic firms. While this study is limited by the relatively short-time period chosen, the following conclusions are derived:

1. The rates of return on the two portfolios are statistically identical. That is, investors holding stocks in either portfolio will receive the same return.

2. The rates of return on the MNC portfolio are less volatile than those on the purely domestic portfolio.

3. The betas of the MNC portfolio are significantly lower and more stable than are those of the purely domestic portfolio.

4. These results indicate that international diversification not only reduces shareholder total risk but also the degree of systematic risk. It was also found that the higher the degree of international involvement, the lower the beta.

226

E. Research by Jacquillat and Solnik (1978) concluded that multinational corporations, although providing some diversification for investors, are poor substitutes for international portfolio diversification. Their results indicate that an internationally diversified portfolio leads to a much greater reduction in variance than does one consisting of firms with internationally diversified activities.

KEY TERMS

Cost of Equity Capital
Capital Asset Pricing Model (CAPM)
Dividend Valuation Model
Marginal Cost of Capital
Cost of Retained Earnings Overseas
Globally Integrated Capital Markets

All-Equity Discount Rate
All-Equity Beta
Unlevering
International Portfolio
   Diversification

CONCEPTUAL QUESTIONS

QUESTION 1: What should be the cost of capital for a foreign project?

ANSWER: One of the major messages of modern financial theory is that the required return on a project is a function of the riskiness of the project itself. The cost of capital for the project should only equal the parent's weighted average cost of capital if the project's risk characteristics are similar to those of the firm's average project. The required return on the project should equal the required return on a similar investment undertaken in the U.S. only if the risks are the same. The minimum return necessary to induce investors to buy or hold the firm's stock depends on the riskiness of the overall returns to equity. This return equals the project cost of capital only if the risks are the same.

QUESTION 2: How should the systematic risk of a project be measured?

ANSWER: The appropriate portfolio against which to measure beta depends on whether shareholders hold a domestically-diversified or globally-diversified portfolio.

QUESTION 3: What alternative approach is there to calculating a project's cost of capital?

ANSWER: Instead of adjusting the parent's weighted average cost of capital for a foreign investment, an alternative is to use the all-equity cost of capital, which abstracts from the project's financial structure and is based solely on the riskiness of the project's cash flows.

PROBLEMS

PROBLEM 1:   A U.S. multinational firm borrows British pounds for one year at 9%, and during the year expects the pound sterling to appreciate against the dollar by 2% annually. What is the approximate before-tax cost of interest in the U.S.?

SOLUTION: The equilibrium dollar interest rate before taxes is

$$r_{us} = 9.0\% \ (1 + 0.02) + 2\%$$
$$= 11.18\%.$$

SELECTED PROBLEMS FROM THE TEXT

PROBLEM 1:   A firm with a corporate-wide debt/equity ratio of 1:2, an after-tax cost of debt of 7%, and a cost of equity capital of 15% is interested in pursuing a foreign project. The debt capacity of the project is the same as for the company as a whole, but its systematic risk is such that the required return on equity is estimated to be about 12%. The after-tax cost of debt is expected to remain at 7%. (a) What is the project's weighted average cost of capital? How does it compare with the parent's WACC? (b) If the project's equity beta is 1.21, what is its unlevered beta?

SOLUTION:

a.   The weighted average cost of capital for the project is

$$k_I = (1 - w) \ x \ k_e' + w \ x \ i_d(1 - t)$$

where w is the ratio of debt to total assets, k_e' is the required risk-adjusted return on project equity, and $i_d(1 - t)$ is the after- tax cost of debt for the project. Substituting in the numbers provided yields

$$k_I = 1/3 \ x \ 12\% + 2/3 \ x \ 7\%$$
$$= 8.67\%.$$

b.   The following approximation is usually used to unlever beta:

$$\text{Unlevered beta} = \text{levered beta}/[1 + (1 - t)D/E]$$

where t is the firm's marginal tax rate and D/E is its debt/equity ratio. Without knowing the firm's marginal tax rate, we cannot unlever beta. Assuming that the marginal tax rate is about 40%, the unlevered beta becomes

$$\text{Unlevered beta} = 1.21/[1 + (1 - .4)1/2]$$
$$= .93.$$

PROBLEM 2: Suppose that a foreign project has a beta of .85, the risk-free return is 12%, and the required return on the market is estimated at 19%. What is the cost of capital for the project?

SOLUTION: The cost of capital for the project is

$$k^* = R_f + \beta^*[E(R_m) - R_f]$$

where R_f is the risk-free required return, β^* is the project beta, and $E(R_m)$ is the expected return on the market. Substituting in the numbers provided in the problem yields

$$k^* = .12 + .85(.19 - .12)$$
$$= 17.95\%.$$

CHAPTER 19

THE MEASUREMENT AND MANAGEMENT OF POLITICAL RISK

Summary: Political risk in the form of currency controls or expropriati
can have both positive and negative impacts on the value of the firm.
Thus, the need for a more formal assessment of political risk and its
implications for corporate decision making is apparent.   This chapter tr
to provide such a framework, focusing primarily on forecasting and manag
the extreme form of political risk, expropriation.

I.   Measuring Political Risk

   A.   Political risk can be viewed from a country-specific perspective
        (macro approach) and a firm-specific perspective (micro approach

   B.   To obtain an indication of the general level of political risk i
        country, a number of forecasting models have been developed whic
        generate country indexes used as a quantitative measure of
        political risk.   Most of these indexes rely on some measures of
        stability of local government.

        1.   The Political Systems Stability Index, developed by Dan
             Haendel, Gerald West, and Robert Meadow, evaluates the
             probability of some political event occurring that would
             change the profit outlook for a given investment.   This
             index, in turn, is composed of three equally weighted
             subindexes:

             a.   The Socioeconomic Characteristics Index, which measures
                  population heterogeneity and prospects for future econom
                  growth.

             b.   The Societal Conflicts Index, which estimates the potent
                  for violent change in a country.

             c.   The Governmental Processes Index, which assesses the
                  prospects for the peaceful transition of political power
                  within a society.

        2.   Various economic variables, such as inflation, balance-of-
             payments deficits of surpluses, and the level and growth rat
             of per capita GNP, are used as indicators of political risk.

        3.   A more subjective measure of political risk is based on the
             perception of a country's attitude toward private enterprise

4. The <u>Business</u> <u>Environment</u> <u>Risk</u> <u>Index</u> (BERI) tries to incorporate all these various economic, social, and political factors into an overall measure of the business climate, including the political environment.

5. One good indicator of the degree of political risk is the seriousness of <u>capital</u> <u>flight</u>, which refers to the transfer of capital abroad in response to fears of political risk.

6. From an economic standpoint, political risk can be defined as the <u>uncertainty</u> <u>over</u> <u>property</u> <u>rights</u>. In this sense, political risk exists if:

   a. The government expropriates legal title to property or the stream of income it generates.

   b. Property owners are constrained in the way they can use their property.

C. While political risk models attempt to quantify the level of political risk in each nation, their usefulness remains problematic.

   1. The major weaknesses of these indexes include the following.

      a. Political instability by itself does not necessarily contribute to political risk.

      b. The degree of political risk is not the same for each firm in a country.

   2. A firm's susceptibility to political risk is largely determined by its characteristics and the effects of that risk on the present value of its foreign investment.

   3. In general, the greater the perceived benefits to the host economy and the more expensive it is to replace a foreign investment with a purely local operation, the smaller the risk of expropriation to the MNC.

   4. Governments tend to select their targets according to nonpolitical criteria which, in turn, suggest that companies can take actions to control their exposure to political risk.

D. Once the possibility of a change in government policy is recognized, the firm must consider its consequences in the context of its investment.

1. Political risk can easily be incorporated in the capital budgeting analysis by:

   a. Shortening the payback period.

   b. Raising the discount rate.

   c. Adjusting project cash flows.

II. Managing Political Risk

   A. After analyzing the political environment of a country and assessing its implications for corporate operations, the company must then decide whether to invest there and, if so, how to structure the investment to minimize political risk.

   B. Once a company has recognized the possible existence of political risk, it can choose from at least four separate, though not necessarily mutually exclusive, policies.

      1. If a country appears to be politically unstable, the firm can simply _avoid_ making its investment there.

      2. An alternative to risk avoidance is to obtain _insurance_ for the firm's assets through:

         a. The _Overseas_ _Private_ _Investment_ _Corporation_ (OPIC) which is a government-operated program to provide insurance against loss due to specific political risks of expropriation, currency inconvertibility, and political violence.

         b. _Lloyd's_ _of_ _London_ which is the only private insurer of consequence against expropriation risk.

      3. With a _concession_ _agreement_ firms try to reach an understanding with the host government before undertaking the investment by defining the rights and responsibilities of both parties.

      4. If the firm has decided to make the investment in a country, it can then try to minimize its exposure to political risk by increasing the cost of nationalization to the host government. This action involves:

         a. Adjusting the operating policies and the financial policies so that the value of the foreign project is closely linked to the multinational firm's continued control.

    b.   Concentrating R & D facilities and proprietary technology in the home country.

    c.   Controlling transportation.

    d.   Developing external stakeholders in the venture's success by raising capital for the venture from the host and other governments, international financial institutions, and customers rather than in the form of parent-guaranteed loans.

    e.   Obtaining unconditional host government guarantees for the amount of the investment so that creditors will be able to threaten or initiate legal action in foreign courts against any commercial transactions between the host country and third parties if a subsequent government fails to honor the nation's obligations.

C. If a company has invested in a project and wants to influence its susceptibility to political risk, it has at least five different policies that can be pursued with varying chances of success.

    1. A multinational company can phase out its ownership of foreign investment over a fixed period of time by selling all or a majority of its equity interest to local shareholders.

    2. If the company needs to divest itself wholly or partially of an equity position, it may respond by attempting to withdraw the maximum amount of cash from the local operation. Short-term profit maximization can be achieved by:

        a.   Deferring maintenance expenditures.

        b.   Cutting investments to a minimum necessary to sustain the desired level of production.

        c.   Curtailing marketing expenditures.

        d.   Producing lower quality goods.

        e.   Setting higher prices.

        f.   Eliminating training programs.

    3. Another alternative is for the multinational company to initiate programs that will reduce the perceived advantage of local ownership and thereby diminish the incentive to expel foreigners. These actions include:

a. Establishing local R & D facilities.

b. Developing export markets for the affiliate's output.

c. Training local workers and managers.

d. Expanding production facilities.

e. Manufacturing a wider range of products locally as substitutes for products.

4. A more positive strategy is to get on good terms with local individuals and groups who have an interest in the affiliate continued existence as a unit of the parent multinational.

5. Some firms choose to pursue a more radical approach to political risk management, which entails adapting to the inevitability of potential expropriation and trying to earn profits on the firm's resource by entering into licensing agreements and management contracts.

III. Postexpropriation Policies

A. A firm that has been notified of being expropriated can open discussions with the host government in an attempt to dissuade from proceeding further. There are four phases of confrontation between the government and the firm in the post-confiscation period.

B. During the first phase, _rational negotiation_, the firm can bargain with the government in an attempt to persuade it that confiscation was a mistake. Mutual concessions may be suggested which will allow the firm to continue its operations.

C. If these concessions do not result in returning the property to the company, it will begin to _apply power_.

1. Political power can take several forms.

a. A positive approach is based on meeting government needs.

b. Applying negative sanctions could take the form of supporting the opposition political party or invoking home government support for the firm's position.

2. Economic power directed at the host government would include cutting off essential components, export markets, technology and management skills.

D. During the first two phases, the firm will begin to pursue <u>legal remedies</u>.

    1. The basic rule of law is that legal relief must be sought first in the courts of the host country and only after having exhausted this avenue can the firm present its case in home country or international courts.

    2. Investors who petition U.S. courts for legal aid and indemnification are faced with two impediments.

        a. The <u>doctrine of sovereign immunity</u> states that a sovereign state may not be tried in the courts of another state without its own consent.

        b. The <u>act of state doctrine</u> states that a nation is sovereign within its own borders, and its domestic actions may not be questioned in the courts of another nation, even if these actions violate international law.

    3. Another possibility of legal redress is to petition the parent country's government agencies to close the home market for raw materials and other products from the host country.

    4. The <u>International Center for Settlement of Investment Disputes</u> provides investors with another alternative to which they can turn in investment disputes in a foreign country.

E. If a company has not been successful during the first three phases, it will surrender to reality and attempt to salvage whatever it can from its investment.

    1. Some firms simply settle for any insurance payments due to them.

    2. Other companies engage in contractual post expropriation relationships with the host government with the purpose to continue generating cash flows from its confiscated property. This can be achieved in at least three ways.

        a. Handling exports as in the past but under a commission arrangement.

        b. Furnishing technical and management skills under a management contract.

        c. Selling raw materials and components to the foreign country.

KEY TERMS

Macro Approach
Micro Approach
Political Systems Stability Index (PSSI)
Business Environment Risk Index (BERI)
Capital Flight
Political Risk
Overseas Private Investment Corporation
(OPIC)
Concession Agreement

Risk Avoidance
Rational Negotiation
Applying Power
Legal Remedies
Doctrine of Sovereign Immuni
Act of State Doctrine
International Center for
   Settlement of Investment
Disputes

CONCEPTUAL QUESTIONS

QUESTION 1: What is meant by political risk?

ANSWER: Political risk is defined as the uncertainty of government intervention that affects the value of the firm.

QUESTION 2: How can a MNC protect itself against the risks of governmer interference?

ANSWER: The basic approach to managing political risk can be broken dov into three steps:

1. Recognizing the existence of political risk and its likely consequences.
2. Developing policies in advance to cope with the possibility of political risk.
3. In the event of expropriation, developing measures to maximize compensation, either in the form of direct payments or through access to the future steam of earnings generated by the expropriated property.

QUESTION 3: Distinguish between the macro approach and the micro appros to measuring political risk.

ANSWER: If political risk is viewed from a country-specific perspective the firm is taking a macro approach to measuring political risk. If it viewed from a firm-specific perspective, the firm is taking a micro approach.

QUESTION 4: Explain the Political Systems Stability Index, as developec Dan Haendel, Gerald West, and Robert Meadow.

ANSWER: The Political Systems Stability Index evaluates the probability some political event occurring that would change the profit outlook for given investment. This index, in turn, is composed of three equally weighted subindexes.

1. The Socioeconomic Characteristic Index measures population heterogeneity and prospects for future economic growth.
2. The Societal Conflict Index estimates the potential for violent change in a country.
3. The Governmental Processes Index assesses the prospects for the peaceful transition of political power within a society.

QUESTION 5:   What are the most appropriate means of managing expropriation risk?

ANSWER: All nations are politically risky to a greater or lesser extent. Hence, avoidance is impossible. Similarly, political risk insurance guarantees only the amount of the initial investment, not its economic value. Planning to divest is also fraught with problems. Assuming that governments behave somewhat rationally in deciding whose assets to expropriate, and respond to the anticipated costs and benefits of their actions.

SELECTED PROBLEMS FROM THE TEXT

PROBLEM 1:   Between 1981 and 1987, direct foreign investment in the Third World plunged by over 50%. The World Bank is concerned about this decline and wants to correct it. Its solution: creating a Multilateral Investment Guarantee Agency (MIGA) that will guarantee foreign investments against expropriation at rates to be subsidized by Western governments. MIGA's defenders argue that it will perform a valuable service in improving the investment climate in Third World countries. (a) Assess the likely consequences of MIGA on both the volume of Western capital flows to Third World nations and the efficiency of international capital allocation. (b) How will MIGA affect the probability of expropriation and respect for property rights in Third World countries? Consider this question from an option pricing perspective. (c) Is MIGA likely to improve the investment climate in Third World nations: (d) According to a senior World Bank official (The Wall Street JOurnal, December 22, 1987, p. 20), "There is vastly more demand for political risk coverage than the sum total available." Is this a valid economic argument for setting up MIGA? (e) Assess the following argument made on behalf of MIGA by a State Department memo: "We should avoid penalizing a good project (by not providing subsidized insurance) for bad government policies over which they have limited influence . . . Restrictions on eligible countries [receiving insurance subsidies because of their doubtful investment policies] will decrease MIGA's volume of business and spread of risk, making it harder to be self-sustaining." (Quoted in the Wall Street Journal, December 22, 1987, p. 20.)

SOLUTION:

a. By lowering the risk-adjusted return required by investors, MIG will increase the flow of Western capital to Third World countries. At the same time, however, subsidizing investment insurance will tend to produce less efficient capital allocation; more money will be channeled to those countries tha have the greatest risk of expropriation (since these are the countries that will receive the greater implicit subsidy from MIGA). Because respect for property rights is critical for economic growth, these are also the nations with the poorest economic prospects. Under MIGA, American taxpayers will wind u subsidizing the expropriation of American property. Thus, MIGA becomes another welfare scheme, not a business venture.

b. Governments always have the option of expropriating foreign property in their nations. The decision of whether to expropriate this property depends on the cost of exercising thi option. By lowering the cost of expropriation, MIGA would make expropriation more advantageous for Third World governments and hence, more likely. Instead of Third World governments compensating MIGA-insured investors, Western governments would provide this compensation.

c. Quite the contrary. MIGA would counter the decline in private investment not by making foreign investment safer, but by havin Western governments pay for the costs of Third World expropriations. If the World Bank really wants to improve the investment climate in the Third World, it could simply stop giving money to Third World governments that subvert their own development by expropriating foreign investors.

d. The problem is not that private insurance is not available--several private entities such as Lloyd's of London offer insurance for foreign investments--but that its costs accurately reflect the true risk of placing one's money in countries where property rights are routinely violated. MIGA w attempt to boost foreign investment in many countries suffering from capital flight. The fact that the countries' own citizens don't trust the government is a clue that investment there is unsafe.

e. MIGA's approach to foreign investments seems to be based more o protection of greedy governments than on a respect for property rights. The World Bank seems to see expropriations as events t involve no human responsibility or blame. The World Bank refus to loudly condemn Third World governments for seizing Western property. Countries throughout Africa that have nationalized foreign corporations have afterward received World Bank loans a subsidized rates to help run the new state-owned industries.

Some countries, like South Korea, Taiwan, and Hong Kong, have done very well at attracting foreign investment. MIGA would play down the differences in how governments treat investors, thus penalizing nations that honor property rights and rewarding nations that violate them. Given the crucial role that property rights play in economic development, this is a perverse set of incentives.

INTERNATIONAL FINANCING AND INTERNATIONAL FINANCIAL MARKETS

Summary: With the growing internationalization of capital markets and th
increased sophistication of companies, the search for financing is made
easier by the wide variety of both internal and external sources of funds
This chapter explores the external medium- and long-term financing
alternatives available to the multinational corporation.

I. Corporate Sources and Uses of Funds

   A. The sources of funds available to the firm consist of internally-
      generated cash, short-term external funds, and long-term external
      funds.

      1. External financing can come from investors (equity) or lender
         (debt).

      2. An alternative to issuing public debt securities is to obtain
         loans from a specialized financial intermediary that issues
         securities of its own in the market.

      3. These alternative debt instruments are commercial bank loans
         or privately-placed bonds.

   B. Companies in different countries follow different financial
      structures.

      1. The financing pattern which has emerged shows a heavy relianc
         on internal funds.

      2. The need for external funds fluctuates with the business cycl
         when profits are high, firms are less reliant on external
         funds.

      3. In the event that a company should need funds, debt securitie
         are issued first before any new stock is issued in the
         financial market.

   C. A substantial amount of corporate borrowing takes the form of
      negotiable securities issued in the public capital markets rather
      than in the form of nonmarketable loans provided by financial
      intermediaries, a process called <u>securitization</u>.

1. Securitization is largely the result of

   a. A reduction in the cost of using financial markets.

   b. A reduction in the cost of accessing the public markets.

2. Globalization has increased the degree of competition among key financial centers and financial institutions which, in turn, has reduced the cost of issuing new securities.

3. International fund flows can take place through international securitization or international financial intermediation.

D. When comparing U.S. leverage with foreign leverage, data compiled by Morgan Stanley Capital International has revealed that financial leverage in Japan and West Germany is considerably higher than in the U.S.

II. National Capital Markets as International Financial Centers

A. The main function of a financial market is the efficient transfer of funds from savers to borrowers that have productive investment opportunities.

B. International financial markets can develop anywhere as long as local regulations permit the market and that potential investors are attracted to it.

   1. The most important international financial centers are located in New York and London.

   2. Countries that have relatively unimportant domestic financial markets are important world financial centers (e.g., Switzerland, Luxembourg, Singapore, Hong King, the Bahamas, Bahrain). The markets of those countries serve as financial entrepots or channels through which foreign funds pass.

   3. In order to become and maintain an important international financial center, especially entrepot centers, host countries must be characterized by political stability and minimal government interventions.

      a. Public or semipublic financial institutions grant loans at below market rates to favored groups by the government.

      b. Other official agencies supply government-backed guarantees, political and economic risk insurance, and rediscounting facilities for certain commercial bank credit.

c. The primary objective of these government interventions to reduce the funds available to other demanders and if interest rates are controlled, to form a waiting list for the remaining funds.

C. Foreigners have difficulty accessing <u>domestic</u> <u>capital</u> <u>markets</u> because of government-imposed or government-suggested restrictions relating to the maturities and amounts of money that they can raise as well as any special taxes. The financial markets of many countries, however, permit foreigners to borrow or invest.

1. The <u>foreign</u> <u>bond</u> <u>market</u> is that part of the domestic bond market that represents issues floated by foreign companies or governments.

   a. Foreign bonds are subject to local laws and must be denominated in the local currency.

   b. These issues may face additional restrictions as well.

2. The <u>foreign</u> <u>banking</u> <u>market</u> represents that part of the domestic bank loans supplied to foreigners abroad. Here again, the government may restrict the amount of funds made available to foreigners.

3. Most major stock exchanges permit sales of <u>foreign</u> <u>equity</u> <u>issues</u> as long as these issues satisfy all the listing requirements of the local market.

   a. Placing stock in the foreign equity market provides a number of advantages to the issuing corporation.

      (1) One attraction is the diversification of equity funding risk.

      (2) Selling stock overseas also increases the potential demand for the company's shares by attracting new shareholders, thereby enhancing the value of the stock.

      (3) Moreover, an international stock offering can make a company's products and name known in the financial markets.

   b. International equity placement can take two forms.

      (1) In the U.S. companies typically do <u>dual</u> <u>syndicated</u> equity offerings, where the offering is split into a domestic and overseas tranche, and each tranche is handled by a separate lead manager.

(2) In Europe, companies most often do <u>Euro-equity</u> <u>issues</u> through a single tranche; that is, a syndicated offering is placed throughout Europe and handled by one lead manager.

D. Medium-term financing usually refers to loans with maturities between one and seven years. Commercial banks provide the majority of this financing in a variety of different forms.

   1. With a <u>renewable overdraft</u>, a customer can write checks in excess of previous deposits up to a predetermined amount that is renewed year after year.

   2. Renewable loans, evidenced by a promissory note, are used to provide <u>bridge</u> <u>financing</u>. The borrowing firm obtains medium- or long-term financing which is sued to pay off the firm's promissory note in a lump sum.

   3. <u>Medium-term</u> <u>loans</u> are usually made on the basis of cash flows that are expected to be generated by the borrower's investment.

   4. Medium-term credit may be provided by <u>rediscounting</u> commercial bank loans either directly or through a semi-public institution.

E. Long-term debt financing can take the following forms.

   1. <u>Long-term</u> <u>loans</u> to industry are provided by commercial banks or their affiliates in many other countries.

   2. Funds from <u>pensions</u> and <u>insurance</u> <u>companies</u> are another important source of long-term debt financing.

   3. <u>Leasing</u> is an important long-term financing technique in most countries. Its value and use depends on the tax regulations relating to depreciation write-offs in a particular country and how important these tax shields are to companies making investment decisions.

   4. In most countries, <u>bond</u> placements are closely controlled either directly by the government or the major commercial and merchant banks.

III. The Euromarkets

A. A <u>Eurocurrency</u> is a dollar or other freely convertible currency deposited in a bank outside its country of origin. These deposits can be placed in a foreign bank or in the foreign branch of a domestic U.S. bank.

B. The <u>Eurocurrency</u> <u>market</u> consists of those banks (Eurobanks) that accept funds for deposits and make loans in foreign currencies.

C. By operating in Eurocurrencies, banks and supplies of funds are able to avoid certain U.S. government regulations and their associated costs.

   1. Eurobanks are not required to set interest rate ceilings on deposits.

   2. Eurobanks are not acquired to maintain reserves against the dollar deposits they take in.

   3. Interest on foreign debt is not subject to any taxes.

   4. There are no restrictions on the use of the funds provided.

D. Eurocurrency operations differ from the structure of domestic banking operations in two ways:

   1. There is a <u>chain</u> <u>of</u> <u>deposits</u> between the original dollar depositor and the U.S. bank.

   2. There is a <u>changing</u> <u>control</u> <u>over</u> <u>the</u> <u>deposits</u> from one Eurobank to another and the use to which the money is put.

E. Eurocurrency lending provides the following characteristics.

   1. Eurocurrency loans are made on a floating-rate basis. Interest rates on loans made to governments and then agencies, corporations, and non-prime banks are set at a fixed margin above LIBOR for a given period (also called rollover period) and currency chosen.

      a. The <u>period</u> chosen is normally six months, but shorter periods, such as one or three months, are possible.

      b. The <u>margin</u> between the lending bank's cost of funds and the interest rate changed the borrower, varies among borrowers due to their perceived riskiness.

      c. The <u>maturity</u> of the loan can vary from three to ten years.

      d. The <u>drawdown</u> and the repayment period vary in accordance with the borrower's needs.

   2. Borrowing can be done in many different currencies, although the dollar is still the dominant currency. Eurodollars have a <u>multi-currency</u> <u>clause</u> which gives the borrower the right switch from one currency to another on any rollover date.

a. This option enables the borrower to match currencies on cash inflows and cash outflows.

b. It also allows a borrower to take advantage of its own expectations, regarding currency changes and shop around for those funds with the lowest effective cost.

3. Arbitrage activities result in a close interdependency between interest rates in national and international money markets.

a. Interest rates in the U.S. and Eurodollar markets differ only in terms of additional costs, controls, or risks associated with moving funds between the U.S. and some other country.

b. Since the cost of shifting fund is relatively insignificant, any difference between domestic and external rates might be explained by currency controls or risk.

c. In general, Eurocurrency spreads are narrower than in domestic money markets.

4. In recent years, a growing number of creditworthy customers are obtaining financing in the Euromarkets at interest rates well below LIBOR. This situation largely reflects the fact that banks have lost much of their appeal to investors.

F. Eurobonds are similar in many respects to the public debt sold in domestic capital markets. The prefix "Euro" refers to the fact that the bonds are sold outside the countries in whose currencies they are denominated.

1. There is a fundamental difference between the Eurobond and Eurocurrency markets.

a. Eurobonds are issued by final borrowers directly, whereas the Eurocurrency market enables investors to hold short-term claims on banks which then act as intermediaries to transform these deposits into long-term claims on final borrowers.

b. In terms of its sure, until recently, the Eurobond market has been substantially smaller than the Eurocurrency market.

c. Borrowers in the Eurobond market must be well known and must have an excellent credit rating.

d. The amounts raised in the Eurobond market is far less than those raised in the Eurocurrency market.

2. Since 1986, the Eurobond market has been in a deep slump which may be attributed to the following factors:

   a. The weakness of the dollar.

   b. The substitution of Euronotes for Eurobonds.

3. A major catalyst for the growth of the Eurobond market has been the use of swaps which are financial transactions in which two counterparties agree to exchange streams of payments over time.

   a. Swaps allow borrowers to raise money in one market and t swap one interest rate structure for another.

   b. They also allow the parties to a contract to arbitrage their relative access to different currency markets.

4. Due to arbitrage activities between the domestic dollar and Eurobond markets, much of the disparity that used to exist between Eurobonds and domestic bonds has been eliminated. A any time, however, Eurobond issuers will take advantage of Eurobond "windows" when a combination of domestic regulations, tax laws, and expectations of international investors enable the issuer to obtain a lower financing cost than that available in the domestic markets.

5. Eurobond issues are arranged through an underwriting group, involving a hundred or more underwriting banks. A growing number of Eurobonds is placed privately for the following reasons:

   a. Simplicity: No prospectus needs to be printed and the offering memorandum is brief.

   b. Speed: The total time it takes to bring in an issue and selling it can be measured in weeks.

   c. Privacy: No lengthy disclosure statements are required.

   d. Lower cost: No need to pay financial intermediaries. Legal costs are lower.

6. About 75% of Eurobond issues have been denominated in U.S. dollars followed by other currencies, such as the German mark which has become more important in the Eurobond market. Other alternatives to denominating issues in the U.S. dollar or German mark include offering bonds whose value is a weighted average or basket of several currencies. The most successful of these currency "cocktails" is the European Currency Unit (ECU) for the following reasons:

   a. Access to markets that might not otherwise be available.

   b. Diversification of currency risk.

   c. A hedge against the dollar.

7. Because of a large number of institutions carrying large portfolios of Eurobonds for trading purposes, the depth and sophistication of the Eurobond secondary market has been increasing. In fact, it has become second only to the U.S. domestic bond market in terms of liquidity.

8. A Eurobond with more than seven years maturity is required to be retired.

   a. A sinking fund requires the borrower to retire a fixed amount of bonds yearly after a specific number of years.

   b. A purchase fund usually starts in the first year, and bonds are retires only if the market price is less than the issue price.

9. In addition, most Eurobonds carry call provisions, giving the borrower the option of retiring bonds prior to maturity should interest rates decline substantially in the future.

10. The rationale for the Eurobond market's existence can be summarized as follows:

   a. The Eurobond market is largely unregulated and untaxed.

   b. Funds can be raised more quickly and more flexibly than in the domestic bond market.

   c. Interest received by investors is tax free.

   d. The borrowing rate on Eurobonds is less than the rate at which the U.S. Treasury can borrow.

   e. Eurobonds are marketed in bearer form, meaning that they are unregistered with no record of the name of the issuer.

f.　As unregistered securities, investors may be able to escape the exchange and other controls imposed by the home government.

g.　Nonresidents can avoid the payment of some taxes.

11.　Because of the size and relatively low interest rates, virtually every treasurer still considers the Eurobond market an important source of financing. But its importance is diminishing, particularly for U.S. companies which have been faced with the repeal of withholding taxes and financia deregulation.

G.　The major differences between Eurobonds and Eurocurrency loans are categorized in five ways:

1.　Cost of borrowing.

a.　Eurobonds are issued in both fixed-rate and floating-rate forms.

b.　Eurocurrency loans are issued in variable-interest rate form, providing a better hedge against noncontractual currency exposure.

2.　Maturity. While the maturity on Eurocurrency loans has lengthened over time, Eurobonds still have longer maturities.

3.　Size of issue. Until recently, the among of loanable funds available at any one time has been much greater in the interbank market than in the bond market. Given the size and price of financing which can be obtained in the Eurobond market, the volume in this market can easily surpass that in the interbank market.

4.　Flexibility

a.　The funds from a Eurobond must be drawn down in one sum on a fixed date and repaid according to a fixed schedule unless the borrower pays an often substantial penalty for early repayment.

b.　Eurocurrency loans issued on a floating-rate basis can be staggered to suit the borrower's needs with a commitment fee on the unused portion of the funds and can be prepaid in whole or in part at any time, without penalty. Moreover, a Eurocurrency loan may include a multi-currency clause.

5. Speed. In the Eurocurrency market, funds can be obtained very quickly, often within two or three weeks of first request. A Eurobond financing generally takes more time to put together.

H. A note issuance facility (NIF) allows borrowers to issue their own short-term notes that are then placed and distributed by the financial institutions providing the NIF.

1. NIFs have some features of the U.S. commercial paper market unsecured short-term debt) and some features of U.S. commercial lines of credit (multiple pricing components).

2. NIFs are more flexible than floating-rate notes and cheaper than syndicated loans.

3. NIFs are like put options, giving borrowers the right to sell their paper to the bank syndicate at a price that yields a prearranged spread over LIBOR.

I. There are several advantages to NIFs compared with the floating-rate note (FRN).

1. Drawdown flexibility. Note issuers have the option to draw down all or part of their total credit whenever their need arises, and they can also rollover portions of its.

2. Timing flexibility. The issuer of a floating-rate note must accept the prevailing rate for the period's duration. By contrast, a Euronote issuer has the option to wait on the issuance depending on the currently prevailing interest rate.

3. Choice of maturities. FRN issuers are generally looked into are maturity setting over the life of the issue. NIFs, on the other hand, give borrowers the choice of issuing notes with different maturities whenever they choose to draw down new debt or roll over old debt.

4. Secondary market. The secondary market for Euronotes is relatively undeveloped compared to the market for FRNs, thus making FRNs highly illiquid.

J. The Asiacurrency market, located in Singapore, has been growing rapidly in terms of both size and range of services provided. Its primary economic function is to channel investment dollars to a number of rapidly growing Southeast Asian countries and to provide deposit facilities for those investors with excess funds.

IV. Development Banks

   A. The U.S. and other countries have established a variety of development banks, whose lending is directed to investments that promote economic backward areas.

      1. Loans, which usually are not made available by private sources, are medium- to long-term and carry concessionary rates.

      2. Lending is done directly to a government.

      3. This type of lending has two implications to the private sector:

         a. The projects require goods and services which can be produced by firms.

         b. By establishing a new infrastructure, new investment opportunities become available for MNCs.

   B. The three different types of development banks include:

      1. The World Bank Group comprising three related financial institutions:

         a. International Bank for Reconstruction and Development.

         b. International Development Association.

         c. International Finance Corporation.

      2. Regional development banks which provide debt and equity financing to aid in the economic development of underdevelope areas.

      3. National development banks which concentrate on a particular region or industry; others are multipurpose.

   C. Development banks are government-owned and government-controlled institutions doing business with other governments.

      1. Thus, it may not be surprising that these banks have been hostile to enforcing stringent Free-market principles as conditions for receiving loans.

      2. Subsequently, these banks have been unable to foster sound economic policies and stable political environments in variou developmental regions.

Securitization

International Financial Center

Entrepot Center

Foreign Bond Market

Foreign Banking Market

Foreign Equity Market

Dual Syndicated Equity Offering

Euro-Equity Issue

Tranche

Renewable Overdraft

Bridge Financing

Rediscountable Medium Term Loans

Eurocurrency

Eurocurrency Market

Eurocurrency Loan

Multicurrency Clause

LIBOR

Currency Cocktail

Sinking Fund

Purchase Fund

Call Provision

Note Issuance Facility (NIF)

Development Banks

Medium-Term Loans

CONCEPTUAL QUESTIONS

QUESTION 1:   Compare and contrast Eurocurrency loans and Eurobonds.

ANSWER: The fundamental distinction between a Eurobond and a Eurocurrency loan stems from the financing mechanism. A Eurobond is issued by the final borrower directly, whereas a Eurocurrency loan is made by a bank. Thus, Eurobond investors hold a claim on the issuer directly, whereas Eurocurrency loans are funded by investors who hold short-term claims on banks that then act as intermediaries to transform these deposits into long-term claims on final borrowers.

SELECTED QUESTIONS FROM THE TEXT

QUESTION 3:   What is securitization? What forces underlie it and how has it affected the financing policies of multinational corporations?

ANSWER: Securitization is the process of matching up borrowers and savers by way of the financial markets. By contrast, financial intermediation involves the use of financial institutions such as banks and thrifts to bring together borrowers and savers. These institutions make a large number of loans and fund them by issuing liabilities (e.g., deposits) in their own name. Securitization largely reflects a reduction in the cost of using financial markets at the same time that the cost of bank borrowing has risen. Multinational companies and other large firms have participated in the securitization process. Instead of raising money in the form of nonmarketable loans provided by financial intermediaries, they are now issuing negotiable securities to the public capital markets.

QUESTION 5:   What is meant by the globalization of financial markets? How has technology affected the process of globalization?

ANSWER: The globalization of financial markets refers to the increasing integration of national financial markets. Markets for U.S. government securities and certain stocks, foreign exchange trading, interbank borrowing and lending--to cite a few examples--operate continuously around the clock and around the world and in enormous size. Foreign financial firms are increasing their participation in the world's leading financial markets. Investors are scanning the globe to place their capital where it can realize the best risk-return combination, while companies are seeking to raise money wherever in the world they can receive the best terms and conditions. In effect, globalization reflects the process of breaking down the artificial barriers that separate domestic from foreign capital markets. True globalization will come when the price of risk and the time value of money are identical worldwide.

Recent technological improvements in such areas as data manipulation and telecommunications have greatly reduced the costs of gathering, processing, and acting on information from anywhere in the world. This has facilitated the process of arbitrage across financial markets. The net result of such arbitrage has been to bring prices of securities with similar risks and returns closer in line with each other and to turn the world into a vast interconnected market.

QUESTION 14: Suppose that the current 180-day interbank Eurodollar rate is 9% (all rates are stated on an annualized basis). If next period's rate is 9.5%, what will a Eurocurrency loan priced at LIBOR plus 1% cost?

ANSWER: Eurodollar loans are made on a floating rate basis, with the rate set at a fixed margin over LIBOR. Thus, if next period's annualized LIBOR is 13%, then the Eurocurrency loan will be at 14% (13% + 1%) on an annualized basis.

QUESTION 20: Why is the NIF described as a put option?

ANSWER: NIFs are put options because they give borrowers the right, but not the obligation, to sell their paper to a bank syndicate at a price that yields the prearranged spread over LIBOR. Borrowers will exercise this right only if they cannot place their notes at a better rate elsewhere.

SPECIAL FINANCING VEHICLES

Summary: This chapter examines three special financing instruments which MNCs can use to finance their foreign investments. These instruments include interest rate and currency swaps, international leasing, and bank loan swaps.

I. Interest Rate and Currency Swaps

    A. The explosive growth experienced in the swap market provides financial risk managers with an additional tool to reduce borrowing costs and increase control over interest rate risk and foreign currency exposure.

    B. An interest rate swap is an agreement between two parties to exchange U.S. dollar interest payments for a specified maturity on an agreed upon notional amount.

        1. An interest rate swap has the following characteristics.

            a. The calculation of the interest payments is based on a theoretical principal.

            b. No principal amount is ever exchanged between the two parties.

            c. Maturities range from less than one year to more than 15 years with the majority of swaps maturing within a two-year to ten-year period.

        2. The major function of the interest rate swap is to transform debt issues, assets, liabilities, or any cash flow from type to type and from currency to currency.

        3. Variations of the basic interest rate swap include:

            a. Coupon swap in which one party pays a fixed rate calculated at the time of trade as a spread to a particular Treasury bond, and the other party pays a floating rate that is adjusted throughout the life of the financial instrument according to a designated index.

            b. Basis swap in which a floating-rate liability tied to one reference rate, e.g., LIBOR, is exchanged for a floating-rate liability with another reference rate, e.g., 90-day Treasury bills.

4. A swap contract can be thought of as a series of forward contracts to protect against an unknown stream of interest payments to service a liability.

C. A <u>currency</u> <u>swap</u> is a contract, arranged across currencies, in whic two parties agree to exchange a principal amount at maturity at a predetermined exchange rate.

   1. Currency swaps solve two potentially serious problems associated with parallel loans:

      a. If there is no <u>right</u> <u>of</u> <u>offset</u>, default by one party does not release the other from making its contractually obligated payments.

      b. The right of offset, which gives each party the right to offset any nonpayment of principal or interest with a comparable nonpayment, is more firmly established with a currency swap.

   2. A currency swap is like a long-dated forward contract, where the forward rate is the current spot rate.

D. There are a number of economic advantages to the use of swaps.

   1. Only if a barrier exists to prevent arbitrage from functioning fully can the transacting parties enjoy the real benefits of a swap. This barrier can take the form of:

      a. Legal restrictions on spot and forward foreign exchange transactions.

      b. Different perceptions by investors of risk and credit worthiness of the two parties.

      c. Appeal or acceptability of one borrower to a certain class of investor.

      d. Tax differentials.

   2. With swaps, firms are able to reduce their cost of foreign exchange risk management.

   3. Firms can use swaps as a long-term financing instruments in foreign currencies.

   4. Swaps provide the opportunity to both parties to engage in some form of tax, regulatory system, or financial market arbitrage.

II. International Leasing

A. With international leasing, a MNC can defer and avoid taxes, safeguard the assets of its foreign affiliates, and avoid currency controls.

B. Because of the tax advantage, international leasing makes a distinction between operating and financial leases.

   1. An _operating lease_, or service lease, is a true lease in that ownership and use of the asset are separated. It is characterized as a lease agreement which:

      a. Covers only part of the useful life of the asset.

      b. May be renewed on a period-by-period basis.

      c. Is cancelable.

   2. A _financial lease_ is one that:

      a. Covers most of the economic life of the asset.

      b. Is noncancelable or is cancelable only with a substantial penalty to the lessor.

   3. Leasing is considered an alternative financing technique.

      a. With a financial lease, the firm has a binding obligation to make all the lease payments, as specified in the lease agreement. Nonpayment legally constitutes default.

      b. Economic ownership of the asset resides with the lessee, which is equivalent to obtaining a loan secured by the asset.

C. Two important issues in any leasing transaction are the tax status of the lease payments and who will be able to deduct depreciation and obtain the benefits of the investment tax credit.

   1. In the U.S., the IRS makes a distinction between operating and financial leases for tax purposes.

      a. If a lease is considered an operating or true lease, its is called a _tax-oriented_ lease, in which the lessor receives the tax benefits of ownership, and the lessee can deduct the full value of the lease payments.

      b. If a lease is considered a financial lease, the lease payments are treated as installments of the purchase price plus interest and are not fully tax-deductible by the lessee.

255

2. International leasing can provide tax benefits if the lease structured as a <u>double-dip</u> <u>lease</u>.

    a. In this lease arrangement, the leasing rules of the lessor's and the lessee's countries allow both parties to be treated as the owner of the leased equipment for tax purposes.

    b. Thus, both the lessor and the lessee are entitled to deduct depreciation and obtain investment tax credits.

    c. If more than two parties are involved in the lease arrangement, it is possible that each party will be entitled to capital allowances.

3. A MNC that incorporates a captive international leasing company in a location characterized by no exchange control restrictions, a stable currency, political stability, and a wide network of tax treaties can enjoy a number of benefits, such as:

    a. Shift income from high-tax to low-tax jurisdictions.

    b. Reduce or eliminate withholding tax on lease payments.

    c. Receive lease income tax free.

    d. Reduce political risk.

    e. More easily recover assets in the case of nationalization

4. In early 1981, Japan introduced the so-called <u>shogun</u> <u>lease</u>, which is a yen-based lease allowing leasing companies, with the help of U.S. banks, to bypass restrictions imposed by Japan's Ministry of Finance on long-term yen loans.

III. Bank Loan Swaps

A. LDC debt swaps allow investors to purchase the external debt of less-developed countries (LDCs) in order to acquire equity or domestic currency in those same countries.

    1. These <u>debt-equity</u> <u>swaps</u> have been selling in the secondary market.

        a. Loans are traded at deep discounts to their face value.

        b. Market discounts are quoted in terms of bids and offers, not single market-clearing transaction prices.

      c. Substantial variations in price quotations are quite common across countries.

2. There are also <u>debt-peso</u> <u>swaps</u>, which enable the residents of a debtor country to purchase their country's foreign debt at a discount and then to convert this debt into domestic currency. These purchases, in turn, are financed with funds held abroad or hard currency obtained from international trade or in the exchange market.

3. The exchange rate offered in the debt swaps market is more favorable than that offered in the official exchange markets, thus providing an opportunity for arbitrage.

4. Debt swaps programs have been initiated by five major debtor nations: Chile, Mexico, Venezuela, Argentina, and the Philippines. Access to these programs, however, is made difficult because of a lot of government red tape.

KEY TERMS

Interest Rate Swap

Coupon Swap

Basis Swap

Currency Swap

Right of Offset

Operating Lease

Financial Lease

Tax-Oriented Lease

Double Dip Lease

Shogun Lease

Debt-Equity Swaps

Debt-Peso Swaps

CONCEPTUAL QUESTIONS

QUESTION 1: What are debt-peso swaps?

ANSWER: Debt-peso swaps enable residents of a debtor country to purchase their country's foreign debt at a discount and to convert this debt into domestic currency. To finance these purchases, residents use funds held abroad or hard currency acquired from international trade or in the exchange market.

QUESTION 2: What is a tax-oriented lease?

ANSWER: A lease that qualifies as a true lease or operating lease for tax purposes is called a tax-oriented lease. In a tax-oriented lease, the lessor receives the tax benefits of ownership, and the lessee gets to deduct the full value of lease payment.

QUESTION 1: What is the difference between a basis swap and a coupon swa

ANSWER: In the coupon swap, one party pays a fixed rate calculated at th time of trade as a spread to a particular Treasury bond, while the other side pays a floating rate that resets periodically throughout the life of the deal against a designated index. In a basis swap, a floating-rate liability tied to one reference rate, say, LIBOR, is exchanged for a floating rate-liability with another reference rate, say, 90-day Treasury bills. Thus, coupon swaps involve converting fixed-rate debt into floating-rate debt (or vice versa), whereas the basis swap involves converting one type of floating-rate debt into another type of floating-rate debt.

QUESTION 3: What factors underlie the economic benefits of swaps?

ANSWER: For swaps to provide economic benefits, they must allow the transacting parties to engage in some form of tax, regulatory system, or financial market arbitrage. Thus, underlying the economic benefits of swaps are barriers that prevent other forms of arbitrage from functioning fully. This impediment must take the form of legal restrictions on spot and forward foreign exchange transactions, different perceptions by investors of risk and creditworthiness of the two parties, appeal or acceptability of one borrower to a certain class of investor, tax differentials, and so forth I the world capital market were fully integrated, the incentive to swap woul be reduced because fewer arbitrage opportunities would exist.

QUESTION 5: How can international lease transactions enable multinational firms to reduce taxes and political risk?

ANSWER: The principal tax advantage from international leasing arises whe it is possible to structure a "double-dip" lease. In a double-dip lease, the different leasing rules of the lessor's and lessee's countries let bot parties be treated as the owner of the leased equipment for tax purposes. Thus, both the lessee and the lessor are entitled to benefits such as fast depreciation and tax credits.

Multinationals can also reduce political risk by investing in politically risky countries via a captive international leasing company incorporated in an appropriate location. Lease financing limits the ownership of assets by subsidiaries in politically unstable countries. Leasing also enables the firm to more easily extract cash from affiliates located in countries where there are exchange controls; lease payments are often a more acceptable method of extracting funds than dividends, interest, or royalty payments. Similarly, there will be more chance of recovering assets (or at least obtaining compensation for them) in the cas of nationalization if they are not owned by the local subsidiary.

SELECTED PROBLEMS FROM THE TEXT

PROBLEM 1: Company A, a low-rated firm, desires a fixed-rate, long-term loan. It presently has access to floating interest rate funds at a margin of 1.5% over LIBOR. Its direct borrowing cost is 13% in the fixed-rate bond market. In contrast, Company B, which prefers a floating-rate loan, has access to fixed-rate funds in the Eurodollar bond market at 11% and floating rate funds at LIBOR + ½%. (a) How can A and B use a swap to advantage? (b) Suppose they split the cost savings. How much would A pay for its fixed-rate funds? How much would B pay for its floating-rate funds?

SOLUTION:

a. Based on the numbers presented, there is an anomaly between the two markets: One judges that the difference in credit quality between the two firms is worth 200 basis points, whereas the other determines that this difference is worth only 100 basis points. The parties can share among themselves the difference of 100 basis points by engaging in a currency swap. This transaction would involve A borrowing floating-rate funds and B borrowing fixed-rate funds and then swapping the proceeds.

b. If they split the cost savings, the resulting costs to the two parties would be as follows:

	Normal Funding Cost	Cost After Swap	Party Difference
Counterparty A	13.00%	12.50	0.50%
Counterparty B	LIBOR +1/2%	LIBOR	0.50%
		Total	1.00%

PROBLEM 2: Chrysler has decided to make a $100 million investment in Mexico via a debt-equity swap. Of that $100 million, $20 million will go to pay off high-interest peso loans in Mexico. The remaining $80 million will go for new capital investment. The government will pay 86 cents on the dollar for debt used to pay off peso loans and 92 cents on the dollar for debt used to finance new investment. If Chrysler can buy Mexican debt in the secondary market for 60 cents on the dollar, how much will it cost Chrysler to make its $100 million investment?

SOLUTION:

The total amount of funds required by Chrysler will consist of:

1. Amount of funds needed to pay off debt

$$\$20,000,000/0.86 = Ps\ 23,255,814.$$

2. Amount of funds needed to finance a new investment

$80,000,000/0.92 = Ps 86,956,522.

3. The total amount of funds needed equals Ps 110,212,336.

At a price of 60 cents on the dollar in the secondary markets, Chrysler will have to pay

$66,127,402 = Ps 110,212,336 (0.60)

for this face value amount of bank debt.

DESIGNING A GLOBAL FINANCING STRATEGY

Summary: This chapter offers an explicit analytical framework to selecting an appropriate strategy for financing the worldwide operations of the MNC. It involves a trade-off between the availability of the different sources of financing and the relative costs and effects of these sources on the firm's operating risk. The approach taken is separated into three main aspects.

I. Exploiting Market Distortions

    A. One of the functions of financial management is to raise funds at a below-market rate.

    B. Arranging positive net present value financing is complicated by the firm's competitive advantages and the fierce competition for funds.

    C. Capital market distortions, in turn, can enable a company to raise funds at below-market rates. These distortions take the following forms.

        1. The different <u>tax</u> treatment of the various components of financial costs translates into unequal after-tax costs, even though the before-tax costs have been the same.

            a. Because interest on debt is tax-deductible, debt financing is considered to be less expensive than equity financing.

            b. This tax advantage does only hold as long as the marginal tax rate to the investor is not equal to the marginal tax rate of the corporation.

            c. The tax incentive for issuing more debt ceases to exist once these two rates are equal.

            d. As long as a firm is able to take advantage of tax distortions, issue tax-exempt debt, or sell debt to investors in marginal tax brackets below 34%, the tax advantage of debt can be preserved.

e. Examples of debt in the respective categories include:

    (1) Bonds denominated in weak currencies.

    (2) Zero-coupon bonds.

    (3) Bearer bonds.

2. A MNC that has access to a variety of different sources of funds is in a unique position to take advantage of deviations in interest rates because of government restrictions and capital controls.

3. Some governments offer a number of incentives to MNCs to influence their production and export sourcing decisions.

    a. Direct investment incentives include interest rate subsidies, loans with long maturities, official repatriation guarantees, grants related to project size, favorable prices for land, favorable terms for the buildi of plants.

    b. Some indirect incentives include corporate income tax holidays, accelerated depreciation, a reduction or elimination of the payment of other business taxes and import duties on capital equipment and raw materials.

    c. Governments of developed nations also have some form of export financing agency, which provides loans with long maturity at concessionary rates and with low-cost politic and economic risk insurance.

II. Reducing Operating Risk

A. After the MNC has taken advantage of the financing sources available to it to reduce its risk-adjusted financing costs, it should arrange any additional financing to reduce the riskiness the operating cash flows.

B. To the extent that the firm's total risk is affected by a particular element of risk, management may want to eliminate tha risk as long as the cost of doing so is reasonable. This action includes the following.

1. A firm can structure its liabilities so as to reduce its exposure to currency risk at no additional cost to shareholders.

    a. With contractual operating cash flows, the strategy to be employed involves matching the net positive cash flows i each currency with borrowing of similar maturity.

b. In the case of <u>noncontractual</u> operating cash flows, assets that generate foreign currency cash flows should be matched with liabilities denominated in those same foreign currencies.

2. Reducing various <u>political</u> <u>risks</u> through financing involves techniques to avoid or reduce the impact of certain risk or to actually change the risk itself.

a. Strategies used by firms to reduce the risk of currency inconvertibility include:

(1) Investing parent funds as debt rather than equity.

(2) Arranging back-to-back and parallel loans.

(3) Using local financing to the maximum extent possible.

b. A firm in an industry most likely to be expropriated may choose to finance its investments with funds from the host and other governments, international development agencies, overseas banks, and from customers.

c. International leasing is another financing alternative that can be sued by MNCs to reduce their political risk.

3. Some firms sell their expected output from the plant or project in advance to customers to reduce the <u>risk</u> <u>of</u> <u>demand</u> <u>fluctuations</u> and then using the sales contracts to obtain financing.

4. A MNC can secure continual <u>access</u> <u>to</u> <u>funds</u> at a reasonable cost and without numerous restrictions by:

a. Maintaining substantial unused debt capacity and liquid assets.

b. Diversifying its fund sources.

c. Indirectly buying insurance through excess borrowing.

III. Establishing a Worldwide Capital Structure

A. For a MNC, the determination of an appropriate mix of debt and equity is complicated by the capital structures of numerous foreign affiliates and the multiplicity of different laws and government regulations.

B. The goal of the multinational enterprise should be to establish a worldwide capital structure that balances the after-tax costs and the benefits of leverage.

C. The optimal capital structure for a foreign affiliate can be arranged in one of the following three ways:

1. The MNC can select a capital structure for its foreign affiliates that conforms to the capital structure of the parent. In this case, the subsidiary:

   a. Does not have an independent capital structure.

   b. Has financial risk that is not determined by its degree of financial leverage.

   c. May forge profitable opportunities to lower its cost of funds.

2. The capital structure of the subsidiaries could be established to reflect the debt norms in each foreign country.

   a. This subsidiary capital structure ignores the strong linkage between U.S.-based MNCs and the U.S. capital market.

   b. The debt/equity level in foreign countries is usually determined by institutional factors that have no bearin on foreign-based MNCs.

3. A cost-minimizing approach to determining foreign affiliate capital structures would be to enable subsidiaries with access to low-cost funds to have a greater debt ratio than the parent company while subsidiaries in higher-capital cos nations would have lower target debt ratios.

D. In determining the overall corporate capital structure, the MNC needs to consider the effects of incomplete information on financial decisions, including potential conflicts with joint partners.

1. Multinational corporations are sometimes reluctant to providing parent-guaranteed loans to their affiliates becaus they believe that:

   a. Subsidiaries should be able to stand along.

   b. Protection against expropriation by issuing a parent-guaranteed loan to the affiliate may be lost.

   c. Lenders should request a guarantee only if the affiliate is operating at a loss or with a debt-heavy capital structure and lending without one when the borrower itself is credit-worthy.

d. Providing support for one operation can lead to demands by lenders in other cases.

e. Non-guaranteed debt would not be included in the parent company's worldwide debt ratio, whereas guaranteed debt would affect the parent's ability to raise debt.

2. In the absence of guarantees:

a. The parent company may convey to investors that its commitment to subsidiary debt is not very strong.

b. The local bank may insist on including various restrictive covenants in the loan agreement with the subsidiary.

c. Borrowing costs are probably higher.

d. The parent company would not be able to take advantage of the tax imposed by the IRS on the imputed income to the guarantor.

3. For multinationals involved in <u>joint ventures</u>, the determination of an appropriate financing mix for this form of investment is an important consideration.

a. Countries that have close relationships between the local banks and corporations, increased leverage will not necessarily lead to increased financial risk.

b. Agency problems associated with this type of ownership can result from differing incentives in such activities as:

(1) Transfer pricing.

(2) Establishment of royalty and licensing fees.

(3) Allocation of production and markets among plants.

c. Lack of complete control over a joint venture's decisions and its profits will cause MNCs, at most, to guarantee joint-venture loans in proportion to their share of ownership.

4. Agency problems do also arise when choosing between bank loans and bond issues.

   a. Bank credit can provide the following advantages:

      (1) Terms and conditions can more readily be custom-tailor made to face-to-face negotiations with the bankers than by trying to deal with a large number smaller investors which the firm never meets.

      (2) It is much easier to renegotiate certain restrictiv covenants in response to changing circumstances.

   b. This banking relationship does not end at the loan agreement, it also includes deposit, payment, and currency services.

   c. The payoff from a long-term banking relationship is tha the bankers tend to have lower costs of monitoring clients activities than do bondholders, who are anonymo and are not interested in this type of relationship, as is a bank.

KEY TERMS

Tax Asymmetry	Parent Capital Structure
Government Restrictions	Subsidiary Capital Structure
Capital Controls	Parent-Guaranteed Loans
Government Subsidies	Joint Ventures
Government Incentives	Agency Costs
Product Market Risk	

CONCEPTUAL QUESTIONS

QUESTION 1: What financial goal is most likely to increase shareholder wealth for a global financing strategy?

ANSWER: A firm that can take advantage of market distortions will surely profit. Reducing the riskiness of operating cash flows and establishing a appropriate financial structure may also create shareholder wealth but so financial economists suggest such actions are irrelevant.

QUESTION 2: What are agency costs?

ANSWER: Although management is legally bound to act as the agent of the shareholders, the separation of ownership and control in the modern corporation results in potential conflicts between the two parties. The agency conflict between managers and outside shareholders stems from two principal sources: Managers tend to (1) consume some of the firm's resources in the form of various perquisites, and (2) to shirk their responsibilities as their equity interest falls.

Agency conflicts also exist between stockholders and creditors. The market value of any firm equals the market value of its debt plus the market value of its stock. This means that managers can create shareholder wealth either by increasing the value of the firm or by reducing the value of its debts. The latter possibility is at the root of stockholder-bondholder conflicts. In order to reduce these conflicts, companies engage in various monitoring and control procedures (e.g., audits, specific reporting systems, restrictive covenants in bond and bank loan agreements). The costs of these activities and constraints, as well the costs of any residual divergence from firm value maximization (given the optimal monitoring and control procedures), are known collectively as agency costs.

QUESTION 3: How should MNCs arrange the capital structures of their foreign affiliates?

ANSWER: There are three options available to establishing subsidiary capital structures.

1. Conform to the capital structure of the parent company. In this situation, an affiliate's degree of leverage does not determine its financial risk. Also, this option is unrelated to shareholder wealth maximization.
2. Reflect the capitalization norms in each foreign country. While this approach may help maintain good relations with the host government, it ignores the linkage between U.S.-based multinationals and the U.S. capital market. Furthermore, the level of foreign debt/equity ratios is usually determined by institutional factors that have no bearing on foreign-based multinationals.
3. Vary to take advantage of opportunities to minimize the MNC's cost of capital. The cost-minimizing approach to determining foreign affiliate capital structures would be to allow subsidiaries with access to low-cost capital markets to exceed the parent company capitalization norm while subsidiaries in higher-capital-cost nations would have lower target debt ratios.

QUESTION 4: What actions should a MNC take in establishing a worldwide financing policy?

ANSWER: The approach taken by a MNC can be separated into three facets.

1. Seek to profit from market distortions, which includes:
   a. Taking advantage of deviations from equilibrium exchange or interest rates that may exist because of government controls and/or subsidies.

b. Exploiting the company's unique position through taxes, exchange controls, and other restrictions, based on its ability to adjust intracorporate fund flows.
2. Arrange financing to reduce the riskiness of the operating cash flows, which includes:
   a. Offsetting the firm's projected economic exposure by borrowing, if cost justified, in appropriate currencies.
   b. Reducing various political risks, either by giving lender a vested interest in the continuing viability of the firm's operations or by decreasing the firm's assets that are exposed.
   c. Selling the output from the plant or project in advance to customers to decrease sales uncertainty and then using the sales contracts to obtain financing.
   d. Securing a continuing supply of financing for corporate activities worldwide by diversifying fund sources and, possibly, borrowing in anticipation of needs.
3. Meet the financial structure goals of the MNC overall, which includes:
   a. Establishing a global capital structure that balances the after-tax costs and benefits of leverage.
   b. Selecting the appropriate affiliate capital structures.
   c. Considering the effects of incomplete information on financi decisions (agency/monitoring costs), including potential conflicts with joint venture partners.

SELECTED QUESTIONS FROM THE TEXT

QUESTION 5: Why do governments provide subsidized financing for some investments?

ANSWER: Governments use subsidized financing to encourage programs and activities that are deemed to be worthy. For example, governments provid subsidized trade financing to boost exports and low-cost financing to projects expected to create jobs in regions with high unemployment.

SELECTED PROBLEMS FROM THE TEXT

PROBLEM 1: Suppose that the cost of borrowing restricted French francs i 7% annually, whereas the market rate for these funds is 12%. If a firm c borrow 10 million French francs of restricted funds, how much will it sav annually in before-tax franc interest expense?

SOLUTION:

By borrowing at 8% when the market interest rate is 15%, Xebec saves 8% annually. This translates into annual before-tax savings of

$$\$12,500,000(.15 - .08) = \$875,000.$$

With a marginal tax rate of 40%, this translates into annual after-tax savings of $525,000.

The value of this ten-year annuity, discounted at Xebec's after-tax debt cost of 9% (15% x .6), is

$$\$525,000 \times 6.4177 = \$3,369,293.$$

PROBLEM 3: Suppose that one of the inducements provided by Taiwan to woo Xidex into setting up a local production facility is a 10-year, $12.5 million loan at 8% interest. The principal is to be repaid at the end of the tenth year. The market interest rate on such a loan is about 15%. With a marginal tax rate of 40%, how much is this loan worth to Xidex?

SOLUTION:

By borrowing at 8% when the market interest rate is 15%, Xidex saves 7% annually. This translates into annual before-tax savings of

$$\$12,500,000 \ (.15 - .08) = \$875,000.$$

With a marginal tax rate of 40%, this translates into annual after-tax savings of $525,000.

The value of this ten-year annuity, discounted at Xidex' after-tax debt cost of 9% (15% x .6), is

$$\$525,000 \times 6.4177 = \$3,369,293.$$

PROBLEM 8: The CFO of Eastman Kodak Company is thinking of borrowing Japanese yen because of their low interest rate, currently at 4.5%. The current interest rate on U.S. dollars is 9%. What is your advice to the CFO?

SOLUTION: My advice would be "Don't speculate." The international Fisher effect says that the 450 basis point differential reflects a 4.5% expected annual appreciation of the yen against the dollar. Thus, the expected costs of dollar and yen financing should be the same. Unless Kodak needs yen financing to offset a yen transaction or operating exposure, it should stick to dollar financing.

CHAPTER 23

INTERNATIONAL BANKING

Summary: This chapter examines several dimensions of international banking. It focuses on the organizational forms and strategies associat with overseas bank expansion and the analysis of country risk.

I. Recent Patterns of International Banking Activities

A. With expanding international trade and the emergence of MNCs, th demand for international financial services increased. Banks located in the traditional financial centers responded by extend loans and developing new, highly innovative financial techniques

B. With the onset of the energy crisis in late 1973, a great need f recycling funds from oil-exporting to oil-importing nations was created. International banks were able to provide the services needed because:

1. They had the broad experience in international lending.

2. They were the recipients of large shares of OPEC's surplus revenues in the form of deposits.

C. Banks located in major financial centers around the world participated in this expansion of international lending.

1. The largest share of the total was handled by banks located the major European centers, particularly in London.

2. Banks in the U.S. became large participants in international lending from their U.S. based offices and through their branches located in financial centers in the Caribbean and i the Far East.

3. The majority of the loans being extended were denominated in U.S. dollars, with the second largest category of loans bein, denominated in the German mark.

4. Loans extended to the governments of less developed countrie were the fastest growing category of loans by international banks during the 1970s.

D. International banking was hit with troubles in 1982 caused by a number of developments.

 1. A vast majority of loans was made in the form of floating-rate loans and denominated in U.S. dollars, thus making borrowers highly vulnerable to:

 a. Increases in real interest rates.

 b. Increases in the real value of the dollar.

 2. In 1979, OPEC implemented an oil price increase resulting in:

 a. Increased balance-of-payments deficits of LDCs.

 b. Increased need of LDCs for external financing.

 3. The catalyst of the crisis was provided by the economic policies of the industrial countries in general, and by the U.S. in particular, in their efforts to deal with rising inflation.

 4. With the recession in the industrial countries, the demand for the LDCs' products was reduced and, thus, the export earnings which were used to service the bank debt.

E. In August 1982, Mexico announced that it was unable to meet the regularly scheduled payments to its international creditors, followed by Brazil and Argentina. By the spring of 1983, about 25 LDCs, accounting for two-thirds of the international banks' claims, were unable to meet their debt payments as scheduled and had entered into loan rescheduling negotiations with their creditor banks.

F. Confronted with interruptions in inflows of funds due to the repayment problem on past loans, a sudden drying up of new sources of funds, and the growing uncertainties as to the capacity of borrowers to service their debt, international banks pulled back sharply on their lending.

G. While the intensity of the International debt crisis has eased off because of the recovery of the world economies and the orderly scheduling of many overdue international loans, the international banking activities continue to be depressed, as compared to the high-growth period of the late 1970s.

II. Organizational Forms and Strategies in Bank Expansion Overseas

A. A bank deciding on how to approach a foreign market must take i
consideration number of variables, such as:

1. Overall financial resources.

2. Level of experience with the markets.

3. Knowledge of the markets.

4. Volume of international business.

5. Strategic plans of the bank.

6. Banking structure of the foreign countries.

B. The possible entry strategies range from facilities with minimal
control and minimum banking services to those with maximum contr
and a full-fledged banking operation, including deposit taking a
bank lending.

1. A great majority of banks maintain correspondent banking
relationships with local banks worldwide. Their main functi
is to help finance the local foreign subsidiaries of their
multinational corporate clients.

a. Advantages: provides low cost market entry, no up-front
investment in staff or facilities, referrals of local
banking opportunities, ability to take advantage of
correspondents' local knowledge and contacts.

b. Disadvantages: correspondents may assign low priority to
servicing the bank's customers on matters such as credit
reports and term loans, restricts the bank's ability to
supply full service to its customers and limits its loca
market penetration.

2. A bank opens a representative office to provide advisory
services to banks and customers and to expedite the services
of the correspondent bank. The representative office,
however, is not authorized to obtain and transfer deposits a
do not provide on-site operating services.

a. Advantages: low-cost means of scouting out the local
market, efficient delivery of services when volume is
small, help attract additional business or prevent loss o
existing business.

b. <u>Disadvantages</u>: inability to gain deep local market penetration, can be expensive, more difficult to attract qualified personnel to work in a representative office than in a foreign branch.

3. As with commercial banks, <u>foreign</u> <u>bank</u> <u>branches</u> serve as lending and deposit-taking institutions.

   a. Many banks choose this form of entry for the following reasons:

      (1) There is a follow-the-customer rationale.

      (2) Foreign branches contribute directly to the bank's earnings which, in turn, help diversify the bank's earnings base.

      (3) Branches provide access to overseas money markets.

   b. <u>Advantages</u>: greater ability to service customers in the foreign country, better access to the local capital market, better ability to gather intelligence about local conditions, more attractive investment opportunities, training ground for executives, easier to attract good personnel eager for overseas experience, ability to provide customers internationally-integrated cash management and other services.

   c. <u>Disadvantages</u>: high cost, requires experienced international lending officers, possibility of alienating correspondent banks.

4. An alternative to expanding overseas by opening new branches is to grow through <u>acquisitions</u>. This form of entry is followed by most foreign banks trying to penetrate U.S. markets. This approach, however, is very expensive, highly risky, and difficult to make work effectively.

   a. <u>Advantages</u>: provides immediate access to the local deposit market, has an established network of local contacts and clients which would be difficult (if not impossible) to duplicate, well-connected executives.

   b. <u>Disadvantages</u>: most banks make the mistake of paying too much for their foreign acquisitions, highly risky, generally not worthwhile unless the acquirer has more to contribute to the acquisition than money.

5. <u>Edge</u> <u>Act</u> <u>and</u> <u>Agreement</u> <u>corporations</u> are subsidiaries of U.S. banks that are permitted to carry on international banking and investment activities.

a. The services provided by the Edge Act institution is limited to foreign customers and to handling the international business of domestic customers.

b. An agreement corporation is functionally similar to the Edge Act corporation. Usually it is state-chartered and enters into an agreement with the Federal Reserve to limit its activities to those of an Edge Act corporation.

6. International banking facilities are U.S.-based subsidiaries which are established to engage in international banking activities.

a. IBFs do not represent new physical banking facilities; instead, they are merely separate sets of books of existing banking facilities.

b. Because they do not transact domestic banking business, they are exempt from reserve and deposit insurance requirements as well as from interest rate limitations, such as Regulation Q.

c. IBF operations are closely linked to the Eurocurrency market, as evidenced by the high proportion of both assets and liabilities due to other banking institutions.

III. Country Risk Analysis

A. Country risk is defined as the possibility that borrowers in a country will be unable or unwilling to service their debt obligations to foreign lenders in a timely manner.

B. Country risk analysis deals with the assessment of factors that affect the likelihood that a country will be able to generate sufficient earnings in order to repay foreign debts as they come due. These factors are both economic and political.

1. Among the economic factors are:

a. The equality and effectiveness of a country's economic and financial management policies.

b. The country's resource base.

c. The country's external financial position.

2. Political factors include:

a. The degree of political stability in a country.

        b.   The extent to which a foreign country will stand behind its external obligations.

C.   The unique characteristics of a sovereign borrower include the following.

    1.   Many of the loan covenants are irrelevant.

    2.   Economic and financial policy restrictions imposed by foreign banks are not accepted.

    3.   In the event of default, seizure of assets is not useful unless the debtor has substantial external assets.

D.   To enforce the debt contracts to sovereign states, foreign banks extend credit in the form of <u>loan syndications</u> and <u>cross-default clauses</u> which ensures that a default to one bank is a default to all banks sharing the loan.

E.   A nation's ability to repay foreign loans is a function of its ability to generate U.S. dollars and other hard currencies. This ability, in turn, is based on the nation's <u>terms of trade</u>, which is a weighted average of a nation's export prices relative to its import prices.

    1.   If the terms of trade increases, the nation will be a better credit risk than if the terms of trade decreases.

    2.   This terms of trade risk can be increased if the government attempts to avoid the necessary economic adjustments to the country's changed wealth position, as evidenced in the decline of the terms of trade.

    3.   When assessing country risk, the key issue is the speed with which a country adjusts to its new wealth position.

    4.   The speed of adjustment, in turn, will be determined in part by the government's perception of the costs and benefits associated with the implementation of austerity policies versus loan default.

        a.   The cost of austerity is determined by the nation's external debt relative to its wealth, as measured by its gross national product. The lower this ratio, the lower the relative amount of consumption that must be sacrificed to meet a nation's foreign debt obligations.

        b.   The cost of default is measured by the possibility of being denied international credit.

5. The <u>bailout</u> <u>decision</u> is largely al political decision and depends on the willingness of citizens of another country t tax themselves on behalf of the country involved.

6. The more volatile a nation's terms of trade and the less stable its political environment, the greater the chances that the government will hold off on any necessary economic adjustments.

F. The enormous outflow of funds, or <u>flight</u> <u>of</u> <u>capital</u>, from debto developing countries is a major factor prolonging the debt crisis.

1. Capital flight occurs for several reasons.

   a. Government regulations, control, and taxes to lower the return on domestic investments.

   b. Investors shifting savings to foreign currencies less likely to depreciate in response to:

      (1) High inflation.

      (2) Interest rates which are artificially held down by the government.

      (3) Devaluation of an overvalued currency.

      (4) Increased political risk.

2. To halt capital flight, the borrowing country needs to implement economic policies, such as:

   a. Cutting budget deficits and taxes.

   b. Removing barriers to investments by foreigners.

   c. Selling off state-owned enterprises.

   d. Allowing for freer trade.

   e. Avoiding currency overvaluation.

   f. Instituting political reforms.

G. When assessing country risk, the following indicators may be quite useful.

1. The government deficit as a percentage of GNP.

2. The correlation between having a controlled exchange rate system and having foreign debt-servicing problems.

3. The degree of waste inherent in the economy; that is, the extent to which the capital from abroad is put to effective use in the borrowing country.

4. The coverage ratio, which is the ratio of exports to debt service.

H. A nation with substantial natural, human, and financial resources is a better economic risk than is one without those resources.

I. While foreign banks try to reduce the riskiness of their international loan portfolios by lending to a large number of nations, they are subject to the following factors:

1. External shocks, such as world recession and falling commodity prices, which affect the borrower's ability to repay its debt.

2. The advent of unexpectedly high real interest rates has shown that the use of floating-rate loans, which were designed to protect banks from interest rate risk, systematically converted this risk into country risk.

3. The increase in the real value of the dollar demonstrated that dollar-denominated loans are subject to exchange rate risk.

J. In addition to identifying the factors that would systematically affect loans to all foreign countries, it is also necessary to determine the susceptibility of the various nations and their debts to the external shocks.

1. This requires a focus on the longer-term issues involving the financial policies and development strategies pursued by different nations.

2. Indicators of the long-run economic health of a nation include:

   a. The structure of incentives that rewards risk-taking in productive ventures.

   b. The legal structure that stimulates the development of free markets.

   c. Minimal regulations and economic distortions.

   d. Clear incentives to save and invest.

K. In order to solve the problems of the current debt crisis, the debtor developing nations need to develop and implement market-oriented reform policies which will lead to:

1. Cutting government spending.

2. Reducing state subsidies to consumer goods and inefficient industries.

3. Removing trade barriers and price controls.

4. Moving interest rates and the exchange rate closer to market levels.

These actions, if implemented, can increase output by making the economy more efficient, can reduce consumption, and thereby can increase the quantity of goods available for exports. They will also discourage savings and investment.

KEY TERMS

International Debt Crisis
Correspondent Banks
Representative Offices
Foreign Branches
Acquisitions
Edge Act and Agreement Corporations
International Banking Facilities (IBF)

Country Risk
Loan Syndication
Cross-Default Clause
Terms of Trade
Terms of Trade Risk
Capital Flight

CONCEPTUAL QUESTIONS

QUESTION 1: What is country risk?

ANSWER: Country risk is defined as the possibility that borrowers in a country will be unable or unwilling to service their debt obligations to foreign lenders in a timely manner.

QUESTION 2: What is the cross-default clause?

ANSWER: A cross-default clause as part of a loan agreement ensures that a default to one bank is a default to all banks.

QUESTION 3: What factors will tend to increase the riskiness of international loans provided by foreign banks?

ANSWER: While foreign banks try to reduce the riskiness of their international loan portfolios by lending to a large number of nations, they are subject to the following factors:

1. External shock, such as world recession and falling commodity prices, which affect the borrower's ability to repay its debt.
2. The advent of unexpectedly high real interest rates has shown that the use of floating-rate loans, which were designed to protect banks from interest rate risk, systematically converted this risk into country risk.
3. The increase in the real value of the dollar demonstrated that dollar-denominated loans are subject to exchange rate risk.

SELECTED QUESTIONS FROM THE TEXT

QUESTION 6: Why is it crucial for banks to prevent several defaults at once?

ANSWER: Banks enforce their loan contracts with sovereign borrowers primarily by threatening to deny further credit to borrowers who repudiate their debts. But this threat is meaningful only so long as the banks can reward with additional credit those nations that do not default. If several nations default simultaneously, then the banks' promise to provide further credit to borrowers who honor their debts is less credible; the erosion in their capital bases caused by several defaults at once will force the banks to curtail their loans. Under these circumstances, even those nations that did not default will suffer a reduction of credit. The lesser penalty for defaulting may induce borrowers to default en masse.

QUESTION 7: What incentive do borrowers have to form a debtors' cartel and simultaneously default? Who would choose not to belong to such a cartel?

ANSWER: Lenders' incentive to form a debtors' cartel and simultaneously default stems from the fact that this action will lower the cost to them of defaulting. The problem, however, is that those borrowers who would like to access the capital markets in the future will also suffer because the banks will not have the resources to extend further credit. Thus, nations that are good credit risks, intend to honor their debt obligations, and intend to raise more money abroad will choose not to join such a cartel.

NEWS ITEMS

Baker Plan

In October 1985, U.S. Treasury Games Baker called on fifteen principal middle-income less developed countries to undertake growth-oriented structural reforms, to be supported by increased financing from the World Bank, continued modest lending from commercial banks, and a pledge by industrial countries to open their markets to LDC exports. The underlying objective of the Baker Plan was to enhance LDC economic growth making these countries more desirable borrowers and restoring their access to international capital markets.

Citicorp

In May 1987 Citicorp announced that it had added $3 billion to its loan loss reserves against its loans to LDCs in response to the deteriorating relations with Brazil and other major debtors. By the end 1987, a total of $23 billion was added to the loss reserves of large U.S. banks and British banks.

The banks who boosted their loan loss reserves are now in a stronge position to demand reforms in countries to which they lend. Moreover, a stronger negotiation stance puts additional pressure on countries to conform to the Baker Plan.

Mexico

By the end of 1987, Mexico, J. P. Morgan, and the U.S. Treasury announced a debt plan involving the exchange of old bank debts for new bonds at a discount. This principal was backed by 20-year zero-coupon U.S Treasury bonds.

Plano Cruzado

On February 28, 1986, President Jose Sarnay of Brazil announced the Plano Cruzado with the purpose of imposing "shock treatment" on the econom and breaking the cycle of "inertial inflation" caused by high inflationary expectations.

CHAPTER 24

EVALUATION AND CONTROL OF FOREIGN OPERATIONS

Summary: This chapter examines how to deal with some of the special problems encountered in evaluating the profitability of foreign operations and the performance of their managers.

I. Developing an Evaluation and Control System

   A. Designing an evaluation system involves four stages.

      1. In the first stage of the system, the purpose of the system must be specified.

         a. A clear distinction needs to be made between the evaluation of subsidiary performance and managerial performance.

         b. The performance of the subsidiary should be evaluated on the basis of how well it is doing as an economic unit.

         c. Because of a number of variables complicating the evaluation of foreign operations, a measure of the affiliate's value from the perspective of corporate headquarters may differ significantly from a fair measure of local management's operating efficiency.

      2. The second stage involves determining what decisions will be made on the basis of this evaluation and the information necessary to support such decisions.

         a. A distinction must be made between uncontrollable and controllable variables.

         b. Different management functions require different measures of subsidiary performance.

      3. The third stage is the design of a reporting system that can provide the required information.

      4. The fourth stage involves conducting a cost/benefit analysis of the evaluation system.

   B. The evaluation system has both costs and benefits which must be weighted against each other.

1. Some of the benefits include:

    a. Greater control over current operations.

    b. More rigorous capital budgeting decisions.

    c. Greater awareness of managerial effectiveness.

2. The costs associated with the evaluation system include:

    a. The time and money involved in redesigning the information system.

    b. Behavioral problems that might be associated with the new evaluation system.

C. The main objectives of the evaluation system include the following:

    1. Providing a rational basis for global resource allocation.

    2. Having an early warning system if something is wrong with current operations.

    3. Evaluating the performance of individual managers.

    4. Providing a set of standards that will motivate managers.

II. Resource Allocation

A. MNCs are continually faced with the decision of allocating capital among its various subsidiaries on a worldwide basis.

B. A measure employed to evaluate potential investments is the expected <u>return on investment</u> (ROI).

    1. As long as proposed investments are comparable to existing or if returns on past investments are indicative of future returns, will the relevant ROI figure for judging the profitability of future investments be appropriate.

    2. However, there two problems involved in allowing returns on past investments to guide this evaluation process.

        a. Problems may arise with measuring the correct <u>investment base</u>.

            (1) According to finance theory, the relevant investment base equals the incremental value of all capital required.

(2) The investment must therefore be measured on a <u>current-cost</u> or <u>replacement-cost</u> basis, rather than a historical-cost basis, and should also include gross fixed assets as well as working capital requirements net of external supplier credits.

    b. There may be difficulties in determining the <u>relevant returns</u>.

        (1) Substantial differences can exist between subsidiary cash flows and parent cash flows.

        (2) According to economic theory, an investment should be evaluated on the basis of its net present value of <u>incremental</u> <u>cash</u> <u>flows</u> back to the investor.

  3. Because of substantial variations in the returns and the investment base, ROI comparisons are misleading.

  4. ROI analysis can be made meaningful, however, by adjusting accounting results according to their economic values.

C. In the <u>post-investment</u> <u>audit</u> comparisons are made between actual results and ex ante budgeted figures. Management is interested in this audit for two reasons:

  1. Some actions may be appropriate with respect to the person(s) responsible for any mistakes.

  2. Correction factors can be included in future investment analysis to prevent a recurrence.

III. The evaluation and Control of Current Operations

A. Operations in uncertain environments should be frequently monitored to determine whether any tactical or strategic changes are warranted. This determination requires formal standards against which to judge performance. There are three types of standards that are used in control systems.

  1. <u>Predetermined</u> <u>standards</u> <u>or</u> <u>budgets</u>, which provide the basis against which actual performance is compared.

  2. <u>Historical</u> <u>standards</u>, which are based on past actual performance have two major drawbacks:

    a. Conditions may have changed between the two periods.

    b. The prior period's performance may not be acceptable to start with.

3. <u>External</u> <u>standards</u>, which are derived from other responsibility centers or other companies.

B. The existence of corporations is based on their ability to generate profits.

    1. Most control systems are designed to measure profitability and to highlight certain key variables.

    2. In evaluating and controlling foreign operations, the appropriate evaluation measure(s) will vary by company and subsidiary and may be different from those used in controlling the domestic business.

    3. <u>Different</u> <u>cost</u> <u>standards</u> are usually necessary for foreign operations because of local value-added requirements, impor tariffs, and government limitation on laying off or firing workers.

C. In a foreign environment, with greater uncertainty, a company m find it helpful to draw up <u>flexible</u> <u>budgets</u>.

    1. Flexible budgeting involves preparing alternative budgets based on different projections of future rates of inflation exchange rate changes, relative price changes, wage settlements, and others.

    2. The major benefit to flexible budgeting is that it may remo many of the economic effects beyond the control of manageme from the performance measures, thereby providing a measure that can better identify management's contribution to the results of the subsidiary.

D. In analyzing the actual results of a subsidiary, <u>ROI</u> <u>comparison</u> can be made for diagnosing areas of profit deficiency and, thus for directing management's attention to potential areas of improvement.

    1. In practice, performance measurement involves comparing the subsidiary's ROI with the ROI of similar businesses, such a local competitors, the firm's subsidiaries and/or competito on a regional or global basis, and parent company operation

    2. Comparisons with local or regional competitors can be meaningless because of:

        a. Different accounting and disclosure requirements.

        b. Different depreciation and earnings reports.

c. Not separating nonrecurring income arising out of the sale of assets from operating income.

d. A high degree of integration and the less-than-arm's length dealings between the units of the MNC.

3. Cross-country comparisons with other affiliates of the MNC are also possible.

IV. Evaluating Managerial Performance

A. In designing a management evaluation system, the company must ensure that the resulting managerial motivations will be consistent with the overall corporate objectives.

1. Managerial performance measures that will emphasize short-run profits include:

a. Current earnings.

b. Return on investment.

c. Return on equity.

2. A manager is properly motivated if his or her performance is judged on the basis of results in those areas over which he or she has control.

a. Both a subsidiary's profitability and ROI would not be appropriate evaluation criteria against which to judge managerial performance, because both measures are subject to uncontrollable events.

b. Instead, it would be more useful to compare actual results with the budgeted figures.

3. Relying on a budget to judge managerial performance requires that the budget:

a. Incorporates reasonable performance objectives.

b. Allows for long-term profit maximization behavior, or at least constrains the use of those short run-oriented policies that may provide immediate benefits to local managers.

4. The MNC should be able to adjust performance standards so as to encourage actions to be taken by subsidiaries to create relationships among subsidiaries that will benefit the overall corporation.

5. In terms of management evaluation, the local manager should be held responsible for net operating income expressed in dollars, using a projected exchange rate.

B. There are three current concerns in performance evaluation.

   1. The task of setting transfer prices corporate-wide should be centralized. In this case, managerial evaluations must be decoupled from the particular transfer prices being used. This involves:

      a. Charging purchasers the marginal cost of production and shipping.

      b. Crediting sellers with a reasonable profit on their sales

   2. Being able to adjust intracorporate fund flows by speeding or slowing payments on intracorporate funds offers potentially great benefits in cash, exchange risk, and blocked-funds management.

      a. Leading and lagging most likely results in distorting the various working capital ratios of a subsidiary.

      b. As a corporate policy, the effects of this tool should not be included when evaluating subsidiary management.

   3. The firm must choose the exchange rate(s) to use when drawing up budget and evaluating performance.

      a. When preparing the operating budget, the following exchange rates are possible:^

         (1) The actual spot rate at the time of setting the budget.

         (2) The forecast rate.

         (3) The updated rate at the time the budget is revised due to exchange rate changes.

      b. In evaluating performance relative to the budget, the following three alternative rates can be used:

         (1) The actual rate at the time the budget is set.

         (2) The projected end-of-period rate.

         (3) The actual end-of-period rate.

c. Of the various combinations of budgeting and evaluation rates, the most desirable combination would be the use of forecasted rates, also called _internal_ _forward_ _rates_, at both stages, because it excludes unplanned currency fluctuations and recognizes expected fluctuations at the budgeting stage.

C. Evaluations of managerial performance will provide the necessary information for promotion and salary decisions.

V. Management Control Systems

A. Management control is the process by which a manager determines that subordinates are making efficient use of the resources available to them in accordance with corporate objectives.

B. The objectives of the control system are essentially the same for both domestic and foreign operations: communication, evaluation, and motivation.

C. In a multinational context, organizing and administering an effective control system will depend partly on environmental factors unique to the MNC.

1. The criteria and the time span over which the subsidiary is evaluated must encourage managers to act in ways that will promote long-term, company-wide profitability.

2. The communication system should be designed to provide an adequate means for coordination among, and control of, the different organizational units at each level in the company hierarchy.

3. Most of all, the managers must be taught the objectives, policies, and expectations of the company.

D. Many MNCs simply export their domestic management control system which has proven to be successful at home.

1. This approach can only work effectively if the firm has similar objectives for its domestic and foreign operations, and that deviations between these operations are not sufficiently great so as to negate the value of the information generated.

2. Otherwise, modifications to the control system and the control standards should reflect the unique environmental variables that exist abroad.

E. The domestic reporting system can be modified in several ways to incorporate the various unique factors abroad.

1. Some companies require more frequent reporting by their foreign affiliates.

2. Smaller subsidiaries may follow a system of reporting and control by exception. In this case, several key performance indicators are monitored.

   a. As long as these indicators stay within clearly defined bounds, no action by corporate headquarters will be necessary.

   b. Only if problems arise will additional controls by imposed

3. A zero-base information system review can help reduce information requirements by auditing all information currently being provided and the uses to which that information is put. Any information that is not used in the decision making process should be discarded.

4. Traveling teams of auditors can provide communications and control within the multinational enterprise.

F. An important concept in organizational design is responsibility reporting, which involves flowing information from each decision area to the manager responsible for the results of these decisions

   1. A general rule in the design of a reporting and control system is to decentralize responsibilities as much as possible.

      a. Decentralization works best for companies that have few linkages between its activity areas.

      b. In the MNC, the interactions among its various organizational units is so great that complete decentralization is suboptimal.

   2. Companies that partially decentralize their operations by establishing regional headquarters for different geographical areas can benefit from:

      a. Shorter lines of communication.

      b. Enhanced dispersal of geographically centered information.

   3. On the other hand, companies that have a limited number of experienced international financial managers benefit the most by centralizing decisions at headquarters.

4. A study by the Conference Board on the level of corporate involvement has identified five key multinational financial key decision areas that are controlled by headquarters. These areas include:

    a. Repatriation of funds.

    b. Inter-subsidiary financing.

    c. Acquisition of funds.

    d. Protection of assets.

    e. Planning and control.

5. In another study, Stobaugh (1979) indicated that significant differences in attitude toward centralization exist among small, medium, and large multinationals.

    a. Small MNCs allowed subsidiaries great freedom in financial management.

    b. Medium-sized MNCs tried to optimize worldwide results by treating each subsidiary as one unit in the global system.

    c. Large MNCs provided subsidiaries with formal guidelines, but within these guidelines they were allowed considerable initiative.

KEY TERMS

Evaluation and Control System
Return on Investment (ROI)
Investment Base
Relevant Returns
Incremental Cash Flows
Postinvestment Audit

Predetermined Standards
Historical Standards
External Standards
Flexible Budgeting
Internal Forward Rates
Responsibility Reporting

CONCEPTUAL QUESTIONS

QUESTION 1: How is an evaluation and control system designed?

ANSWER: Designing an evaluation and control system involves four stages:

1. In the first stage of the system, the purpose of the system must be clearly specified.
2. The second stage involves determining what decisions will be made on the basis of this evaluation and the information that is necessary to support such decisions.

3. The third stage is the design of a reporting system that can provide the required information.
4. The fourth stage involves conducting a cost/benefit analysis of t evaluation system.

QUESTION 2:   What is responsibility reporting?

ANSWER: Responsibility reporting is an important concept in organization design which involves flowing information from each decision area to the manager responsible for the results of these decisions.

SELECTED QUESTIONS FROM THE TEXT

QUESTION 2:   What are the key benefits of an evaluation system?

ANSWER: The key benefits of an evaluation system include:

1. **Greater control over current operations.** The company will have a early warning system if something is wrong with current operations.
2. **More rigorous capital budgeting decisions.** An evaluation system should provide a rational basis for global resource allocation.
3. **Greater awareness of managerial effectiveness.** The company should be able to evaluate the performance of individual managers. **Increase managerial initiative.**
4. An evaluation system should provide a set of standards that will motivate managers to work in the company's best interest.

QUESTION 5:   What is flexible budgeting and why might it be particularly useful to the MNC?

ANSWER: Flexible budgeting involves drawing up alternative budgets based on different projections of future rates of inflation, exchange rate changes, relative price changes, wage settlements, and so on. Two key benefits are 1) the firm should have an advantage in coping with foreseeable changes in its operating environment and 2) by removing from performance measures many of the effects of general economic events beyond management's control, the company can better identify management's contribution to subsidiary results. This benefit is especially valuable to the MNC given the wider range of possible economic scenarios it is likely to face abroad.

QUESTION 10: Top management of Siemens, the giant West German electronics firm, is worried. Siemens's return on equity slid from 10.7% in 1984 to 8% in 1987. How serious a problem is this? German inflation fell from 2.4% in 1984 to 0.1% in 1987.

ANSWER: This problem illustrates how the distinction between real and nominal returns can affect a company's measured profitability. The real return on equity in 1984 was approximately

$$8.3\% \ (10.7 - 2.4);$$

by 1987, Siemens' real ROE had declined to

$$7.9\% \ (8 - .1).$$

Although Siemens didn't do as well in 1987 as in 1984, the real difference was only 0.4%, not the 2.7% that it seems to be based on examining nominal returns per annum.

CHAPTER 25

INTERNATIONAL TAX MANAGEMENT

Summary: The purpose of this chapter is to present an overview of international taxation, including tax treatment of foreign-source earning tax credits, effects of bilateral tax treaties to avoid double taxation, tax havens, special incentives to reduce taxes, and benefits of organizin foreign operations in the form of a branch or a subsidiary.

I. The Theoretical Objectives of Taxation

    A. Tax <u>neutrality</u> and <u>tax equity</u> are two concepts of taxation that a characteristic of most tax systems.

        1. The objective of each concept is to achieve a status of equit within the tax system.

        2. The economic difference between the two concepts lies in thei effect on decision making.

            a. Tax neutrality is accomplished by ensuring that decisions are unaffected by the tax laws.

            b. Tax equity is achieved by ensuring that equal sacrifices are made in bearing the tax burden.

    B. A <u>neutral tax</u> is defined as one that will not influence any aspect of the investment decision. Its basic justification is economic efficiency. There are two types of tax neutrality: domestic and foreign neutrality.

        1. <u>Domestic neutrality</u> in taxation is that U.S. citizens investin at home and U.S. citizens investing abroad are treated equally

            a. This form of neutrality involves:

                (1) Uniformity in both the applicable tax rate and the determination of taxable income.

                (2) Equalization of all taxes on profits.

            b. Because of differences in accounting methods and governmental policies equal tax rates do not lead to equal tax burdens.

            c. <u>Indirect taxation</u> is another important issue because this type of tax is imposed more heavily in foreign countries than in the U.S.

d.   In the U.S., foreign income is taxed at the same rate as domestic income, with a credit for any taxes paid to a foreign government.

e.   Departures from the theoretical norm of tax neutrality include the following.

   (1) An investment tax credit has never been allowed on foreign investments, and the rules on carrybacks and carryforwards are less liberal on foreign operations.

   (2) The tax credit for taxes paid to a foreign governments is limited to the amount of tax that would have been due if the income had been earned in the U.S. If the tax rate in the foreign country is higher than that of the U.S., no additional tax credits are provided.

   (3) The Foreign Sales Corporation (FSC) sells special tax incentives for U.S. exports.

   (4) Taxation of income earned in foreign subsidiaries is defined until it is returned to the U.S. in the form of a dividend. This deferral becomes important only if the effective foreign tax is below that of the U.S.

2. _Foreign neutrality_ in taxation states that the tax burden placed on the foreign subsidiaries of U.S. firms should equal that imposed on foreign-owned competitors operating in the same country, which include:

   a. Firms owned by residents of the host country.

   b. Foreign subsidiaries of non-U.S. corporations.

3. The major capital exporting countries follow a mixed policy of foreign and domestic tax neutrality whereby:

   a. The home government taxes foreign branch profits but defers taxation of foreign subsidiary earnings until these earnings are repatriated.

   b. The host taxes on branch or subsidiary earnings may be credited against the home tax; this credit is limited by the home tax or host tax, whichever is lower.

4. Several home countries fully or partially exempt foreign subsidiary and/or branch earnings from domestic taxation.

5. In other countries, a portion of the foreign income is excluded when the domestic tax liability is calculated.

C. <u>Tax equity</u> is based on the criterion that all taxpayers in a similar situation be subject to the same rules. This means that:

    1. All U.S. corporations be taxed on income, no matter where it earned.

    2. The income of a foreign branch be taxed in the same manner as that earned by a domestic branch.

D. A number of countries have developed a network of bilateral tax treaties with the purpose of avoiding double taxation of income b the two taxing jurisdictions. In addition, treaties allocate certain types of income to specific countries and reduce or eliminate withholding taxes.

II. U.S. Taxation of Multinational Corporations

A. According to U.S. tax law, <u>domestic corporations</u>, which are incorporated within the U.S., are taxed on their income earned i the U.S. In the case that a foreign-based affiliate of a U.S. company is not a branch but a separate incorporated entity under the host country's law, its earnings would not be subject to U.S taxation unless, and until, these earnings are repatriated.

B. U.S. tax laws also make a distinction between branches and subsidiaries.

    1. Because a branch is regarded as part of the parent's own operations, its profits are fully taxed as foreign income in the year in which they are earned, even though they may not remitted to the U.S. parent company.

    2. The earnings from a subsidiary can be deferred until the yea they are transferred to the parent in the form of a dividend or payment for corporate services.

C. The U.S. and other home countries allow a credit against domesti income tax for foreign income taxes already paid to eliminate double taxation of foreign-source earnings.

    1. A <u>direct tax credit</u> can be taken for taxes paid on the earnings of a foreign branch of a U.S. company and any forei withholding taxes deducted from remittances to a U.S. investor.

    2. An <u>indirect tax credit</u> is allowed on dividends received from foreign operation in which U.S. shareholders have at least a 10% ownership interest.

3. The formula for computing the indirect tax credit is given as follows:

$$\frac{\text{Dividend (including withholding tax)}}{\text{Earnings net of foreign income taxes}} \times \text{Foreign tax.}$$

D. The rule of <u>overall</u> <u>limitation</u> on tax credit states that the credit for taxes paid abroad in a given year cannot exceed the U.S. tax due on total foreign-source income for the same year.

1. The overall limitation can be calculated as:

$$\frac{\text{Consolidated foreign profits and losses}}{\text{Worldwide taxable income}} \times \text{Amount of U.S. tax liability} = \text{Maximum total credit.}$$

2. If the overall limitation is applicable, any excess foreign credits may be carried back two years and carried forward five years.

E. The Tax Reform Act of 198655 has created five new and distinct <u>baskets</u> or limitations for which separate tax credits will be calculated.

1. The first four baskets apply to foreign corporations with more than a 50% ownership interest and include:

a. Passive income.

b. Financial services income.

c. Shipping income.

d. High withholding-tax interest income.

2. The fifth is a separate basket for dividends from minority foreign subsidiaries.

3. The major benefits of this approach include:

a. Preventing MNCs to average the rates on highly-taxed and low-taxed classes of income.

b. Preventing foreign taxes paid in high-tax jurisdictions to be used to offset U.S. tax owed on certain types of lower tax income.

F. Once a taxpaying corporation and the IRS have agreed on the total amount of worldwide deductions, the <u>allocation</u> of these deductions between foreign-source and domestic-source income becomes important.

    1. The current U.S. tax law obliges companies to transfer certain interest, R & D, and general and administrative expenses incurred in the U.S. to the books of foreign subsidiaries.

    2. The U.S. source of income rules are important to U.S. companies because foreign-source taxable income is a major variable in the calculation of foreign tax credits.

G. The IRS adjusts transactions between related parties to reflect arm's-length prices, which are prices that would be reached by two independent firms in normal dealings.

H. Subpart F of the 1962 Revenue Act subjects U.S. company affiliates with majority ownership and incorporated abroad to U.S. taxation whenever they engage in intracorporate international trade of goods, factors, or services and regardless of where their profits originate or accumulate.

III. United States Tax Incentives for Foreign Trade

A. To encourage certain types of business activity in different regions of the world, a number of tax incentives have been added to the tax code.

B. The <u>Foreign</u> <u>Sales</u> <u>Corporation</u> (FSC) was created by the Tax Reform Act of 1984 as the U.S. government's primary incentive for exporting U.S.-produced goods overseas.

    1. The FSC is a corporation that is incorporated, and maintains an office, in a possession in the U.S. (including Guam, American Samoa, the Commonwealth of Northern Mariana Islands and the U.S. Virgin Islands) or in a foreign country that has an IRS-approved exchange of tax information program with the U.S.

    2. The following criteria must be met by the FSC to qualify for tax benefits under the law:

        a. 25 or fewer shareholders must be maintained at all times.

        b. No preferred stock.

        c. Certain tax and accounting records must be maintained at a location within the U.S.

      d.   At least one member of the Board of Directors must be a non-U.S. resident.

      e.   The FSC must not be a member of a controlled group of corporations having a DISC as a member.

      f.   An election to be treated as an FSC must be filed within the 90-day period immediately preceding the beginning of a taxable year.

  3. The FSC must generate foreign trading gross receipts which are derived from

      a.   Sale, exchange, or other disposition of export property.

      b.   Lease or rental of export property for use outside the U.S. by unrelated parties.

      c.   Performance of services related and subsidiary to, the sale or lease of export property.

      d.   Performance of managerial services for unrelated FSCs, provided that at least 50% of the FSC's gross receipts are derived from the first three activities above.

  4. Export property includes property manufactured, produced, grown, or extracted in the U.S. by a person other than the FSC.

  5. To derive foreign trading gross receipts, there are foreign management and foreign economic process requirements that must be met by the FSC.

  6. In determining the FSC's income from the sale or other disposition of export property, it is not necessary to apply the normal arm's length transfer pricing rules.

C. An alternative to the FSC is a small FSC which is the same as an FSC except that the small FSC does not have to fulfill the foreign management or foreign economic process requirements.

D. An interest-charge DISC is a domestic corporation controlled by firms that did not establish an FSC. Its benefits include:

  1. Deferring taxes on income attributable to qualified export receipts.

  2. Providing a financing device.

E. A <u>U.S.</u> <u>possessions</u> <u>corporation</u> is a domestic operation that mee
    the following requirements:

    1. At least 80% of its gross income has been derived from
        sources in a U.S. possession or possessions (excluding the
        Virgin Islands).

    2. At least 75% of gross income is derived from the active
        conduct of trade.

    These requirements must be met for three years preceding the
    close of the taxable year in which the corporation will become :
    U.S. possessions corporation.

IV. Tax Havens and the Multinational Corporation

    A. <u>Tax</u> <u>havens</u> include countries whose moderate level of taxation an
        liberal tax incentives enable multinationals to substantially
        reduce or defer taxation on income that is channeled through
        these countries.

    B. The decision to use a tax haven is based on the following
        framework:

        1. Selecting the type of tax haven based on an evaluation of
            projected needs against the advantages of the various tax
            havens.

        2. Considering the form of organization outside the U.S., which
            entails choosing between the branch or subsidiary as well as
            the use of any tax incentive organization. Three key factor:
            underlying this decision include:

            a. The projected cash flows in the country under
                consideration.

            b. The attitude of the U.S. parent company toward
                repatriation of funds.

            c. The alternative uses of funds.

        3. Making a selective examination of possible locations based on
            the preceding considerations and factors. The focus is on
            the relative advantages and disadvantages of each country
            given its tax laws.

V. Taxation and Corporate Organization

    A. The decision about the form of organization to use abroad require
        a careful analysis of many complex issues.

1. The major issues of such an analysis include:

   a. The objective of the firm.

   b. The cash flows of the particular unit under consideration.

2. The basic decision about the organizational form lies on whether to use a branch or an incorporated subsidiary. The key consideration would be the alternative uses of excess tax credits.

   a. If the sum of the foreign tax credits is greater than the U.S. tax rate and if the excess tax credits cannot be used, then a branch may be preferred.

   b. If the U.S. tax rate is greater than the foreign rates, a subsidiary may be preferred.

3. These conclusions can be quickly changed by many factors.

   a. There can be alternative uses for the excess tax credits.

   b. The cash flow and tax situation change from country to country.

   c. Problems may arise if part of the subsidiary cash flows include income of a controlled foreign operation under Subpart F.

4. Other possible forms of organization involve the special corporations, such as:

   a. The FSC.

   b. U.S. possessions corporations.

   c. Tax haven corporations.

KEY TERMS

Tax Neutrality	Indirect Tax Credit
Tax Equity	Overall Limitation
Neutral Tax	Subpart F
Domestic Neutrality	Foreign Sales Corporation (FSC)
Indirect Taxation	Small FSC
Foreign Neutrality	Interest-Charge DISC
Tax Treaties	U.S. Possessions Corporation
Direct Tax Credit	Tax Havens

CONCEPTUAL QUESTIONS

QUESTION 1: What major decisions must be included in global tax planning

ANSWER: The major decisions which must be made in global tax planning include:

1. Determining the legal form of organization for the firm's foreign operations.
2. Deciding when, how, and from where to bring back funds.
3. Arranging for the optimal use of tax havens, bilateral tax treaties, and special corporate tax incentive vehicles.

QUESTION 2: Distinguish between domestic neutrality and foreign neutrality.

ANSWER: Domestic neutrality in taxation is that U.S. citizens investing home and u>S. citizens investing broad are treated equally. On the other hand, foreign neutrality in taxation states that the tax burden place on the foreign subsidiaries of U.S. firms should equal that imposed on foreign-owned competitors operating in the same country, which include firms owned by residents of the host country and foreign subsidiaries of non-U.S. corporations.

QUESTION 3: Explain the rule of overall limitation on tax credit.

ANSWER: The rule of overall limitation on tax credit states that the credit for taxes paid abroad in a given year cannot exceed the U.S. tax d» on total foreign-source income for the same year. Any excess tax credits can be carried back two years and carried forward five years.

QUESTION 4: What factors can influence the decision about the form of organization to use abroad?

ANSWER: Any decision made about the form of organization to use abroad c₃ be quickly changed by the following factors:

1. There are alternative uses for any excess tax credit.
2. The cash flow and tax situation change from country to country.
3. Problems may arise if part of the subsidiary cash flows include income of a controlled foreign operation under Subpart F.

QUESTION 5: What is the purpose of bilateral tax treaties?

ANSWER: A number of countries have developed a network of bilateral tax treaties designed to avoid double taxation of income by two taxing jurisdictions. Although foreign tax credits help to some extent, the treaties go further in that they allocate certain types of income to specific countries and also reduce or eliminate withholding taxes.